TOTAL RECALL™

VOLUME ONE: LIFE ON MARS

DYNAMITE® ENTERTAINMENT

TOTAL RECALL™

VOLUME ONE: LIFE ON MARS

WRITTEN BY
VINCE MOORE

ART BY
CEZAR RAZEK

COLORS BY
SALVATORE AIALA ISSUES 1-3
INLIGHT STUDIO ISSUE 4

LETTERS AND COLLECTION DESIGN BY
BILL TORTOLINI

COLLECTION COVER BY
DARICK ROBERTSON

SPECIAL THANKS TO
THE LICENSING GROUP

DYNAMITE® ENTERTAINMENT

NICK BARRUCCI • PRESIDENT
JUAN COLLADO • CHIEF OPERATING OFFICER
JOSEPH RYBANDT • EDITOR
JOSH JOHNSON • CREATIVE DIRECTOR
RICH YOUNG • DIRECTOR BUSINESS DEVELOPMENT
JASON ULLMEYER • SENIOR DESIGNER
JOSH GREEN • TRAFFIC COORDINATOR
CHRIS CANIANO • PRODUCTION ASSISTANT

ISBN10: 1-60690-223-7 ISBN13: 978-1-60690-223-3

10 9 8 7 6 5 4 3 2 1

TOTAL RECALL ™ VOLUME ONE: LIFE ON MARS. First printing. Contains materials originally published in Total Recall #1-4. Published by Dynamite Entertainment. 155 Ninth Ave. Suite B, Runnemede, NJ 08078.

For media rights, foreign rights, promotions, licensing, and advertising: marketing@dynamite.net

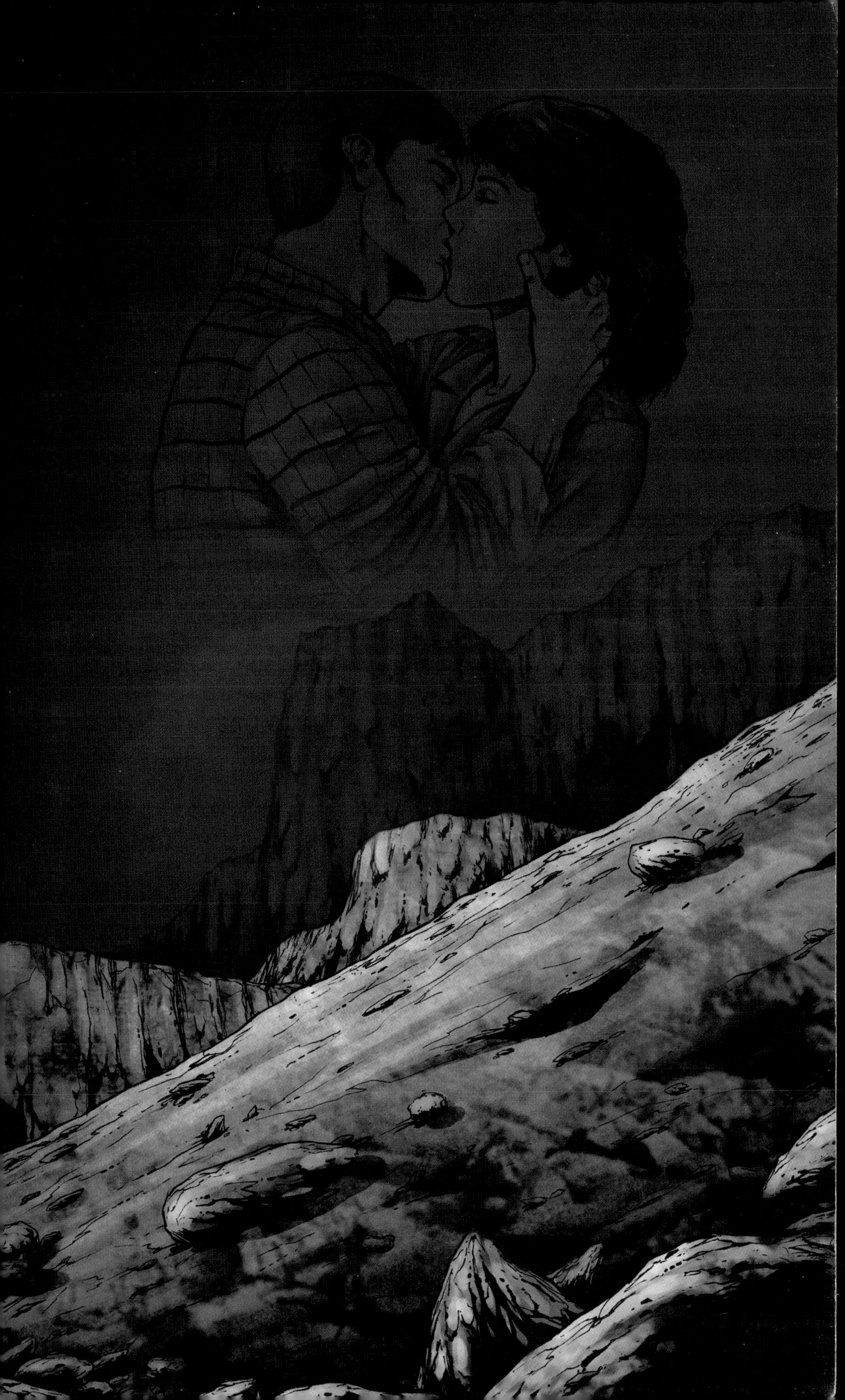

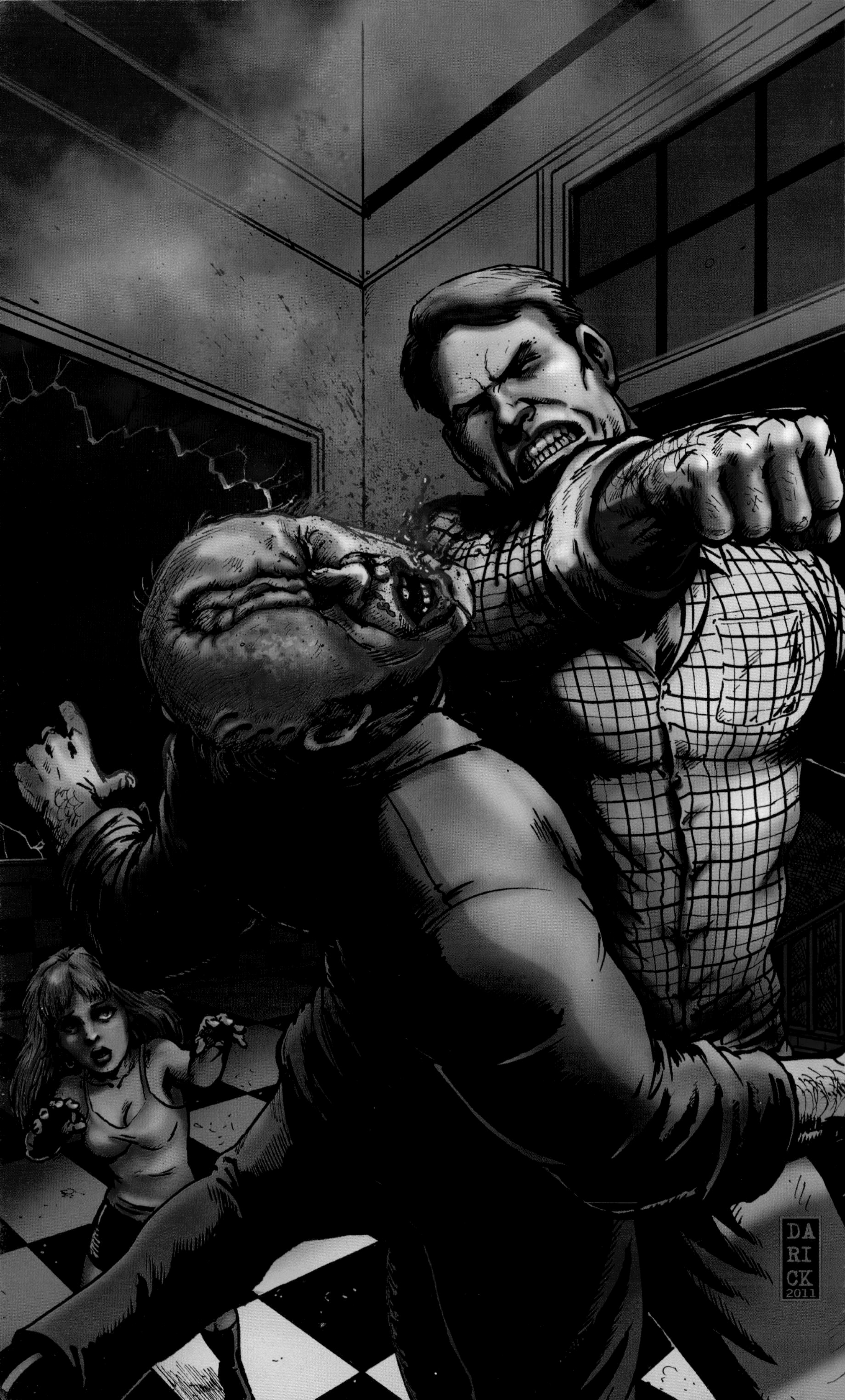
DA
RI
CK
2011

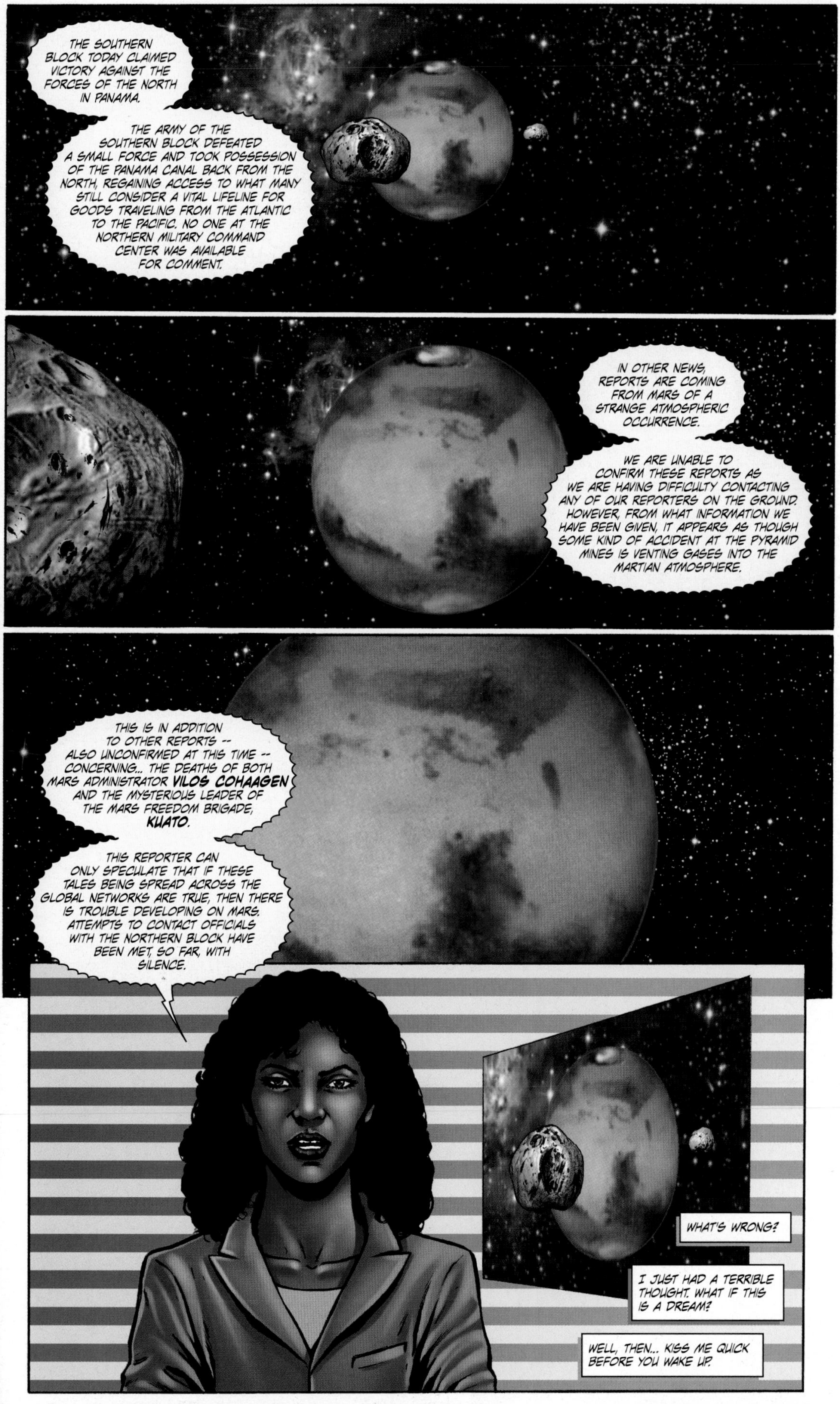
THE SOUTHERN BLOCK TODAY CLAIMED VICTORY AGAINST THE FORCES OF THE NORTH IN PANAMA.
THE ARMY OF THE SOUTHERN BLOCK DEFEATED A SMALL FORCE AND TOOK POSSESSION OF THE PANAMA CANAL BACK FROM THE NORTH, REGAINING ACCESS TO WHAT MANY STILL CONSIDER A VITAL LIFELINE FOR GOODS TRAVELING FROM THE ATLANTIC TO THE PACIFIC. NO ONE AT THE NORTHERN MILITARY COMMAND CENTER WAS AVAILABLE FOR COMMENT.
IN OTHER NEWS, REPORTS ARE COMING FROM MARS OF A STRANGE ATMOSPHERIC OCCURRENCE.
WE ARE UNABLE TO CONFIRM THESE REPORTS AS WE ARE HAVING DIFFICULTY CONTACTING ANY OF OUR REPORTERS ON THE GROUND. HOWEVER, FROM WHAT INFORMATION WE HAVE BEEN GIVEN, IT APPEARS AS THOUGH SOME KIND OF ACCIDENT AT THE PYRAMID MINES IS VENTING GASES INTO THE MARTIAN ATMOSPHERE.
THIS IS IN ADDITION TO OTHER REPORTS -- ALSO UNCONFIRMED AT THIS TIME -- CONCERNING... THE DEATHS OF BOTH MARS ADMINISTRATOR **VILOS COHAAGEN** AND THE MYSTERIOUS LEADER OF THE MARS FREEDOM BRIGADE, **KUATO**.
THIS REPORTER CAN ONLY SPECULATE THAT IF THESE TALES BEING SPREAD ACROSS THE GLOBAL NETWORKS ARE TRUE, THEN THERE IS TROUBLE DEVELOPING ON MARS. ATTEMPTS TO CONTACT OFFICIALS WITH THE NORTHERN BLOCK HAVE BEEN MET, SO FAR, WITH SILENCE.
WHAT'S WRONG?
I JUST HAD A TERRIBLE THOUGHT. WHAT IF THIS IS A DREAM?
WELL, THEN... KISS ME QUICK BEFORE YOU WAKE UP.

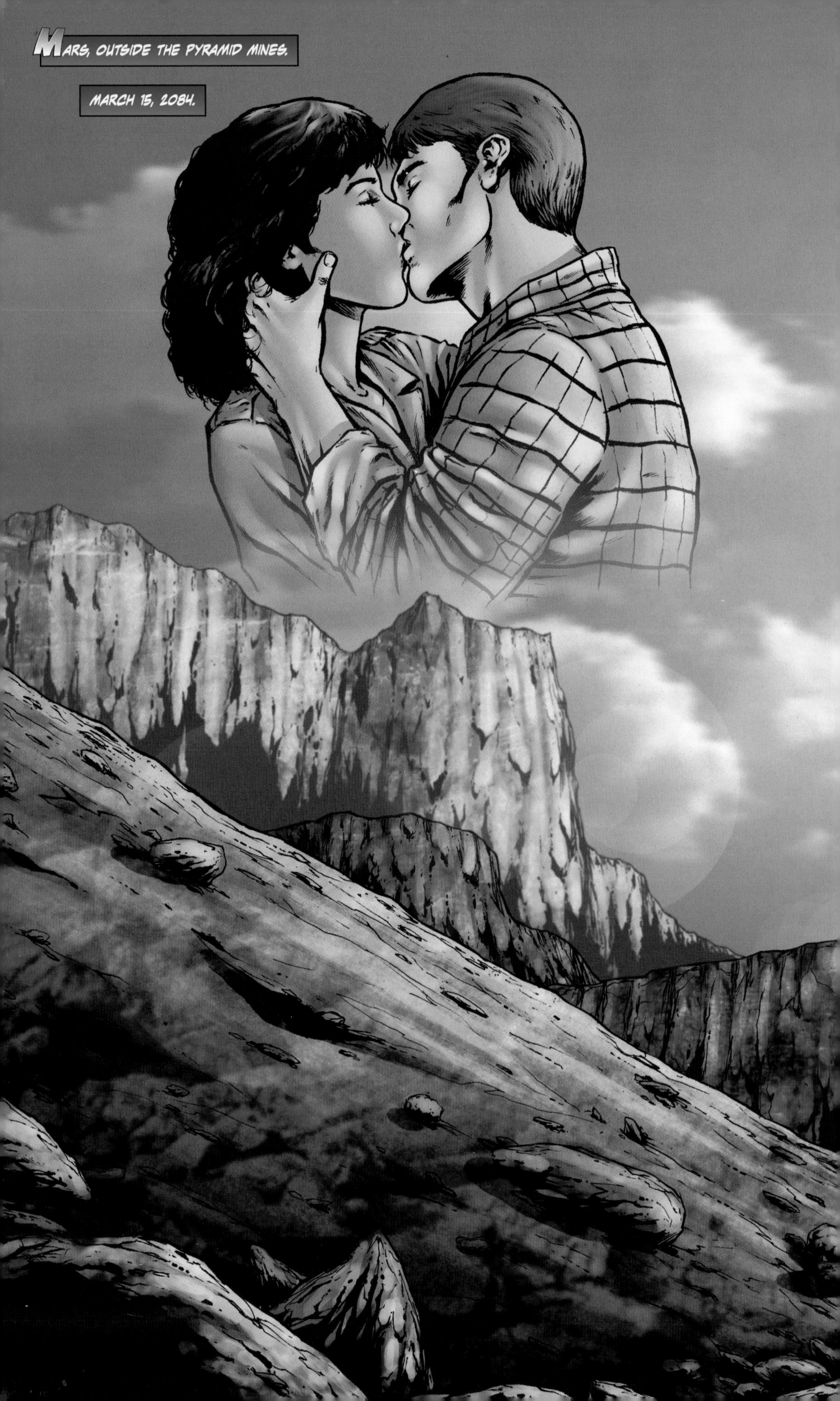
MARS, OUTSIDE THE PYRAMID MINES.
MARCH 15, 2084.

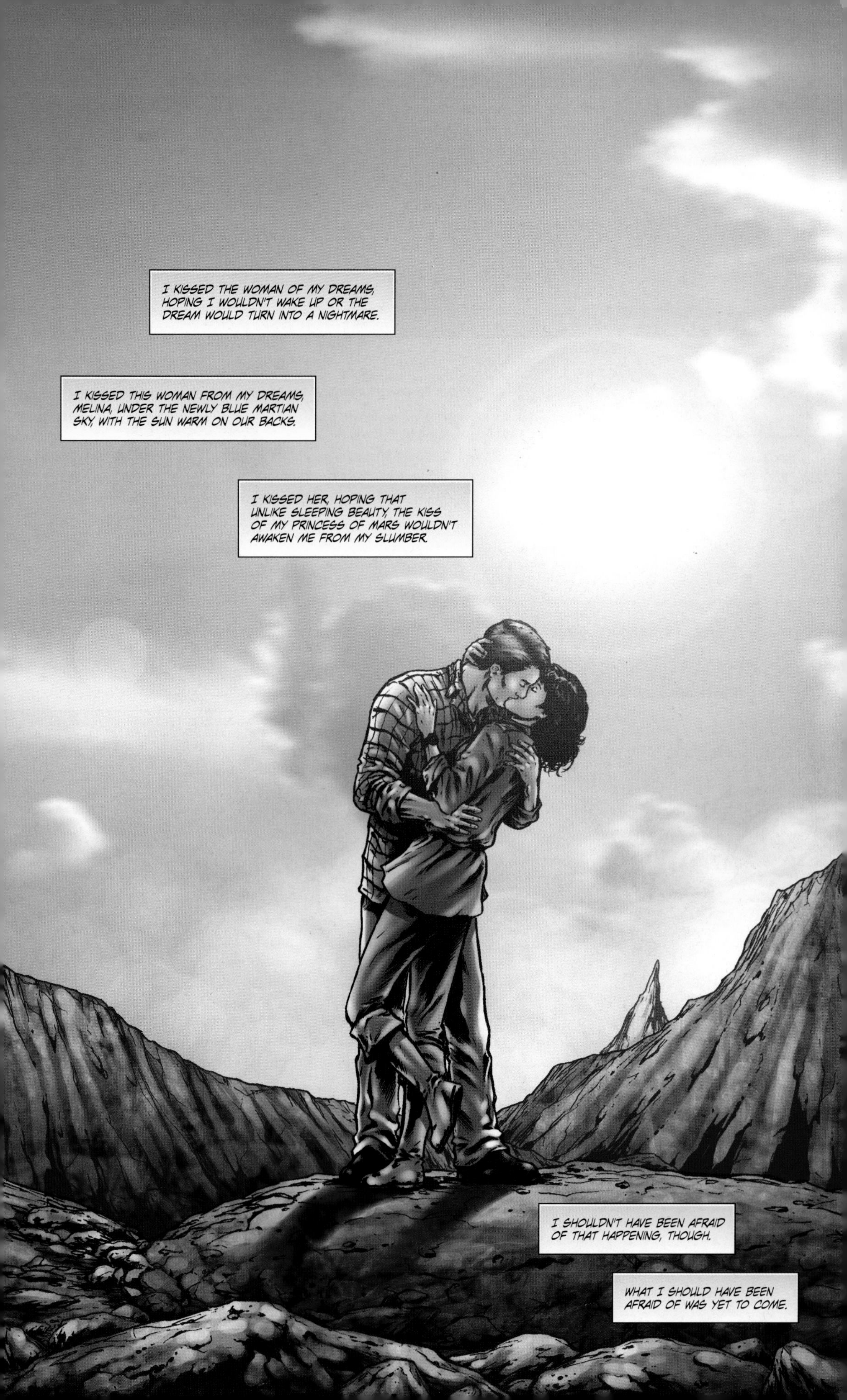
I KISSED THE WOMAN OF MY DREAMS, HOPING I WOULDN'T WAKE UP OR THE DREAM WOULD TURN INTO A NIGHTMARE.
I KISSED THIS WOMAN FROM MY DREAMS, MELINA, UNDER THE NEWLY BLUE MARTIAN SKY, WITH THE SUN WARM ON OUR BACKS.
I KISSED HER, HOPING THAT UNLIKE SLEEPING BEAUTY, THE KISS OF MY PRINCESS OF MARS WOULDN'T AWAKEN ME FROM MY SLUMBER.
I SHOULDN'T HAVE BEEN AFRAID OF THAT HAPPENING, THOUGH.
WHAT I SHOULD HAVE BEEN AFRAID OF WAS YET TO COME.

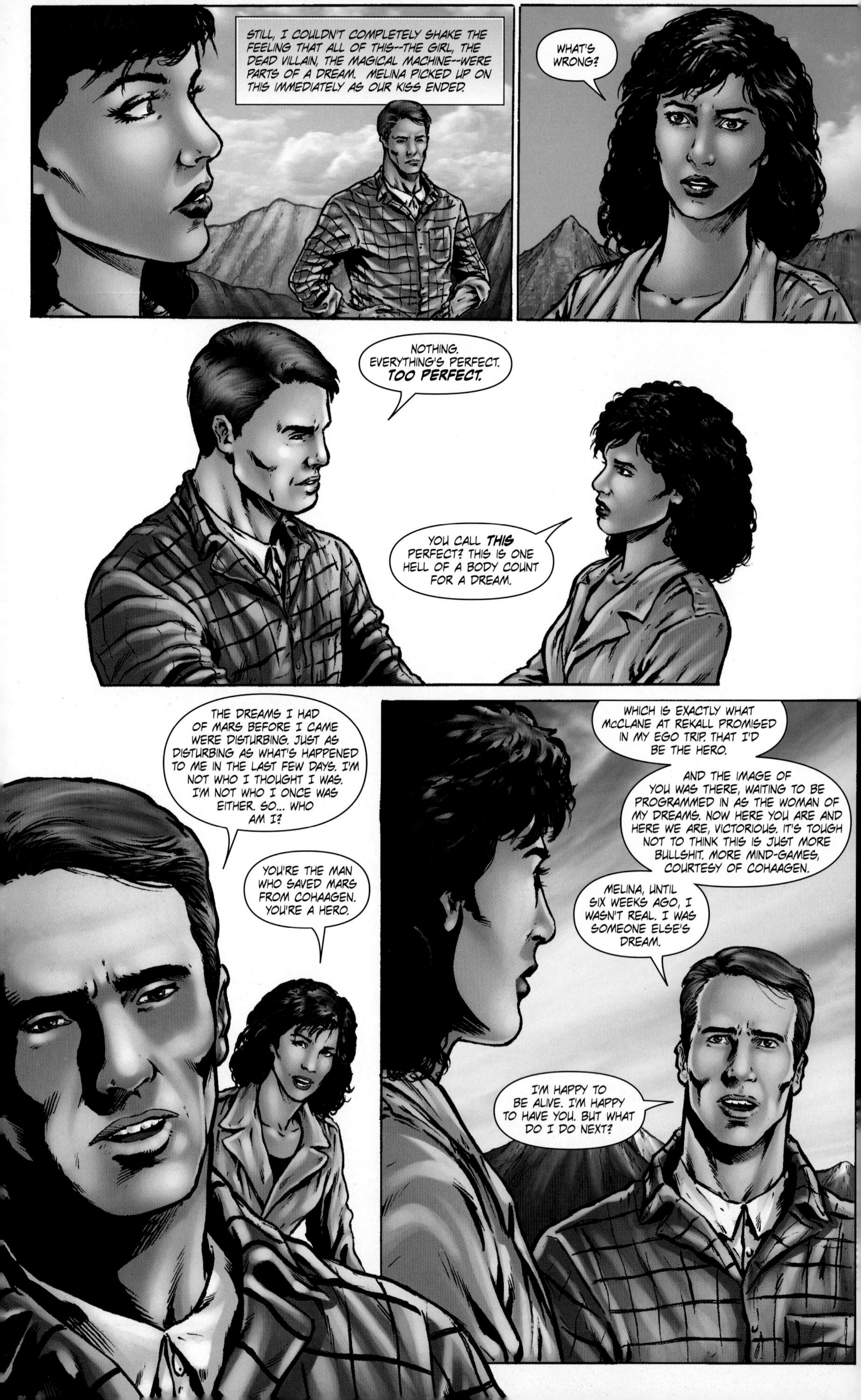
STILL, I COULDN'T COMPLETELY SHAKE THE FEELING THAT ALL OF THIS--THE GIRL, THE DEAD VILLAIN, THE MAGICAL MACHINE--WERE PARTS OF A DREAM. MELINA PICKED UP ON THIS IMMEDIATELY AS OUR KISS ENDED.
WHAT'S WRONG?
NOTHING. EVERYTHING'S PERFECT. TOO PERFECT.
YOU CALL THIS PERFECT? THIS IS ONE HELL OF A BODY COUNT FOR A DREAM.
THE DREAMS I HAD OF MARS BEFORE I CAME WERE DISTURBING. JUST AS DISTURBING AS WHAT'S HAPPENED TO ME IN THE LAST FEW DAYS. I'M NOT WHO I THOUGHT I WAS. I'M NOT WHO I ONCE WAS EITHER. SO... WHO AM I?
YOU'RE THE MAN WHO SAVED MARS FROM COHAAGEN. YOU'RE A HERO.
WHICH IS EXACTLY WHAT McCLANE AT REKALL PROMISED IN MY EGO TRIP. THAT I'D BE THE HERO.
AND THE IMAGE OF YOU WAS THERE, WAITING TO BE PROGRAMMED IN AS THE WOMAN OF MY DREAMS. NOW HERE YOU ARE AND HERE WE ARE, VICTORIOUS. IT'S TOUGH NOT TO THINK THIS IS JUST MORE BULLSHIT. MORE MIND-GAMES, COURTESY OF COHAAGEN.
MELINA, UNTIL SIX WEEKS AGO, I WASN'T REAL. I WAS SOMEONE ELSE'S DREAM.
I'M HAPPY TO BE ALIVE. I'M HAPPY TO HAVE YOU. BUT WHAT DO I DO NEXT?

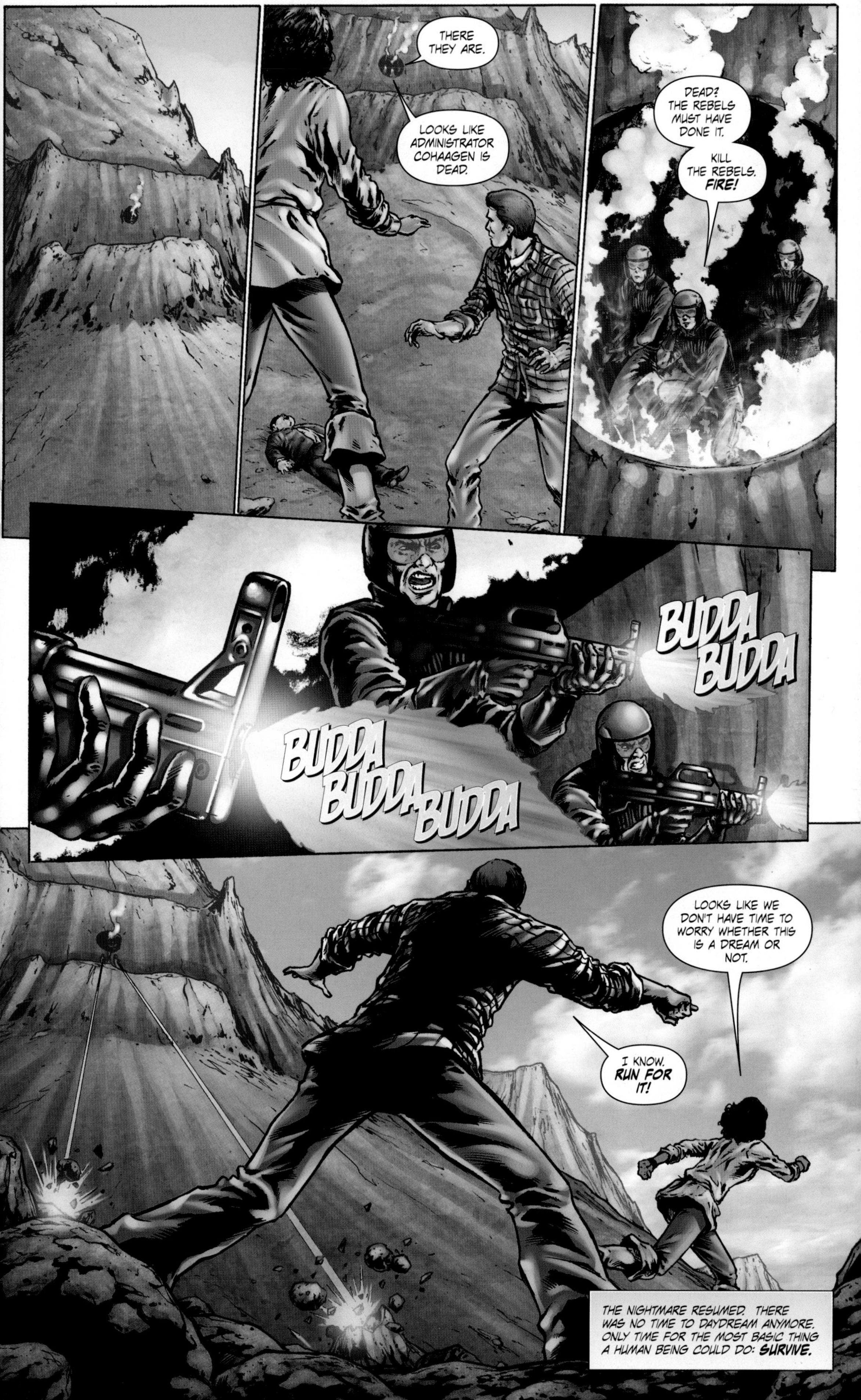
THERE THEY ARE.
LOOKS LIKE ADMINISTRATOR COHAAGEN IS DEAD.
DEAD? THE REBELS MUST HAVE DONE IT.
KILL THE REBELS. **FIRE!**
BUDDA BUDDA
BUDDA BUDDA BUDDA
LOOKS LIKE WE DON'T HAVE TIME TO WORRY WHETHER THIS IS A DREAM OR NOT.
I KNOW. **RUN FOR IT!**
THE NIGHTMARE RESUMED. THERE WAS NO TIME TO DAYDREAM ANYMORE. ONLY TIME FOR THE MOST BASIC THING A HUMAN BEING COULD DO: **SURVIVE.**

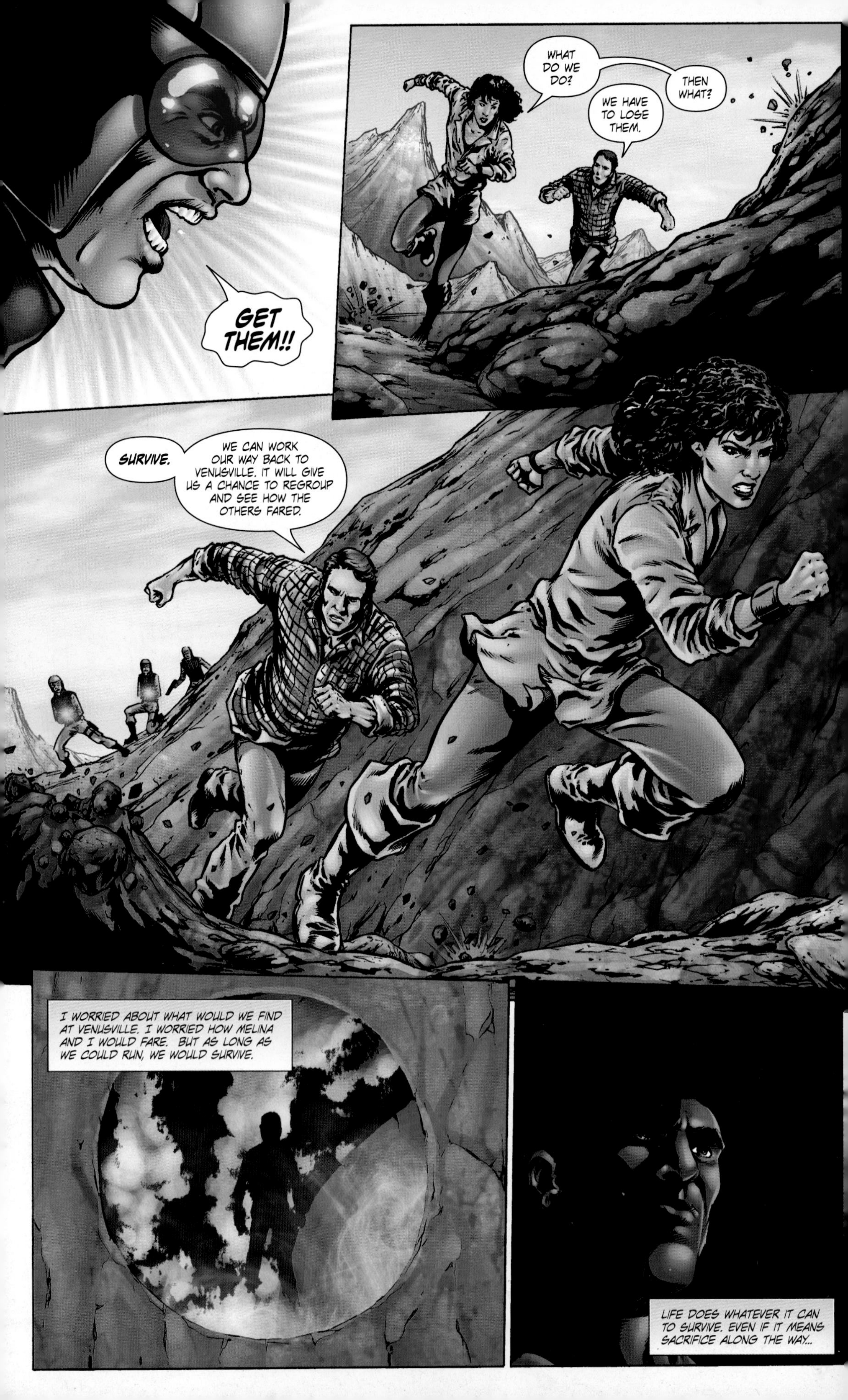
GET THEM!!
WHAT DO WE DO?
WE HAVE TO LOSE THEM.
THEN WHAT?
SURVIVE.
WE CAN WORK OUR WAY BACK TO VENUSVILLE. IT WILL GIVE US A CHANCE TO REGROUP AND SEE HOW THE OTHERS FARED.
I WORRIED ABOUT WHAT WOULD WE FIND AT VENUSVILLE. I WORRIED HOW MELINA AND I WOULD FARE. BUT AS LONG AS WE COULD RUN, WE WOULD SURVIVE.
LIFE DOES WHATEVER IT CAN TO SURVIVE. EVEN IF IT MEANS SACRIFICE ALONG THE WAY...

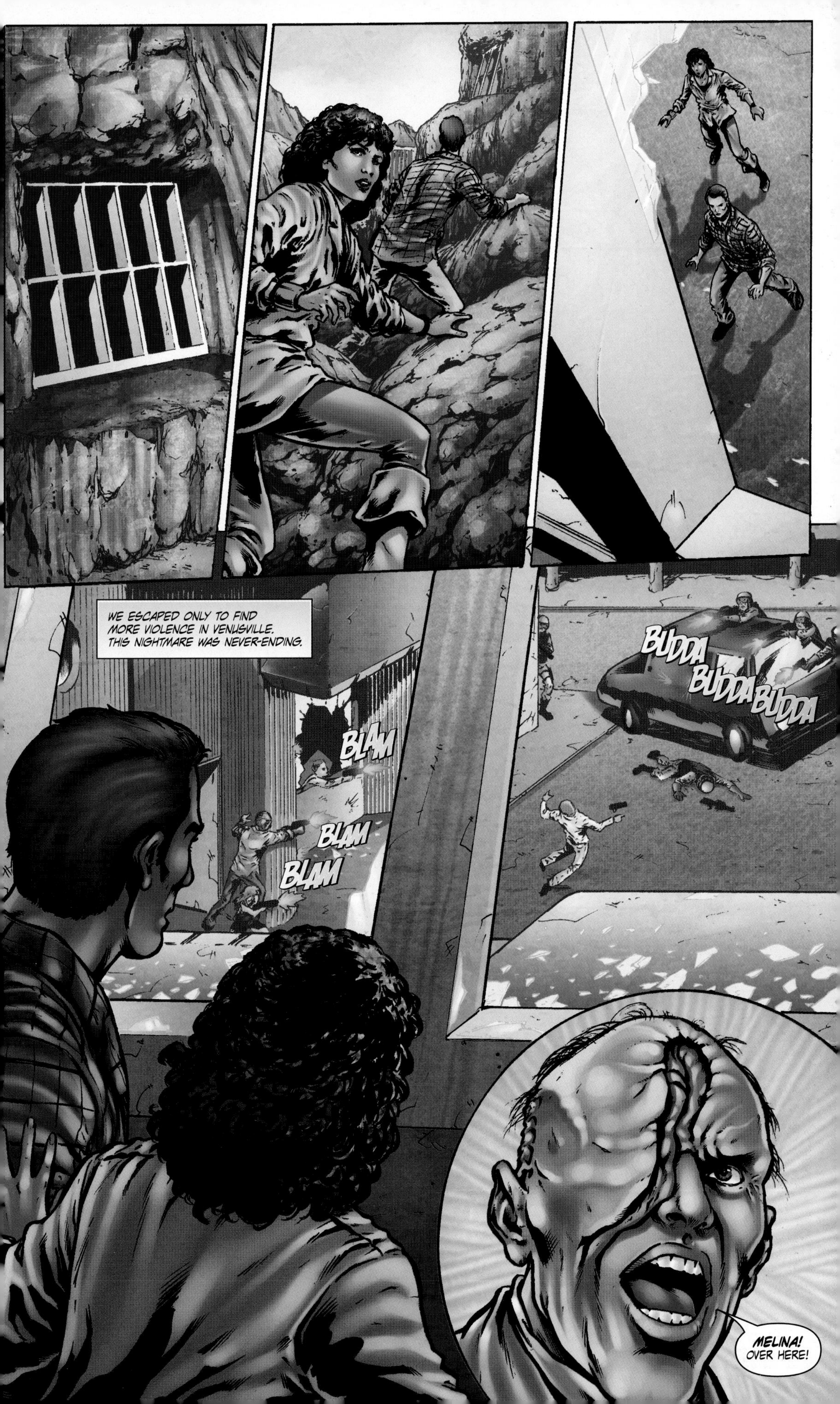

WE ESCAPED ONLY TO FIND MORE VIOLENCE IN VENUSVILLE. THIS NIGHTMARE WAS NEVER-ENDING.
BLAM
BLAM
BLAM
BUDDA
BUDDA
BUDDA
MELINA! OVER HERE!

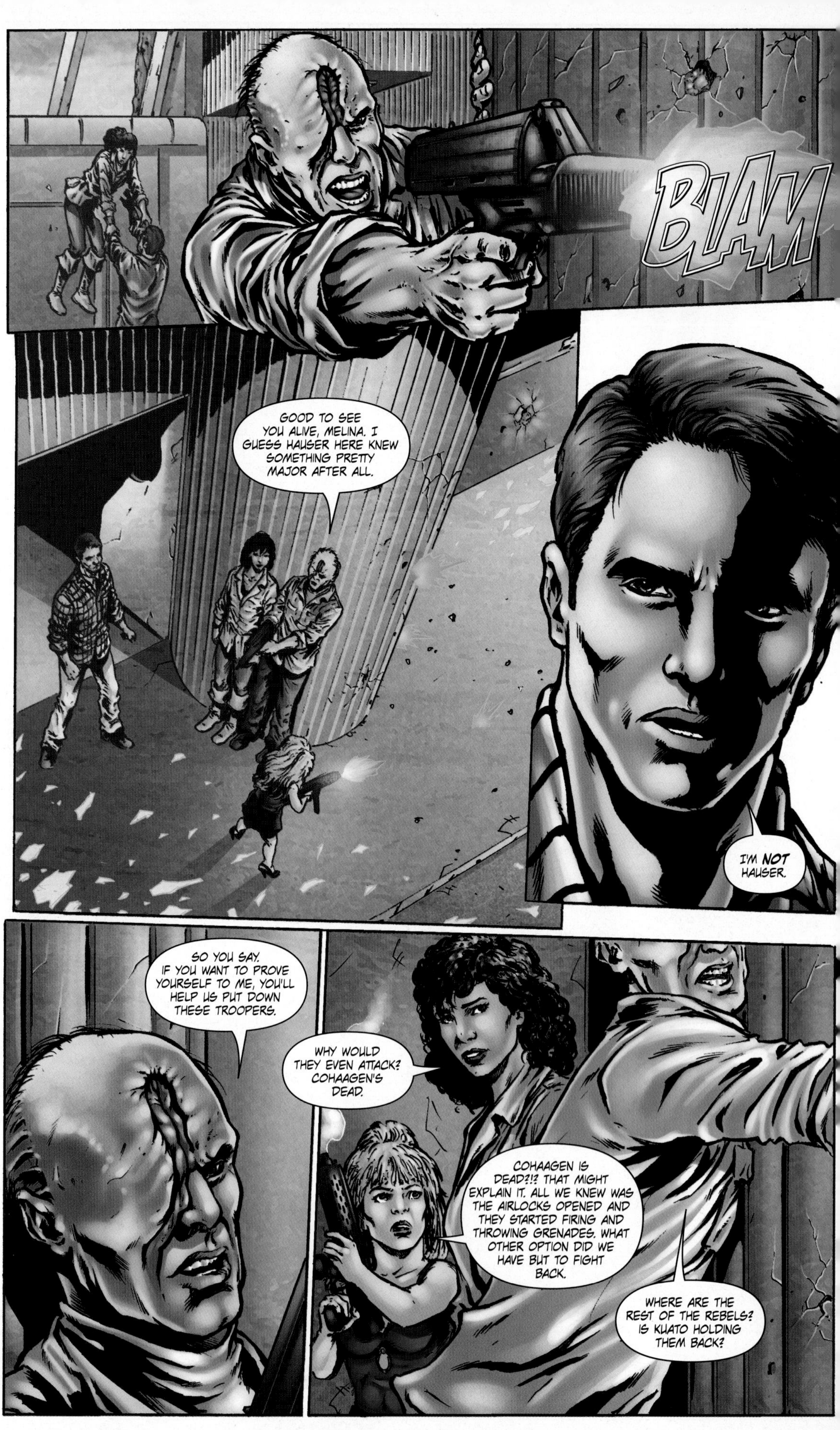
BLAM
GOOD TO SEE YOU ALIVE, MELINA. I GUESS HAUSER HERE KNEW SOMETHING PRETTY MAJOR AFTER ALL.
I'M **NOT** HAUSER.
SO YOU SAY. IF YOU WANT TO PROVE YOURSELF TO ME, YOU'LL HELP US PUT DOWN THESE TROOPERS.
WHY WOULD THEY EVEN ATTACK? COHAAGEN'S DEAD.
COHAAGEN IS DEAD?!? THAT MIGHT EXPLAIN IT. ALL WE KNEW WAS THE AIRLOCKS OPENED AND THEY STARTED FIRING AND THROWING GRENADES. WHAT OTHER OPTION DID WE HAVE BUT TO FIGHT BACK.
WHERE ARE THE REST OF THE REBELS? IS KUATO HOLDING THEM BACK?

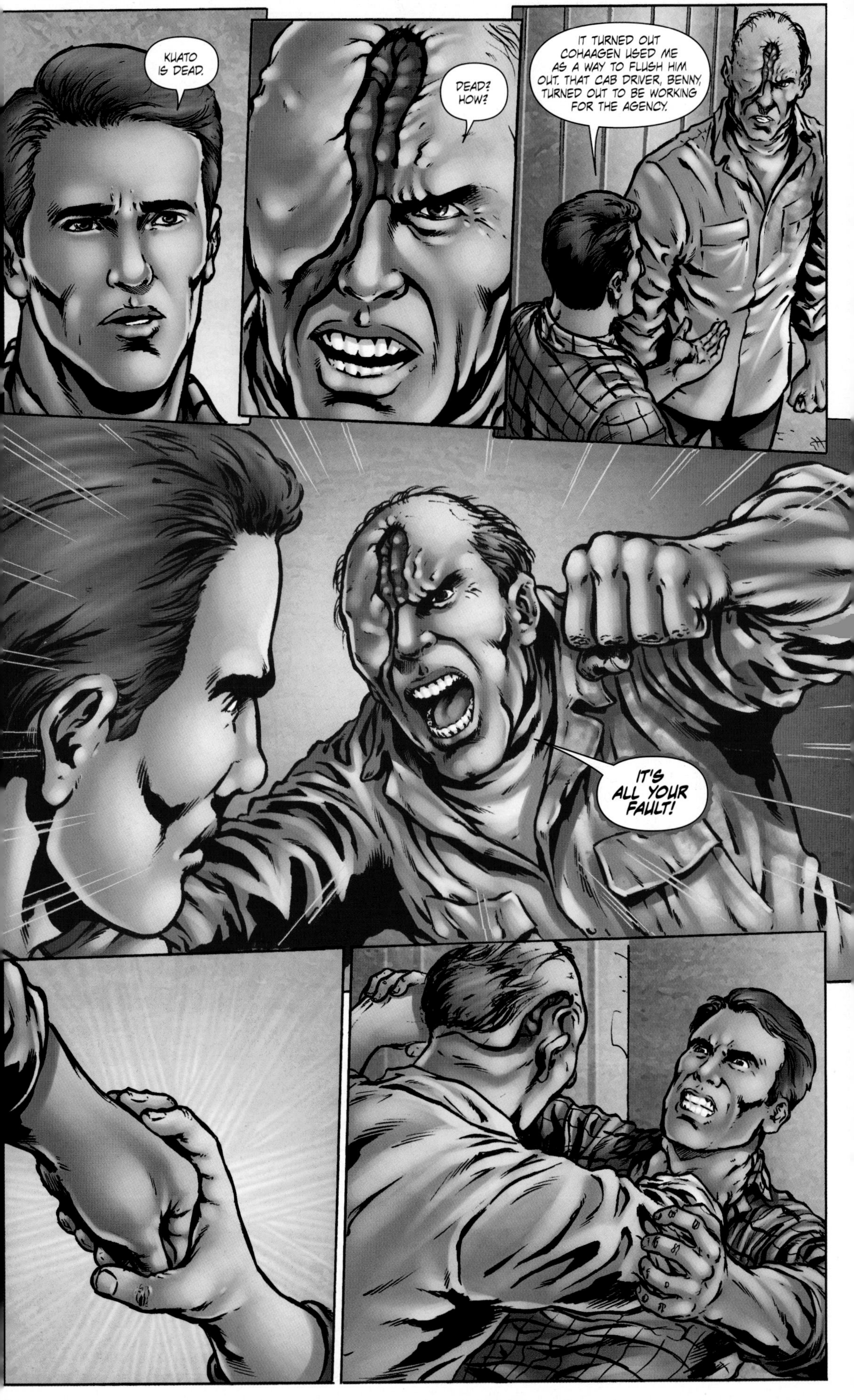
KUATO IS DEAD.
DEAD? HOW?
IT TURNED OUT COHAAGEN USED ME AS A WAY TO FLUSH HIM OUT. THAT CAB DRIVER, BENNY, TURNED OUT TO BE WORKING FOR THE AGENCY.
IT'S ALL YOUR FAULT!

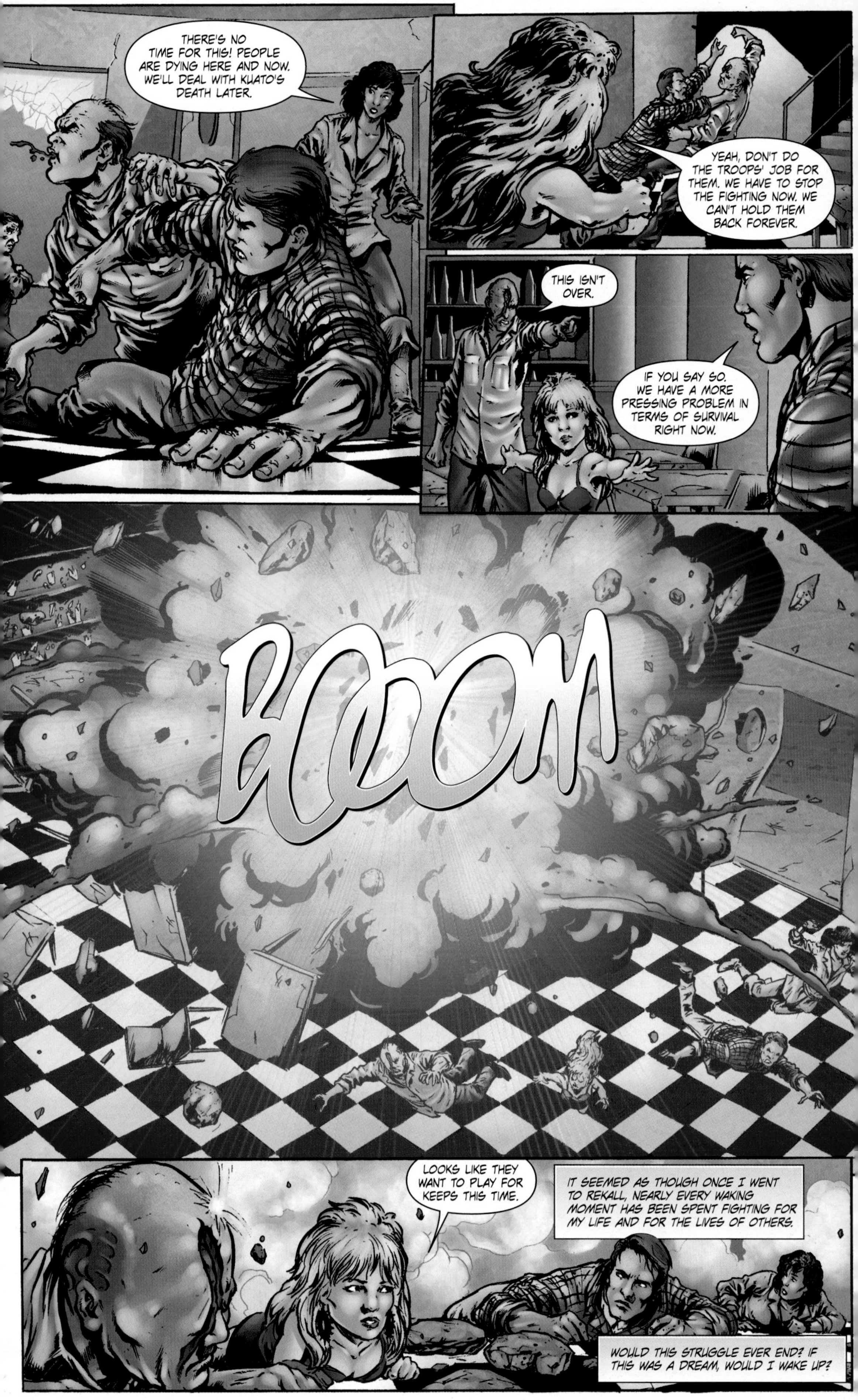
THERE'S NO TIME FOR THIS! PEOPLE ARE DYING HERE AND NOW. WE'LL DEAL WITH KUATO'S DEATH LATER.
YEAH, DON'T DO THE TROOPS' JOB FOR THEM. WE HAVE TO STOP THE FIGHTING NOW. WE CAN'T HOLD THEM BACK FOREVER.
THIS ISN'T OVER.
IF YOU SAY SO. WE HAVE A MORE PRESSING PROBLEM IN TERMS OF SURVIVAL RIGHT NOW.
BOOOM
LOOKS LIKE THEY WANT TO PLAY FOR KEEPS THIS TIME.
IT SEEMED AS THOUGH ONCE I WENT TO REKALL, NEARLY EVERY WAKING MOMENT HAS BEEN SPENT FIGHTING FOR MY LIFE AND FOR THE LIVES OF OTHERS.
WOULD THIS STRUGGLE EVER END? IF THIS WAS A DREAM, WOULD I WAKE UP?

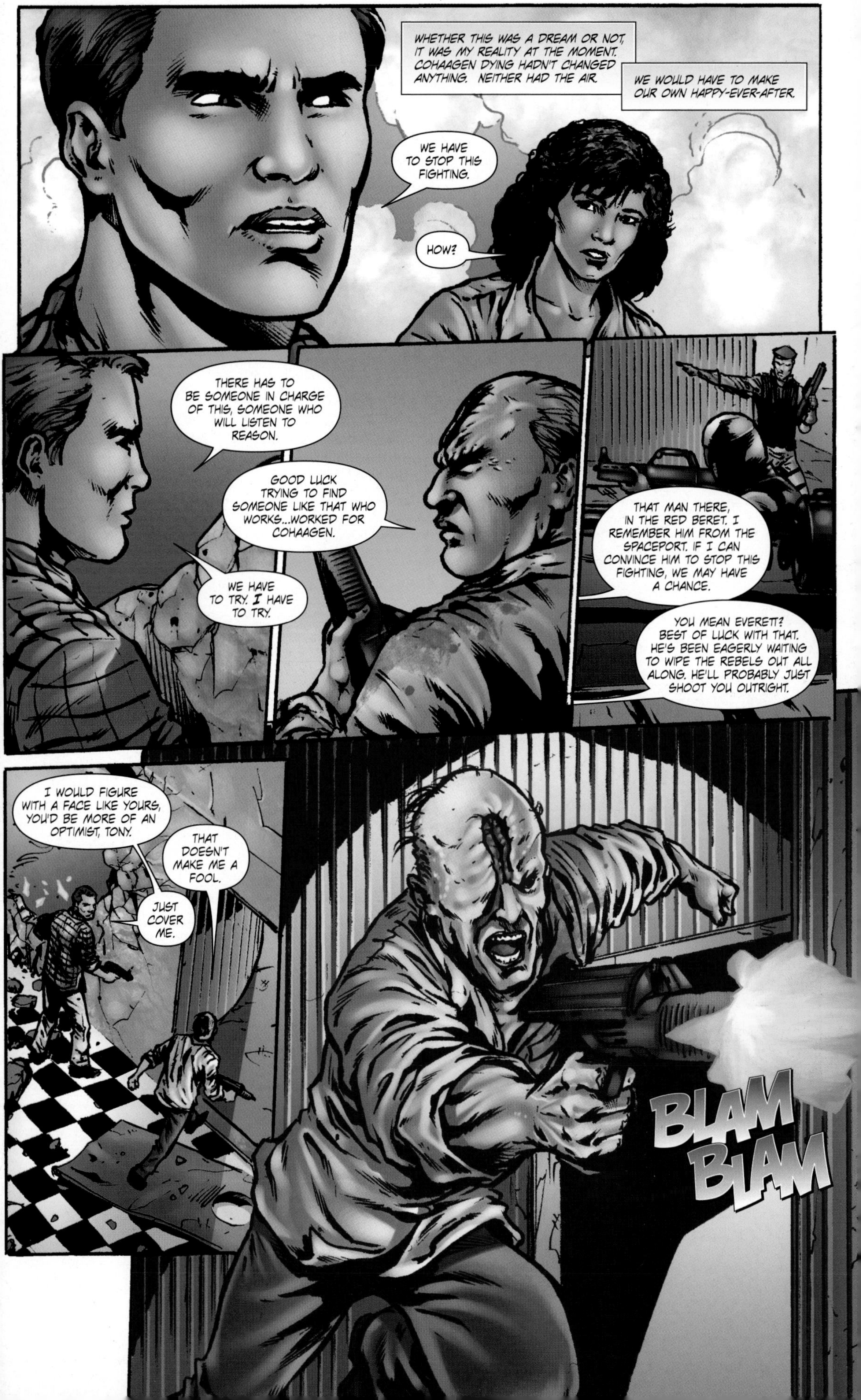
WHETHER THIS WAS A DREAM OR NOT, IT WAS MY REALITY AT THE MOMENT. COHAAGEN DYING HADN'T CHANGED ANYTHING. NEITHER HAD THE AIR.
WE WOULD HAVE TO MAKE OUR OWN HAPPY-EVER-AFTER.
WE HAVE TO STOP THIS FIGHTING.
HOW?
THERE HAS TO BE SOMEONE IN CHARGE OF THIS, SOMEONE WHO WILL LISTEN TO REASON.
GOOD LUCK TRYING TO FIND SOMEONE LIKE THAT WHO WORKS...WORKED FOR COHAAGEN.
WE HAVE TO TRY. I HAVE TO TRY.
THAT MAN THERE, IN THE RED BERET. I REMEMBER HIM FROM THE SPACEPORT. IF I CAN CONVINCE HIM TO STOP THIS FIGHTING, WE MAY HAVE A CHANCE.
YOU MEAN EVERETT? BEST OF LUCK WITH THAT. HE'S BEEN EAGERLY WAITING TO WIPE THE REBELS OUT ALL ALONG. HE'LL PROBABLY JUST SHOOT YOU OUTRIGHT.
I WOULD FIGURE WITH A FACE LIKE YOURS, YOU'D BE MORE OF AN OPTIMIST, TONY.
THAT DOESN'T MAKE ME A FOOL.
JUST COVER ME.
BLAM BLAM

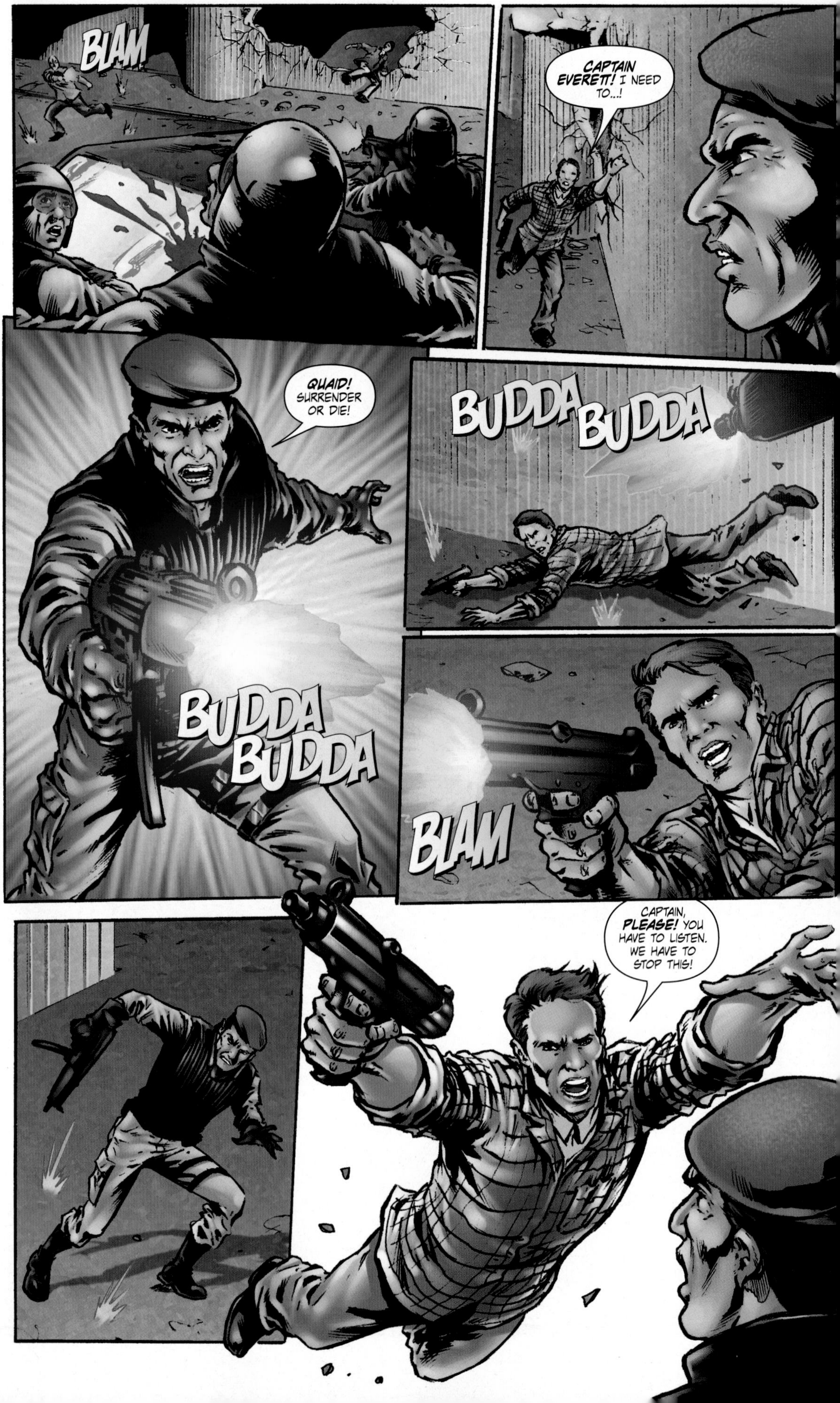
BLAM
CAPTAIN EVERETT! I NEED TO...!
QUAID! SURRENDER OR DIE!
BUDDA BUDDA
BUDDA BUDDA
BLAM
CAPTAIN, PLEASE! YOU HAVE TO LISTEN. WE HAVE TO STOP THIS!

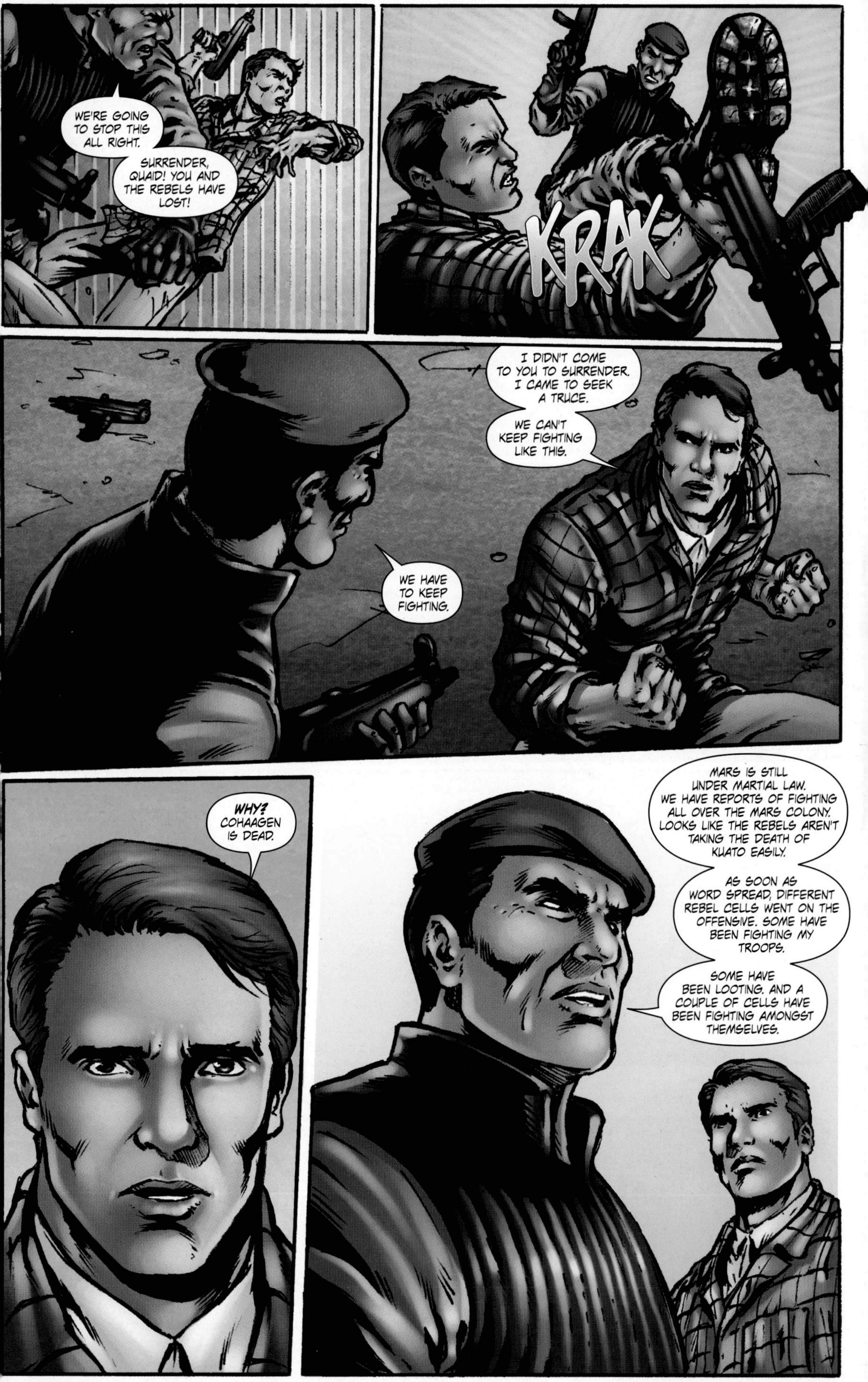
WE'RE GOING TO STOP THIS ALL RIGHT.
SURRENDER, QUAID! YOU AND THE REBELS HAVE LOST!
KRAK
I DIDN'T COME TO YOU TO SURRENDER. I CAME TO SEEK A TRUCE.
WE CAN'T KEEP FIGHTING LIKE THIS.
WE HAVE TO KEEP FIGHTING.
WHY? COHAAGEN IS DEAD.
MARS IS STILL UNDER MARTIAL LAW. WE HAVE REPORTS OF FIGHTING ALL OVER THE MARS COLONY. LOOKS LIKE THE REBELS AREN'T TAKING THE DEATH OF KUATO EASILY.
AS SOON AS WORD SPREAD, DIFFERENT REBEL CELLS WENT ON THE OFFENSIVE. SOME HAVE BEEN FIGHTING MY TROOPS.
SOME HAVE BEEN LOOTING. AND A COUPLE OF CELLS HAVE BEEN FIGHTING AMONGST THEMSELVES.

KUATO MUST HAVE BEEN KEEPING THE DIFFERING VOICES OF THE REBELLION IN CHECK.

EXACTLY, AND WITHOUT THAT STRONG LEADER, ALL HELL HAS BROKEN LOOSE.

BUT WHAT ABOUT YOUR SIDE?

ABOUT THE SAME. A FEW SOLDIERS ARE AFRAID OF BEING ON THE LOSING SIDE, SO THEY ARE EITHER TRYING TO JOIN THE REBELS TO SAVE THEIR OWN SKINS, OR PLANNING ON GOING DOWN FIGHTING. LEADING TO MORE FIGHTING. IT'S A MESS.

AT LEAST MARS HAS AIR. THAT SHOULD SOLVE SOME PROBLEMS.

CREATE MORE PROBLEMS THAN IT SOLVES MORE LIKELY.

BUT WE SHOULD STILL TRY TO STOP THE FIGHTING. ORDINARY PEOPLE ARE GETTING HURT IN ALL OF THE CHAOS.

THINK ABOUT IT. WE'RE ALL ON THE SAME PLANET. WE SHOULD WORK TOGETHER TO BRING PEACE.

WHAT KIND OF GUARANTEES CAN YOU GIVE ME?

ALL I CAN PROMISE IS THAT IF YOUR TROOPS STOP FIGHTING, I WILL CONVINCE THE REBELS TO DO THE SAME. THEN WE CAN WORK TOGETHER TO PICK UP THE PIECES.

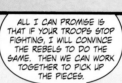

I'M RELUCTANT TO TRUST THE REBELS, BUT IT COULD WORK. AT LEAST UNTIL THE NEW ADMINISTRATORS ARRIVE.

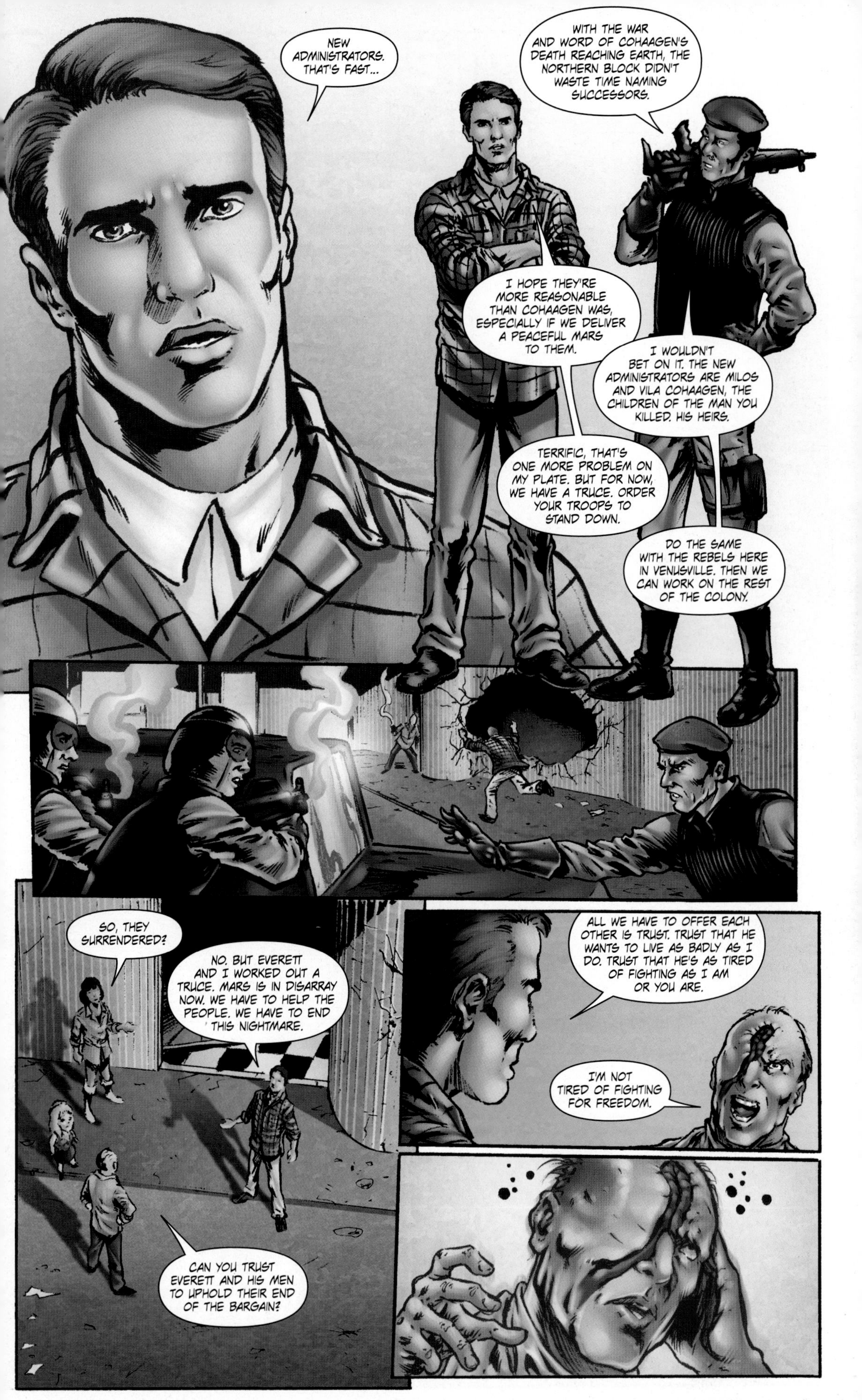
NEW ADMINISTRATORS. THAT'S FAST...
WITH THE WAR AND WORD OF COHAAGEN'S DEATH REACHING EARTH, THE NORTHERN BLOCK DIDN'T WASTE TIME NAMING SUCCESSORS.
I HOPE THEY'RE MORE REASONABLE THAN COHAAGEN WAS, ESPECIALLY IF WE DELIVER A PEACEFUL MARS TO THEM.
I WOULDN'T BET ON IT. THE NEW ADMINISTRATORS ARE MILOS AND VILA COHAAGEN, THE CHILDREN OF THE MAN YOU KILLED. HIS HEIRS.
TERRIFIC, THAT'S ONE MORE PROBLEM ON MY PLATE. BUT FOR NOW, WE HAVE A TRUCE. ORDER YOUR TROOPS TO STAND DOWN.
DO THE SAME WITH THE REBELS HERE IN VENUSVILLE. THEN WE CAN WORK ON THE REST OF THE COLONY.
SO, THEY SURRENDERED?
NO. BUT EVERETT AND I WORKED OUT A TRUCE. MARS IS IN DISARRAY NOW. WE HAVE TO HELP THE PEOPLE. WE HAVE TO END THIS NIGHTMARE.
CAN YOU TRUST EVERETT AND HIS MEN TO UPHOLD THEIR END OF THE BARGAIN?
ALL WE HAVE TO OFFER EACH OTHER IS TRUST. TRUST THAT HE WANTS TO LIVE AS BADLY AS I DO. TRUST THAT HE'S AS TIRED OF FIGHTING AS I AM OR YOU ARE.
I'M NOT TIRED OF FIGHTING FOR FREEDOM.

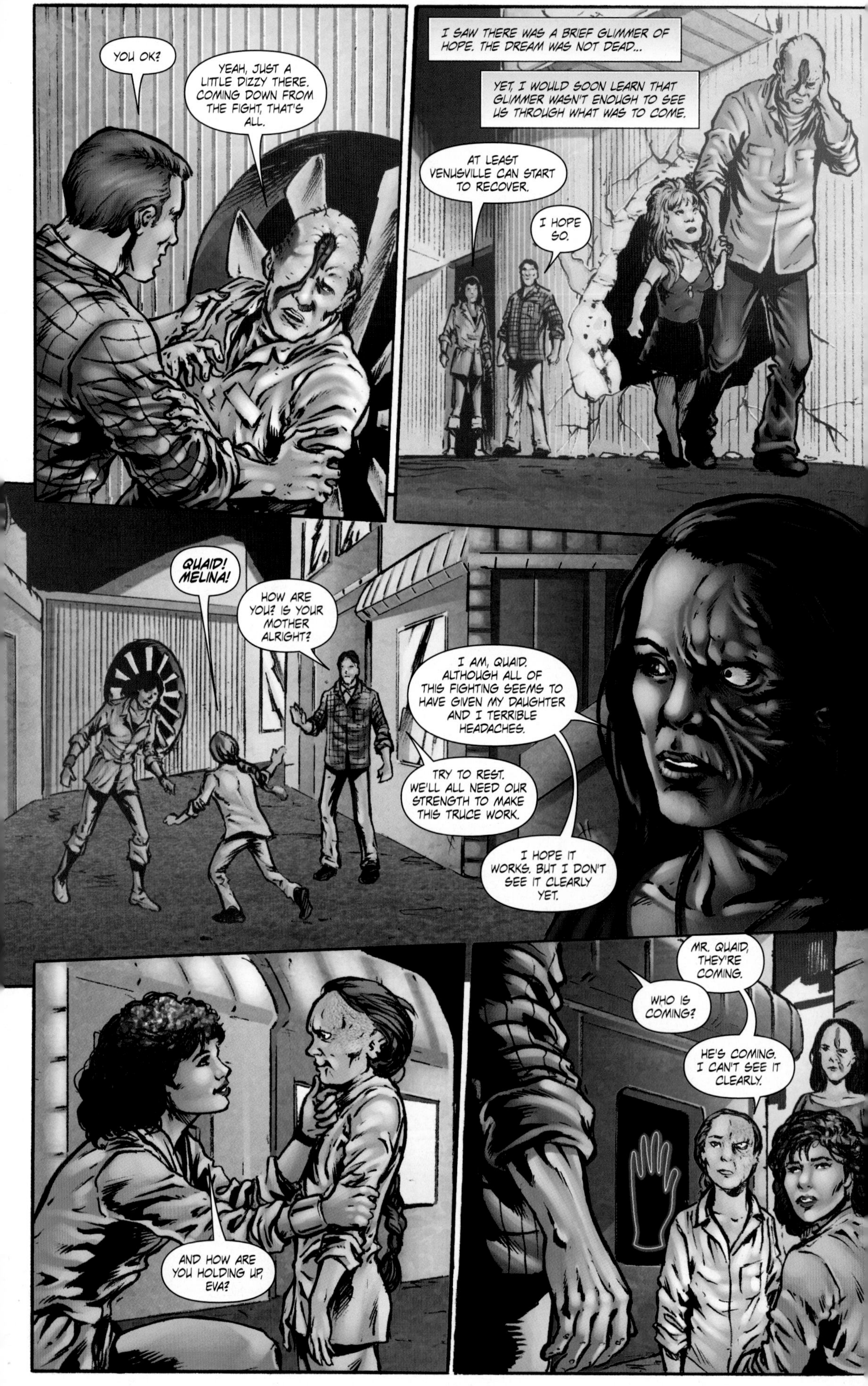
YOU OK?
YEAH, JUST A LITTLE DIZZY THERE. COMING DOWN FROM THE FIGHT, THAT'S ALL.
I SAW THERE WAS A BRIEF GLIMMER OF HOPE. THE DREAM WAS NOT DEAD...
YET, I WOULD SOON LEARN THAT GLIMMER WASN'T ENOUGH TO SEE US THROUGH WHAT WAS TO COME.
AT LEAST VENUSVILLE CAN START TO RECOVER.
I HOPE SO.
QUAID! MELINA!
HOW ARE YOU? IS YOUR MOTHER ALRIGHT?
I AM, QUAID. ALTHOUGH ALL OF THIS FIGHTING SEEMS TO HAVE GIVEN MY DAUGHTER AND I TERRIBLE HEADACHES.
TRY TO REST. WE'LL ALL NEED OUR STRENGTH TO MAKE THIS TRUCE WORK.
I HOPE IT WORKS. BUT I DON'T SEE IT CLEARLY YET.
AND HOW ARE YOU HOLDING UP, EVA?
MR. QUAID, THEY'RE COMING.
WHO IS COMING?
HE'S COMING. I CAN'T SEE IT CLEARLY.

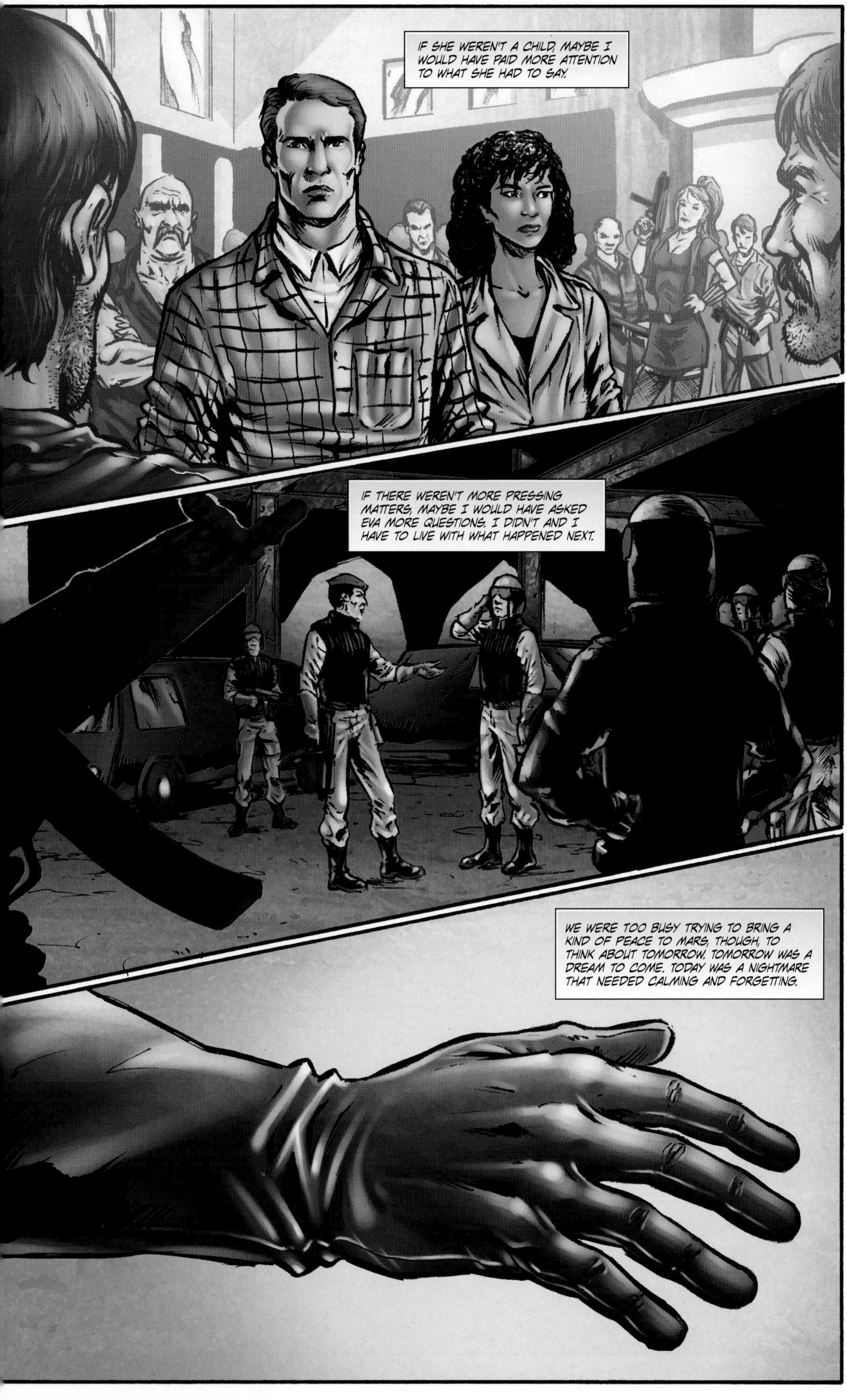
IF SHE WEREN'T A CHILD, MAYBE I WOULD HAVE PAID MORE ATTENTION TO WHAT SHE HAD TO SAY.
IF THERE WEREN'T MORE PRESSING MATTERS, MAYBE I WOULD HAVE ASKED EVA MORE QUESTIONS. I DIDN'T AND I HAVE TO LIVE WITH WHAT HAPPENED NEXT.
WE WERE TOO BUSY TRYING TO BRING A KIND OF PEACE TO MARS, THOUGH, TO THINK ABOUT TOMORROW. TOMORROW WAS A DREAM TO COME. TODAY WAS A NIGHTMARE THAT NEEDED CALMING AND FORGETTING.

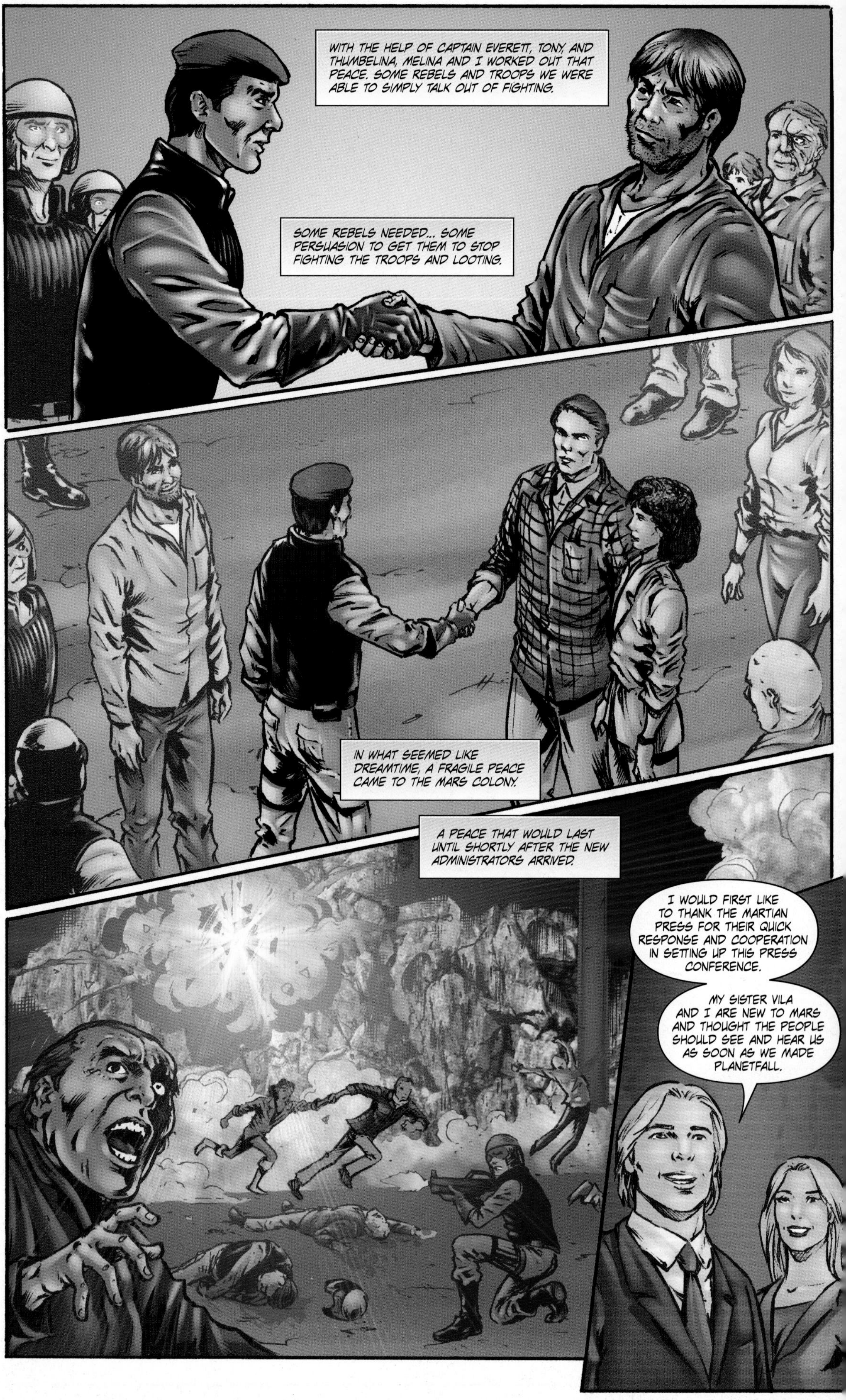
WITH THE HELP OF CAPTAIN EVERETT, TONY, AND THUMBELINA, MELINA AND I WORKED OUT THAT PEACE. SOME REBELS AND TROOPS WE WERE ABLE TO SIMPLY TALK OUT OF FIGHTING.
SOME REBELS NEEDED... SOME PERSUASION TO GET THEM TO STOP FIGHTING THE TROOPS AND LOOTING.
IN WHAT SEEMED LIKE DREAMTIME, A FRAGILE PEACE CAME TO THE MARS COLONY.
A PEACE THAT WOULD LAST UNTIL SHORTLY AFTER THE NEW ADMINISTRATORS ARRIVED.
I WOULD FIRST LIKE TO THANK THE MARTIAN PRESS FOR THEIR QUICK RESPONSE AND COOPERATION IN SETTING UP THIS PRESS CONFERENCE.
MY SISTER VILA AND I ARE NEW TO MARS AND THOUGHT THE PEOPLE SHOULD SEE AND HEAR US AS SOON AS WE MADE PLANETFALL.

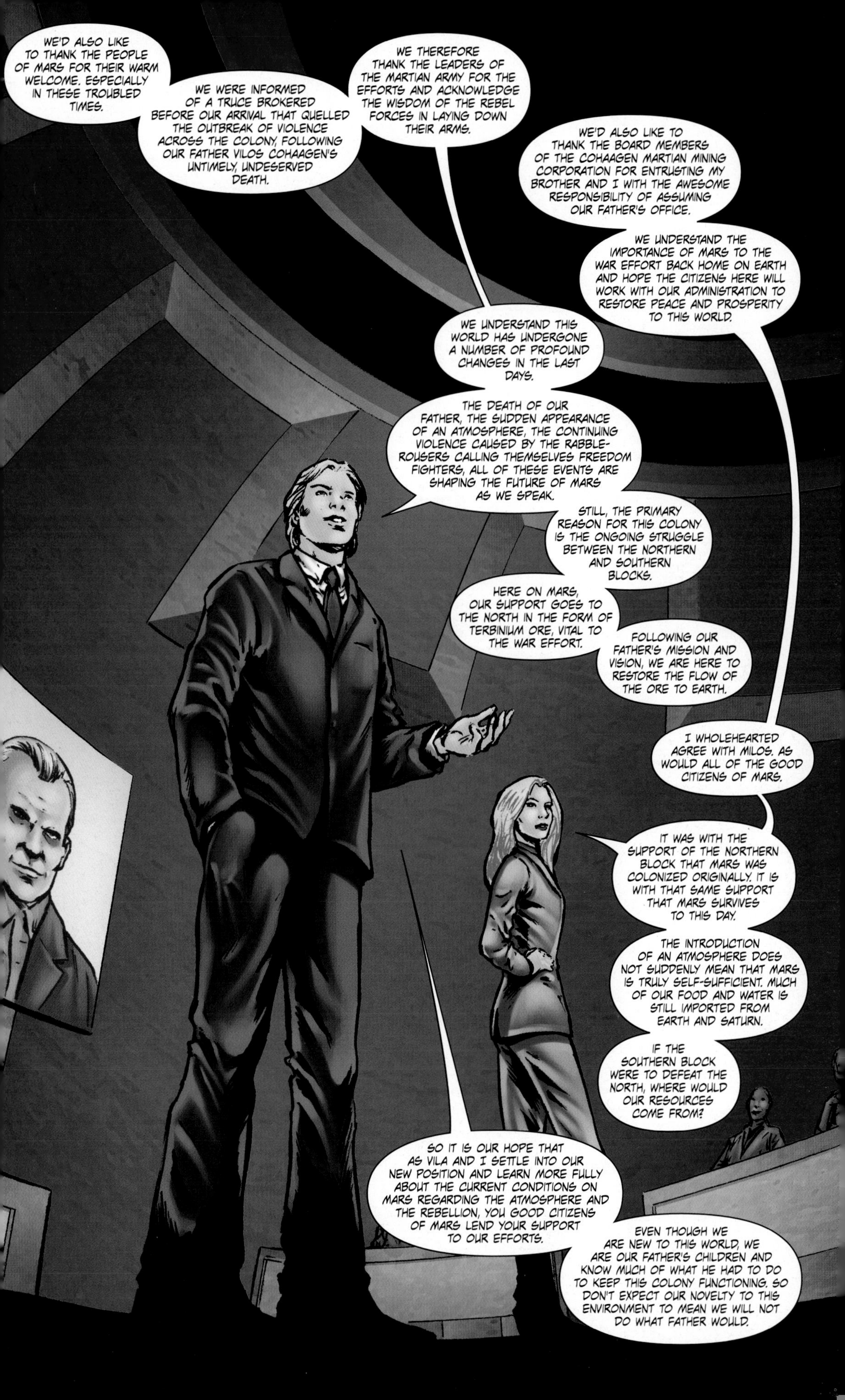
WE'D ALSO LIKE TO THANK THE PEOPLE OF MARS FOR THEIR WARM WELCOME. ESPECIALLY IN THESE TROUBLED TIMES.
WE WERE INFORMED OF A TRUCE BROKERED BEFORE OUR ARRIVAL THAT QUELLED THE OUTBREAK OF VIOLENCE ACROSS THE COLONY, FOLLOWING OUR FATHER VILOS COHAAGEN'S UNTIMELY, UNDESERVED DEATH.
WE THEREFORE THANK THE LEADERS OF THE MARTIAN ARMY FOR THE EFFORTS AND ACKNOWLEDGE THE WISDOM OF THE REBEL FORCES IN LAYING DOWN THEIR ARMS.
WE'D ALSO LIKE TO THANK THE BOARD MEMBERS OF THE COHAAGEN MARTIAN MINING CORPORATION FOR ENTRUSTING MY BROTHER AND I WITH THE AWESOME RESPONSIBILITY OF ASSUMING OUR FATHER'S OFFICE.
WE UNDERSTAND THE IMPORTANCE OF MARS TO THE WAR EFFORT BACK HOME ON EARTH AND HOPE THE CITIZENS HERE WILL WORK WITH OUR ADMINISTRATION TO RESTORE PEACE AND PROSPERITY TO THIS WORLD.
WE UNDERSTAND THIS WORLD HAS UNDERGONE A NUMBER OF PROFOUND CHANGES IN THE LAST DAYS.
THE DEATH OF OUR FATHER, THE SUDDEN APPEARANCE OF AN ATMOSPHERE, THE CONTINUING VIOLENCE CAUSED BY THE RABBLE-ROUSERS CALLING THEMSELVES FREEDOM FIGHTERS, ALL OF THESE EVENTS ARE SHAPING THE FUTURE OF MARS AS WE SPEAK.
STILL, THE PRIMARY REASON FOR THIS COLONY IS THE ONGOING STRUGGLE BETWEEN THE NORTHERN AND SOUTHERN BLOCKS.
HERE ON MARS, OUR SUPPORT GOES TO THE NORTH IN THE FORM OF TERBINIUM ORE, VITAL TO THE WAR EFFORT.
FOLLOWING OUR FATHER'S MISSION AND VISION, WE ARE HERE TO RESTORE THE FLOW OF THE ORE TO EARTH.
I WHOLEHEARTED AGREE WITH MILOS. AS WOULD ALL OF THE GOOD CITIZENS OF MARS.
IT WAS WITH THE SUPPORT OF THE NORTHERN BLOCK THAT MARS WAS COLONIZED ORIGINALLY. IT IS WITH THAT SAME SUPPORT THAT MARS SURVIVES TO THIS DAY.
THE INTRODUCTION OF AN ATMOSPHERE DOES NOT SUDDENLY MEAN THAT MARS IS TRULY SELF-SUFFICIENT. MUCH OF OUR FOOD AND WATER IS STILL IMPORTED FROM EARTH AND SATURN.
IF THE SOUTHERN BLOCK WERE TO DEFEAT THE NORTH, WHERE WOULD OUR RESOURCES COME FROM?
SO IT IS OUR HOPE THAT AS VILA AND I SETTLE INTO OUR NEW POSITION AND LEARN MORE FULLY ABOUT THE CURRENT CONDITIONS ON MARS REGARDING THE ATMOSPHERE AND THE REBELLION, YOU GOOD CITIZENS OF MARS LEND YOUR SUPPORT TO OUR EFFORTS.
EVEN THOUGH WE ARE NEW TO THIS WORLD, WE ARE OUR FATHER'S CHILDREN AND KNOW MUCH OF WHAT HE HAD TO DO TO KEEP THIS COLONY FUNCTIONING. SO DON'T EXPECT OUR NOVELTY TO THIS ENVIRONMENT TO MEAN WE WILL NOT DO WHAT FATHER WOULD.

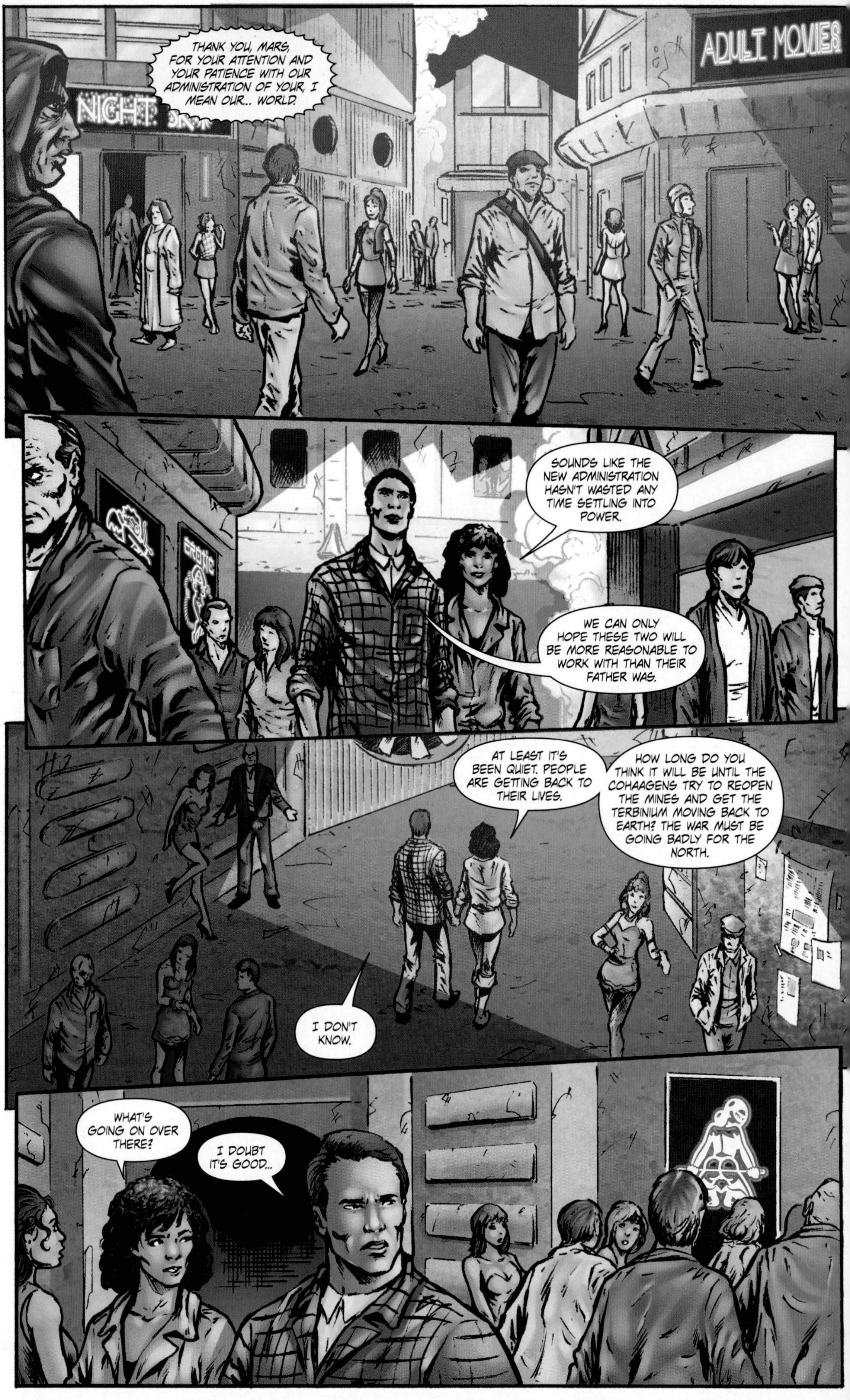
ADULT MOVIES
NIGHT
THANK YOU, MARS, FOR YOUR ATTENTION AND YOUR PATIENCE WITH OUR ADMINISTRATION OF YOUR, I MEAN OUR... WORLD.
EROTIC
SOUNDS LIKE THE NEW ADMINISTRATION HASN'T WASTED ANY TIME SETTLING INTO POWER.
WE CAN ONLY HOPE THESE TWO WILL BE MORE REASONABLE TO WORK WITH THAN THEIR FATHER WAS.
AT LEAST IT'S BEEN QUIET. PEOPLE ARE GETTING BACK TO THEIR LIVES.
HOW LONG DO YOU THINK IT WILL BE UNTIL THE COHAAGENS TRY TO REOPEN THE MINES AND GET THE TERBINIUM MOVING BACK TO EARTH? THE WAR MUST BE GOING BADLY FOR THE NORTH.
I DON'T KNOW.
WHAT'S GOING ON OVER THERE?
I DOUBT IT'S GOOD...

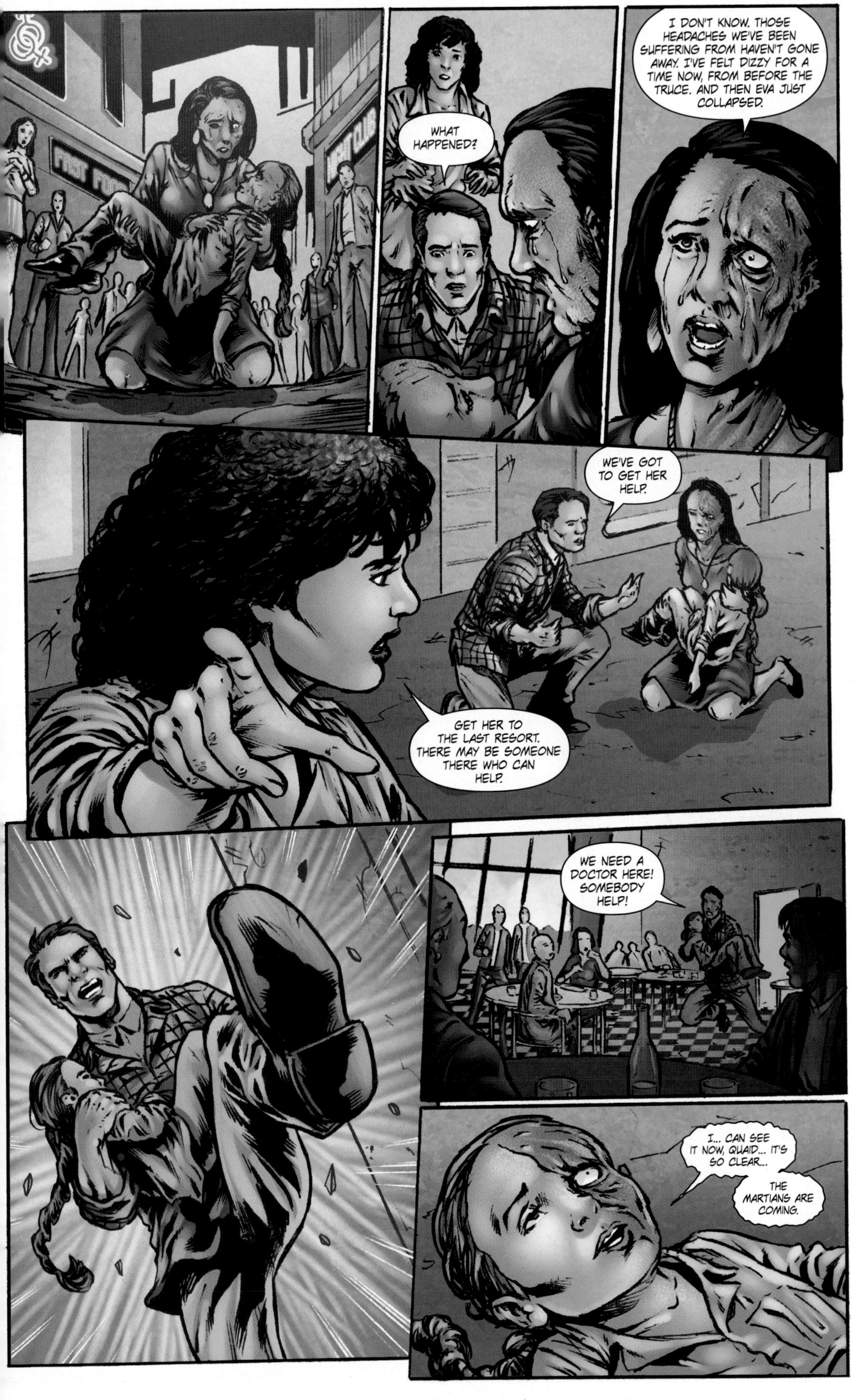
FAST FOOD
NIGHT CLUB
WHAT HAPPENED?
I DON'T KNOW. THOSE HEADACHES WE'VE BEEN SUFFERING FROM HAVEN'T GONE AWAY. I'VE FELT DIZZY FOR A TIME NOW, FROM BEFORE THE TRUCE. AND THEN EVA JUST COLLAPSED.
WE'VE GOT TO GET HER HELP.
GET HER TO THE LAST RESORT. THERE MAY BE SOMEONE THERE WHO CAN HELP.
WE NEED A DOCTOR HERE! SOMEBODY HELP!
I... CAN SEE IT NOW, QUAID... IT'S SO CLEAR...
THE MARTIANS ARE COMING.

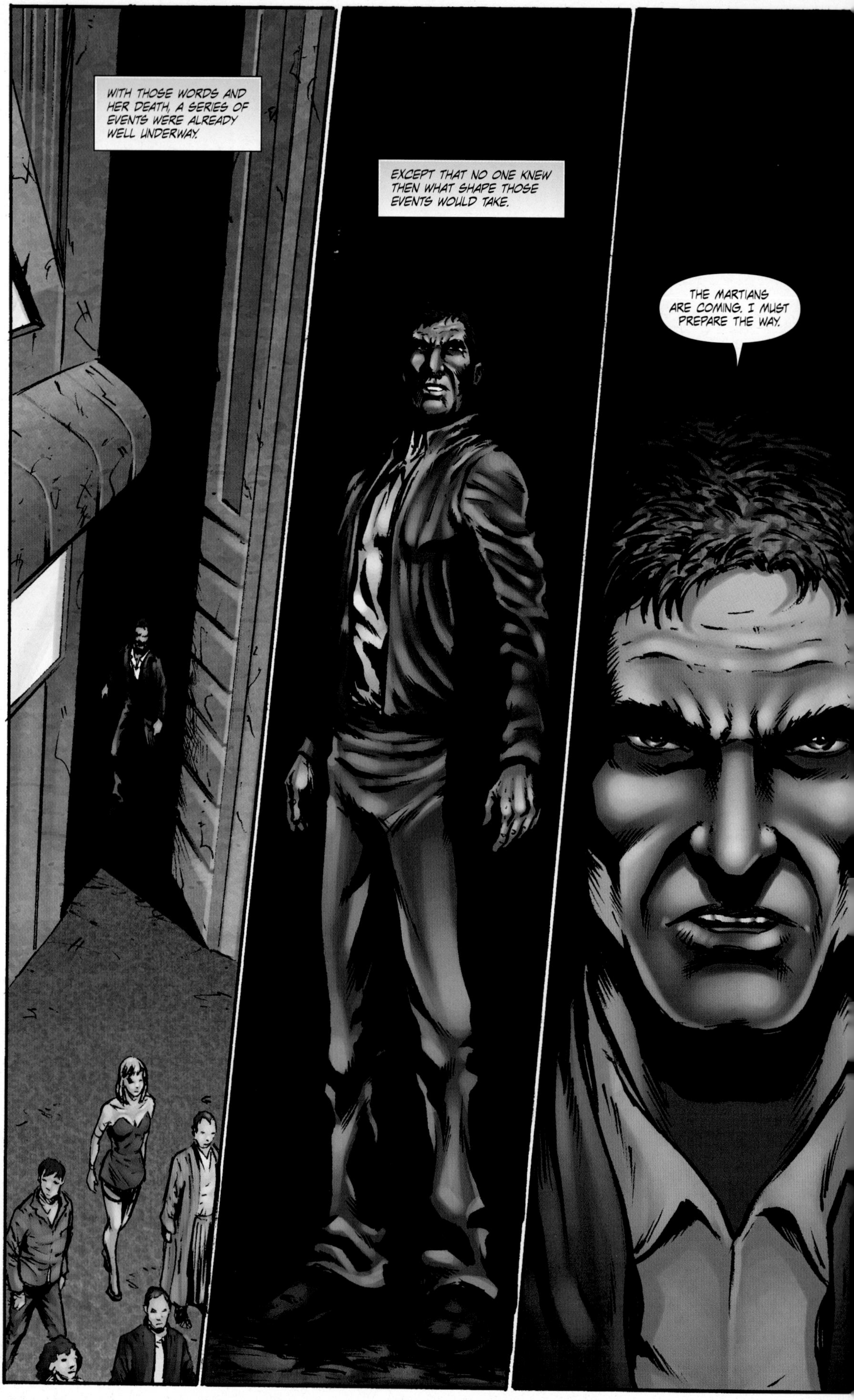
WITH THOSE WORDS AND HER DEATH, A SERIES OF EVENTS WERE ALREADY WELL UNDERWAY.
EXCEPT THAT NO ONE KNEW THEN WHAT SHAPE THOSE EVENTS WOULD TAKE.
THE MARTIANS ARE COMING. I MUST PREPARE THE WAY.

ISSUE 2 COVER BY
DARICK
ROBERTSON

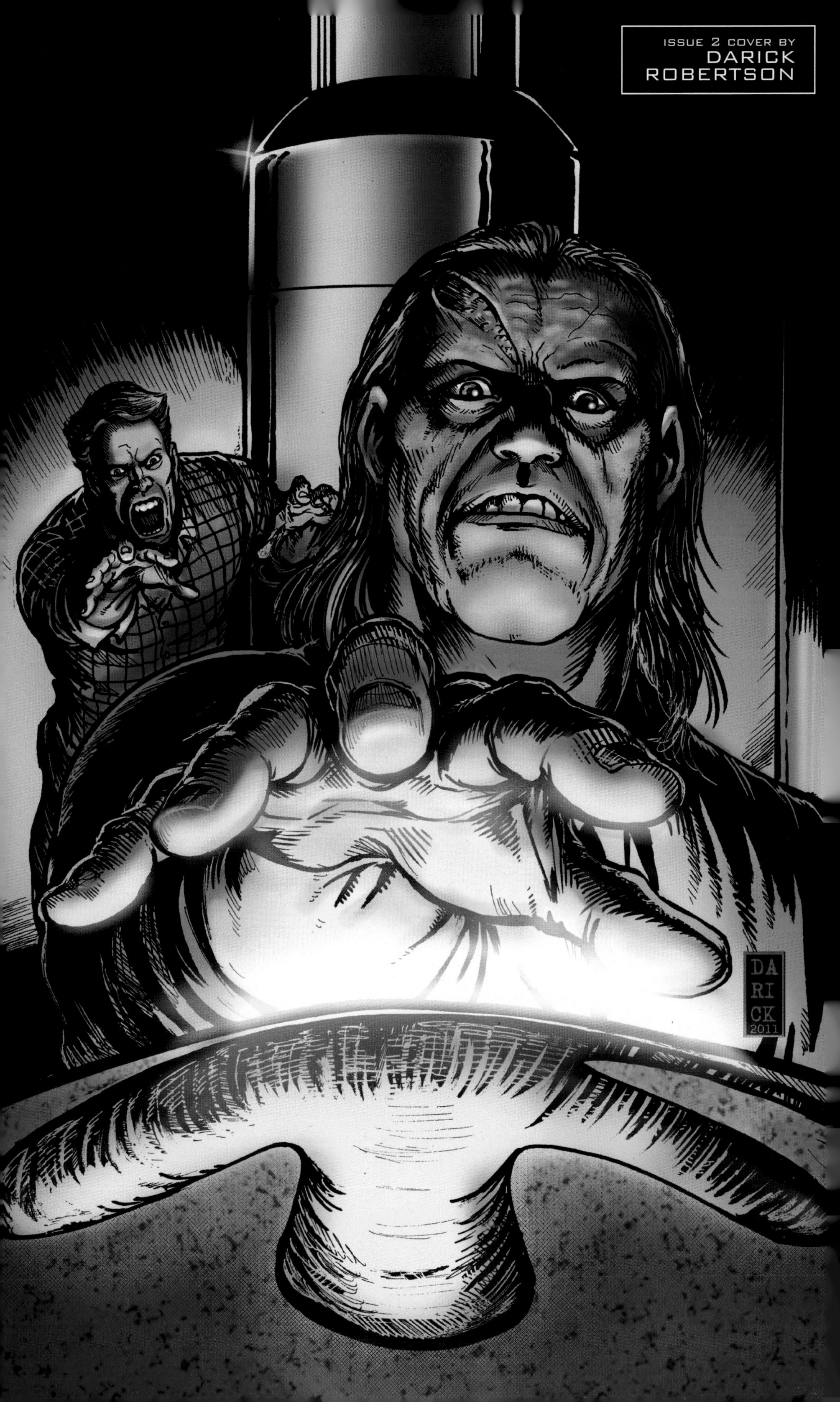
DA
RI
CK
2011

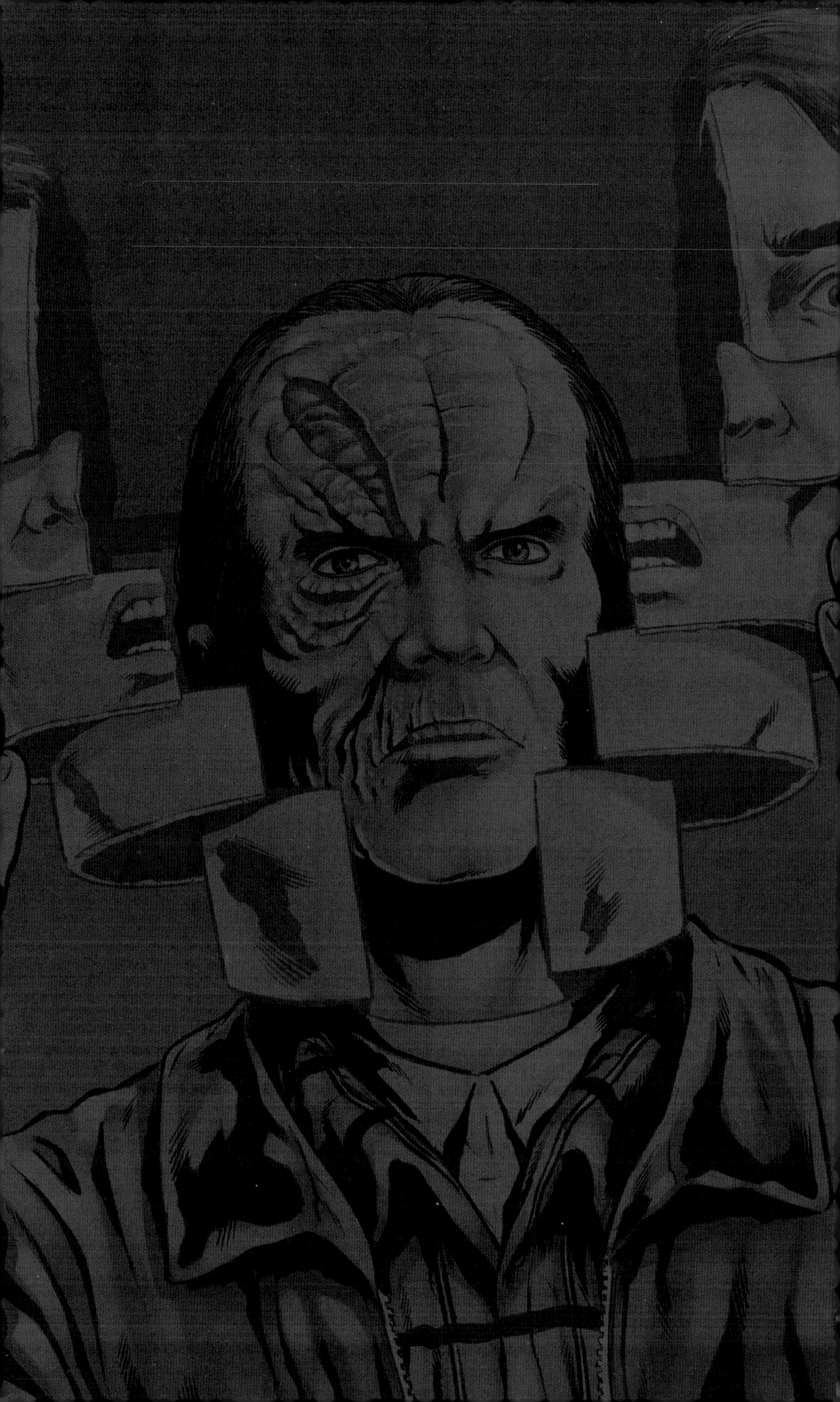

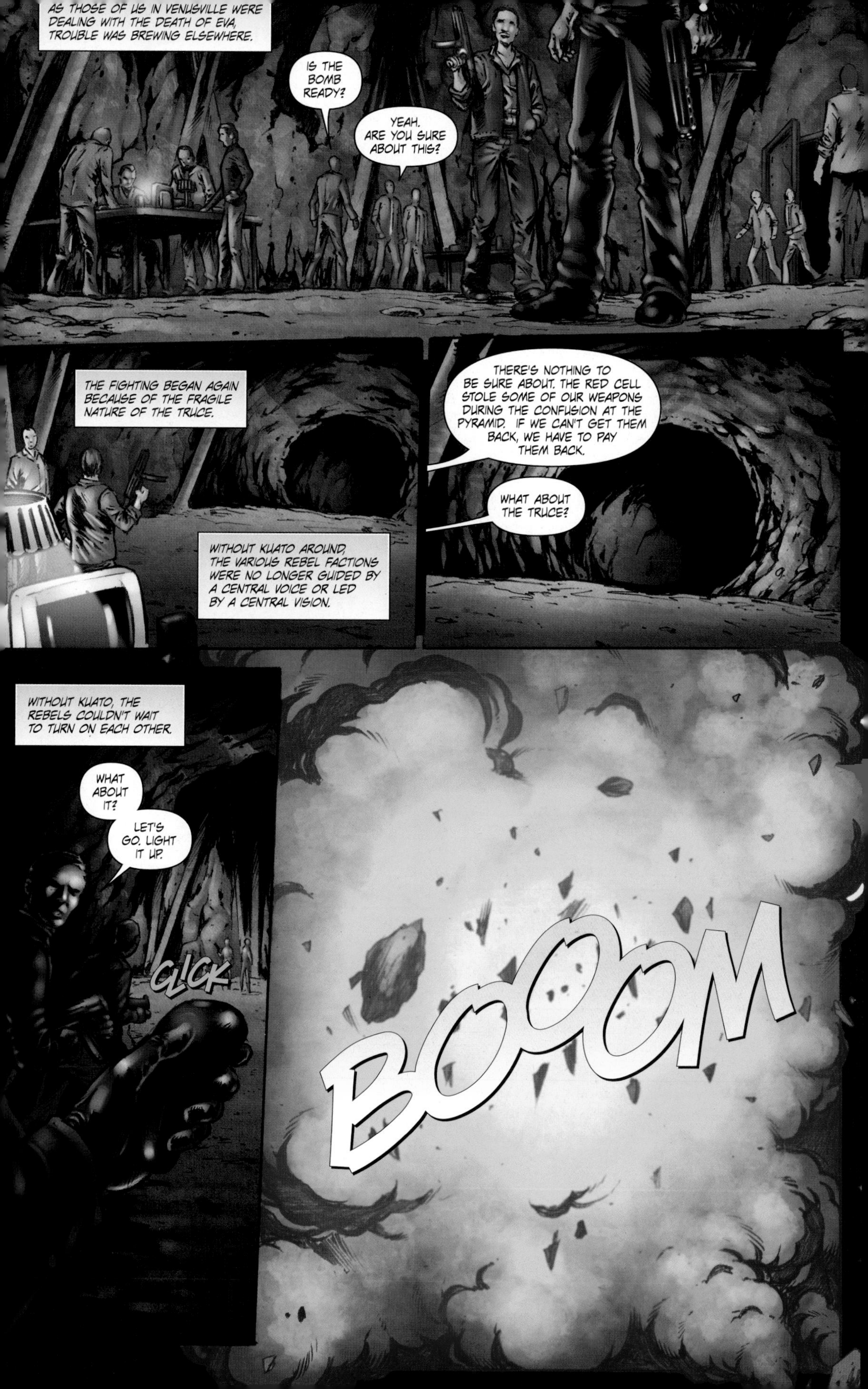
AS THOSE OF US IN VENUSVILLE WERE DEALING WITH THE DEATH OF EVA, TROUBLE WAS BREWING ELSEWHERE.
IS THE BOMB READY?
YEAH. ARE YOU SURE ABOUT THIS?
THE FIGHTING BEGAN AGAIN BECAUSE OF THE FRAGILE NATURE OF THE TRUCE.
WITHOUT KUATO AROUND, THE VARIOUS REBEL FACTIONS WERE NO LONGER GUIDED BY A CENTRAL VOICE OR LED BY A CENTRAL VISION.
THERE'S NOTHING TO BE SURE ABOUT. THE RED CELL STOLE SOME OF OUR WEAPONS DURING THE CONFUSION AT THE PYRAMID. IF WE CAN'T GET THEM BACK, WE HAVE TO PAY THEM BACK.
WHAT ABOUT THE TRUCE?
WITHOUT KUATO, THE REBELS COULDN'T WAIT TO TURN ON EACH OTHER.
WHAT ABOUT IT?
LET'S GO. LIGHT IT UP.
CLICK
BOOOOM

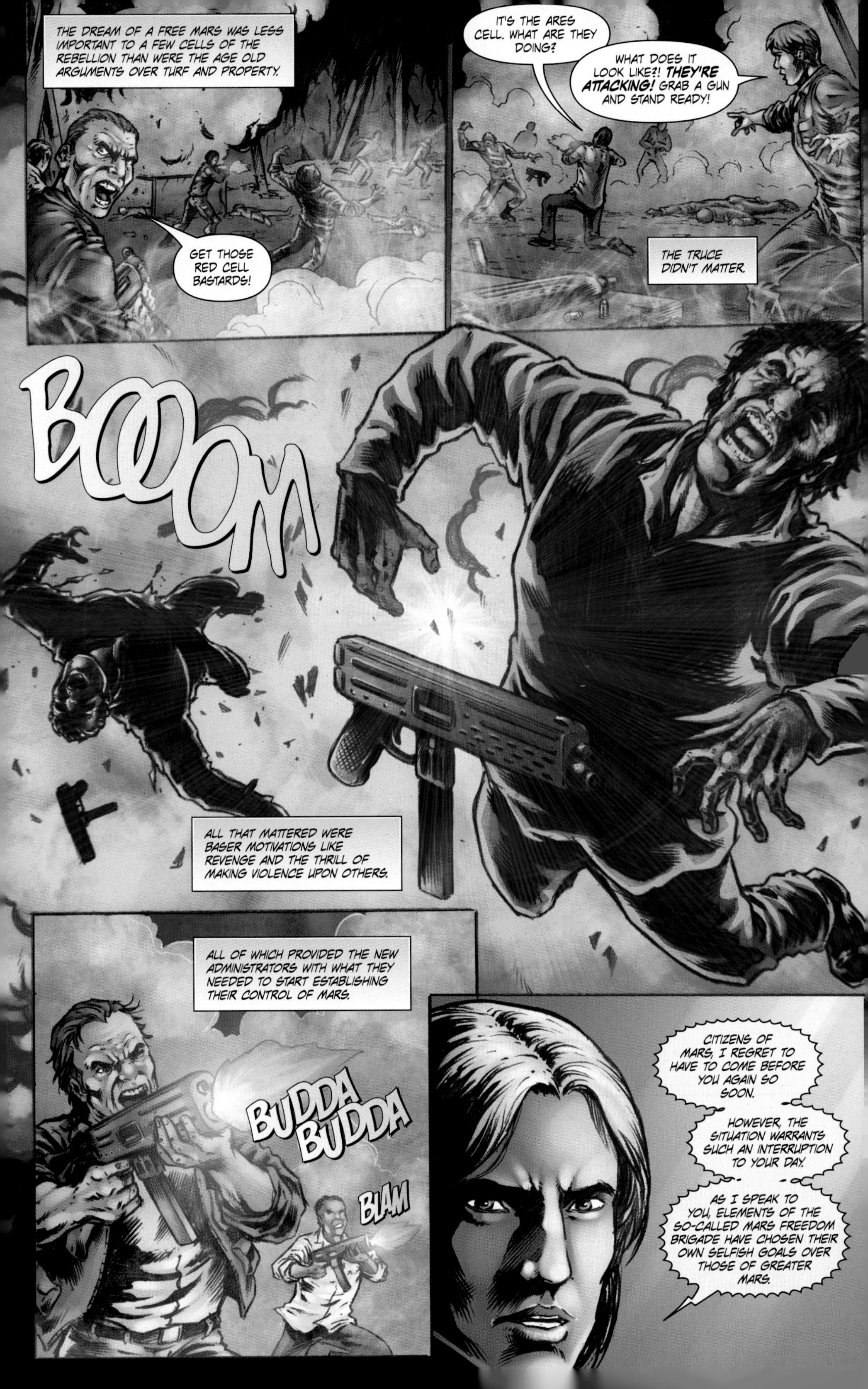
THE DREAM OF A FREE MARS WAS LESS IMPORTANT TO A FEW CELLS OF THE REBELLION THAN WERE THE AGE OLD ARGUMENTS OVER TURF AND PROPERTY.
GET THOSE RED CELL BASTARDS!
IT'S THE ARES CELL. WHAT ARE THEY DOING?
WHAT DOES IT LOOK LIKE?! **THEY'RE ATTACKING!** GRAB A GUN AND STAND READY!
THE TRUCE DIDN'T MATTER.
BOOOM
ALL THAT MATTERED WERE BASER MOTIVATIONS LIKE REVENGE AND THE THRILL OF MAKING VIOLENCE UPON OTHERS.
ALL OF WHICH PROVIDED THE NEW ADMINISTRATORS WITH WHAT THEY NEEDED TO START ESTABLISHING THEIR CONTROL OF MARS.
BUDDA BUDDA
BLAM
CITIZENS OF MARS, I REGRET TO HAVE TO COME BEFORE YOU AGAIN SO SOON.
HOWEVER, THE SITUATION WARRANTS SUCH AN INTERRUPTION TO YOUR DAY.
AS I SPEAK TO YOU, ELEMENTS OF THE SO-CALLED MARS FREEDOM BRIGADE HAVE CHOSEN THEIR OWN SELFISH GOALS OVER THOSE OF GREATER MARS.

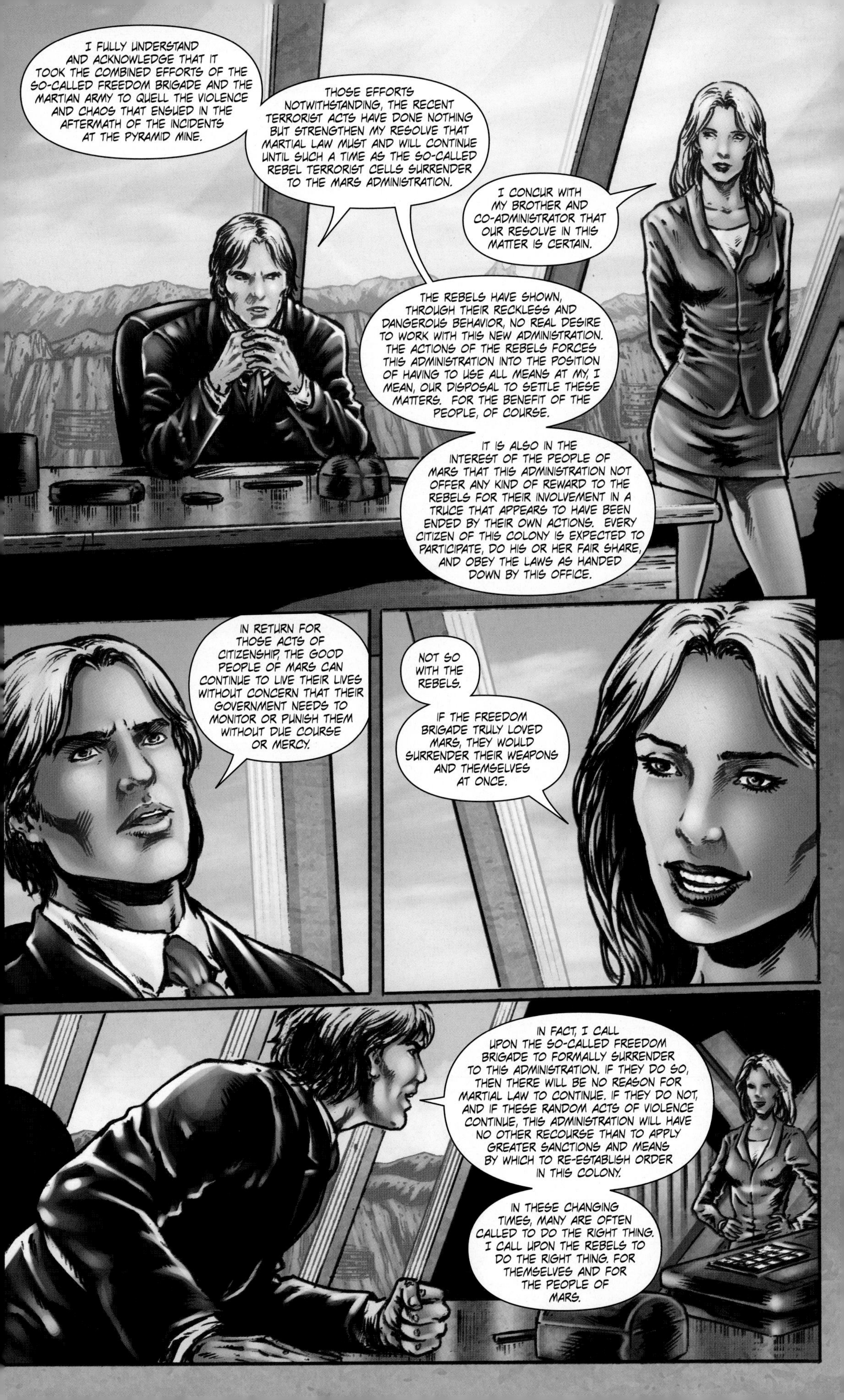
I FULLY UNDERSTAND AND ACKNOWLEDGE THAT IT TOOK THE COMBINED EFFORTS OF THE SO-CALLED FREEDOM BRIGADE AND THE MARTIAN ARMY TO QUELL THE VIOLENCE AND CHAOS THAT ENSUED IN THE AFTERMATH OF THE INCIDENTS AT THE PYRAMID MINE.
THOSE EFFORTS NOTWITHSTANDING, THE RECENT TERRORIST ACTS HAVE DONE NOTHING BUT STRENGTHEN MY RESOLVE THAT MARTIAL LAW MUST AND WILL CONTINUE UNTIL SUCH A TIME AS THE SO-CALLED REBEL TERRORIST CELLS SURRENDER TO THE MARS ADMINISTRATION.
I CONCUR WITH MY BROTHER AND CO-ADMINISTRATOR THAT OUR RESOLVE IN THIS MATTER IS CERTAIN.
THE REBELS HAVE SHOWN, THROUGH THEIR RECKLESS AND DANGEROUS BEHAVIOR, NO REAL DESIRE TO WORK WITH THIS NEW ADMINISTRATION. THE ACTIONS OF THE REBELS FORCES THIS ADMINISTRATION INTO THE POSITION OF HAVING TO USE ALL MEANS AT MY, I MEAN, OUR DISPOSAL TO SETTLE THESE MATTERS. FOR THE BENEFIT OF THE PEOPLE, OF COURSE.
IT IS ALSO IN THE INTEREST OF THE PEOPLE OF MARS THAT THIS ADMINISTRATION NOT OFFER ANY KIND OF REWARD TO THE REBELS FOR THEIR INVOLVEMENT IN A TRUCE THAT APPEARS TO HAVE BEEN ENDED BY THEIR OWN ACTIONS. EVERY CITIZEN OF THIS COLONY IS EXPECTED TO PARTICIPATE, DO HIS OR HER FAIR SHARE, AND OBEY THE LAWS AS HANDED DOWN BY THIS OFFICE.
IN RETURN FOR THOSE ACTS OF CITIZENSHIP, THE GOOD PEOPLE OF MARS CAN CONTINUE TO LIVE THEIR LIVES WITHOUT CONCERN THAT THEIR GOVERNMENT NEEDS TO MONITOR OR PUNISH THEM WITHOUT DUE COURSE OR MERCY.
NOT SO WITH THE REBELS.
IF THE FREEDOM BRIGADE TRULY LOVED MARS, THEY WOULD SURRENDER THEIR WEAPONS AND THEMSELVES AT ONCE.
IN FACT, I CALL UPON THE SO-CALLED FREEDOM BRIGADE TO FORMALLY SURRENDER TO THIS ADMINISTRATION. IF THEY DO SO, THEN THERE WILL BE NO REASON FOR MARTIAL LAW TO CONTINUE. IF THEY DO NOT, AND IF THESE RANDOM ACTS OF VIOLENCE CONTINUE, THIS ADMINISTRATION WILL HAVE NO OTHER RECOURSE THAN TO APPLY GREATER SANCTIONS AND MEANS BY WHICH TO RE-ESTABLISH ORDER IN THIS COLONY.
IN THESE CHANGING TIMES, MANY ARE OFTEN CALLED TO DO THE RIGHT THING. I CALL UPON THE REBELS TO DO THE RIGHT THING. FOR THEMSELVES AND FOR THE PEOPLE OF MARS.

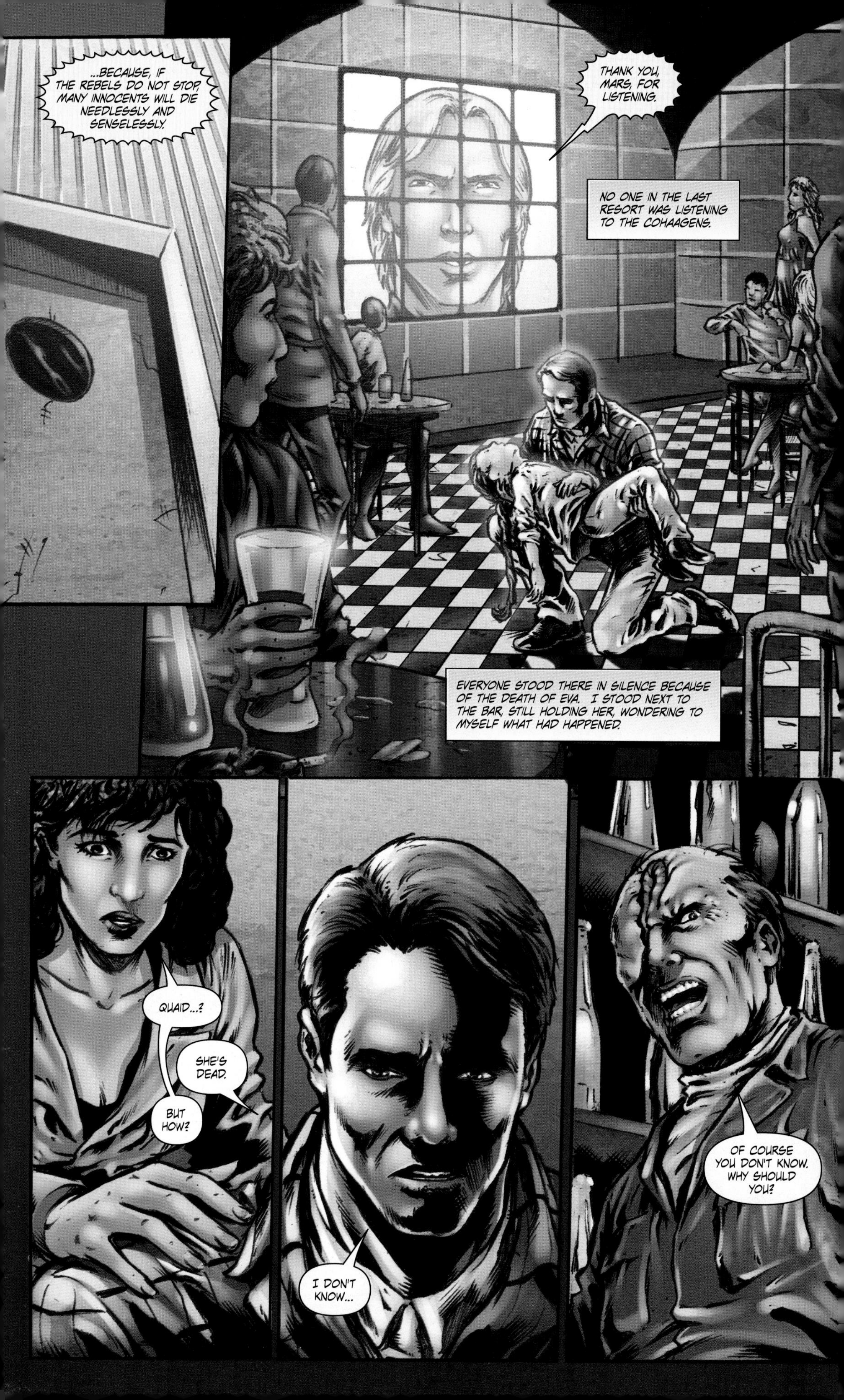
...BECAUSE, IF THE REBELS DO NOT STOP, MANY INNOCENTS WILL DIE NEEDLESSLY AND SENSELESSLY.
THANK YOU, MARS, FOR LISTENING.
NO ONE IN THE LAST RESORT WAS LISTENING TO THE COHAAGENS.
EVERYONE STOOD THERE IN SILENCE BECAUSE OF THE DEATH OF EVA. I STOOD NEXT TO THE BAR, STILL HOLDING HER, WONDERING TO MYSELF WHAT HAD HAPPENED.
QUAID...?
SHE'S DEAD.
BUT HOW?
I DON'T KNOW...
OF COURSE YOU DON'T KNOW. WHY SHOULD YOU?

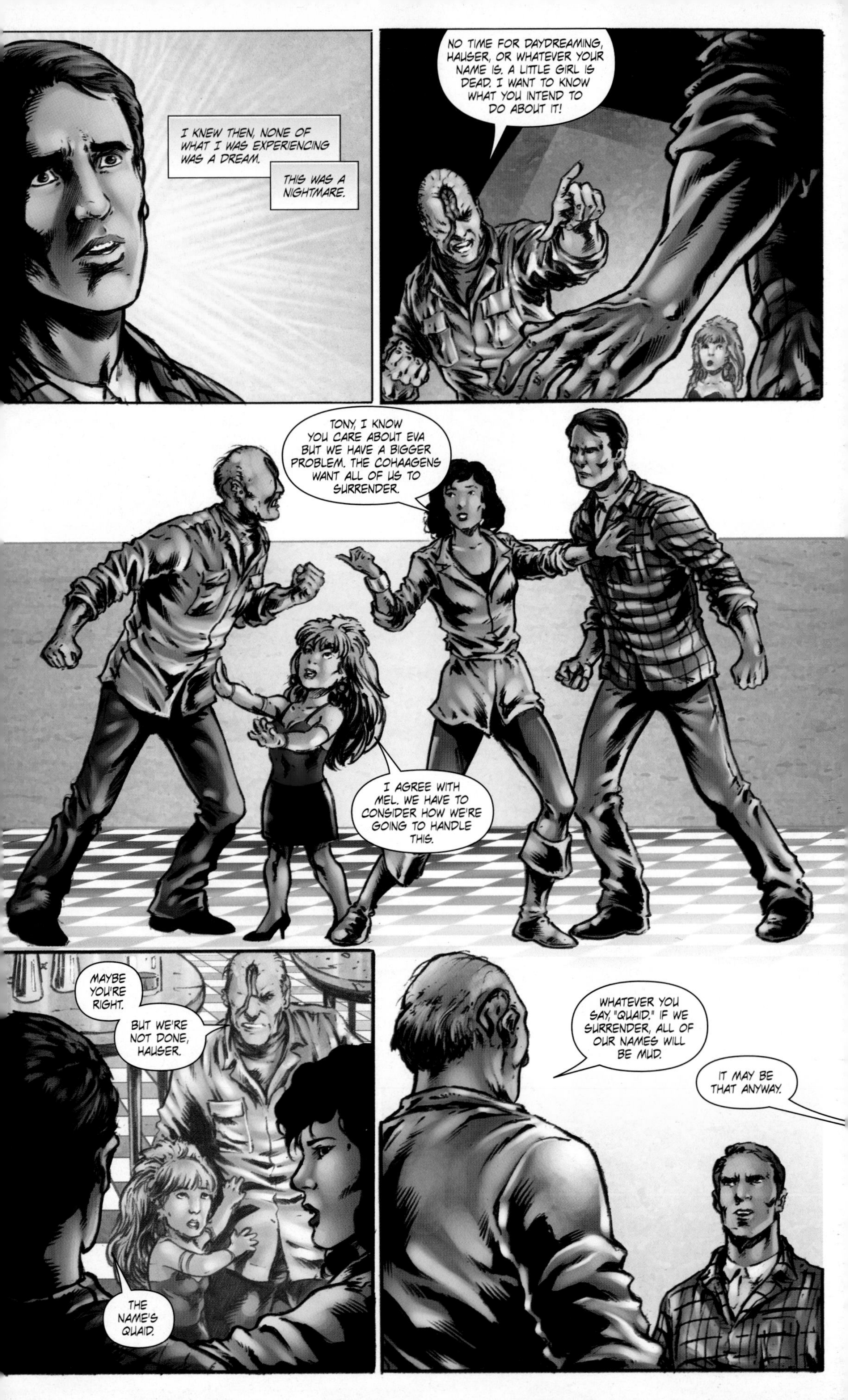

I KNEW THEN, NONE OF WHAT I WAS EXPERIENCING WAS A DREAM.
THIS WAS A NIGHTMARE.
NO TIME FOR DAYDREAMING, HAUSER, OR WHATEVER YOUR NAME IS. A LITTLE GIRL IS DEAD. I WANT TO KNOW WHAT YOU INTEND TO DO ABOUT IT!
TONY, I KNOW YOU CARE ABOUT EVA BUT WE HAVE A BIGGER PROBLEM. THE COHAAGENS WANT ALL OF US TO SURRENDER.
I AGREE WITH MEL. WE HAVE TO CONSIDER HOW WE'RE GOING TO HANDLE THIS.
MAYBE YOU'RE RIGHT.
BUT WE'RE NOT DONE, HAUSER.
THE NAME'S QUAID.
WHATEVER YOU SAY, "QUAID." IF WE SURRENDER, ALL OF OUR NAMES WILL BE MUD.
IT MAY BE THAT ANYWAY.

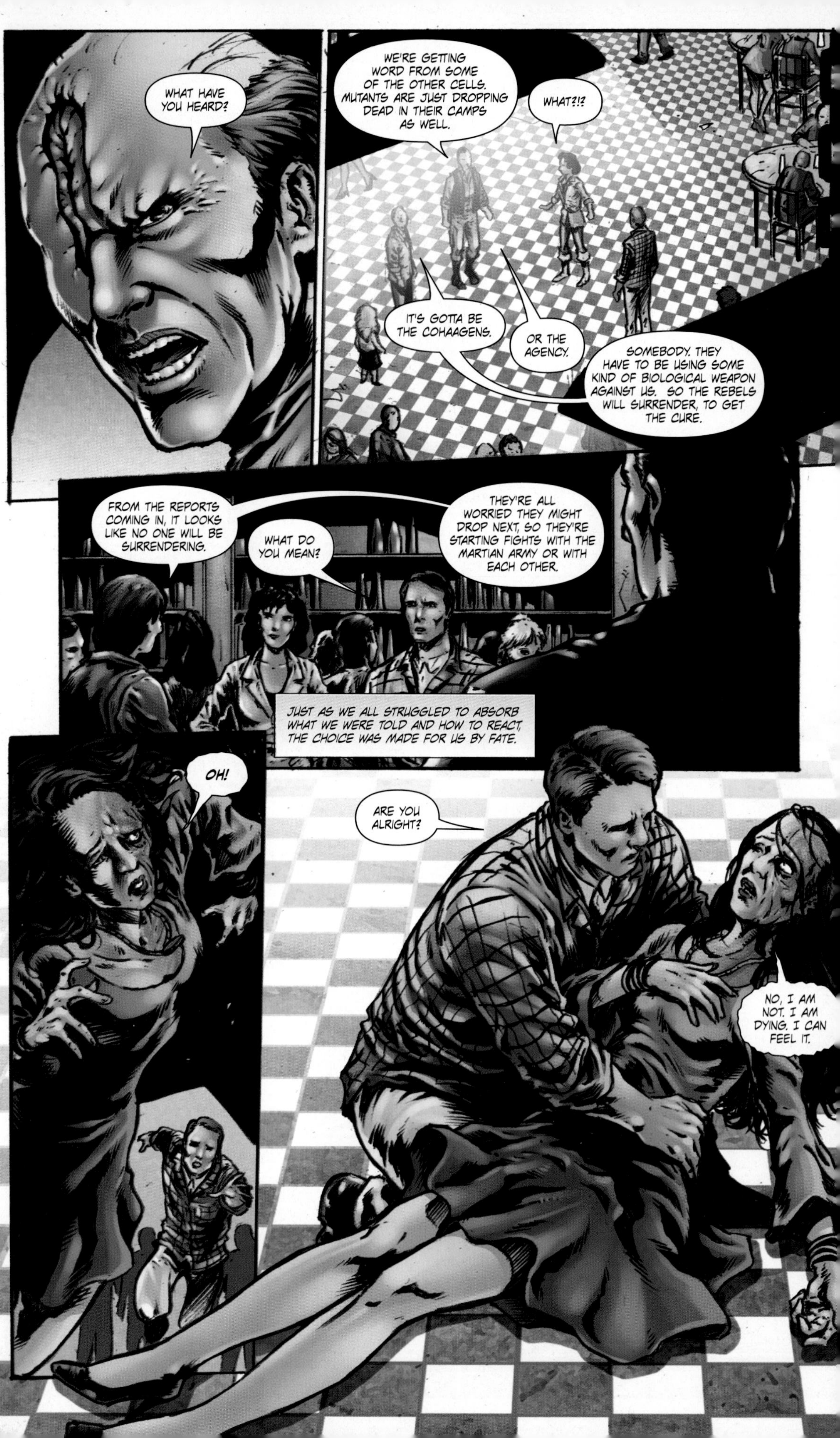
WHAT HAVE YOU HEARD?
WE'RE GETTING WORD FROM SOME OF THE OTHER CELLS. MUTANTS ARE JUST DROPPING DEAD IN THEIR CAMPS AS WELL.
WHAT?!?
IT'S GOTTA BE THE COHAAGENS.
OR THE AGENCY.
SOMEBODY. THEY HAVE TO BE USING SOME KIND OF BIOLOGICAL WEAPON AGAINST US. SO THE REBELS WILL SURRENDER, TO GET THE CURE.
FROM THE REPORTS COMING IN, IT LOOKS LIKE NO ONE WILL BE SURRENDERING.
WHAT DO YOU MEAN?
THEY'RE ALL WORRIED THEY MIGHT DROP NEXT, SO THEY'RE STARTING FIGHTS WITH THE MARTIAN ARMY OR WITH EACH OTHER.
JUST AS WE ALL STRUGGLED TO ABSORB WHAT WE WERE TOLD AND HOW TO REACT, THE CHOICE WAS MADE FOR US BY FATE.
OH!
ARE YOU ALRIGHT?
NO, I AM NOT. I AM DYING. I CAN FEEL IT.

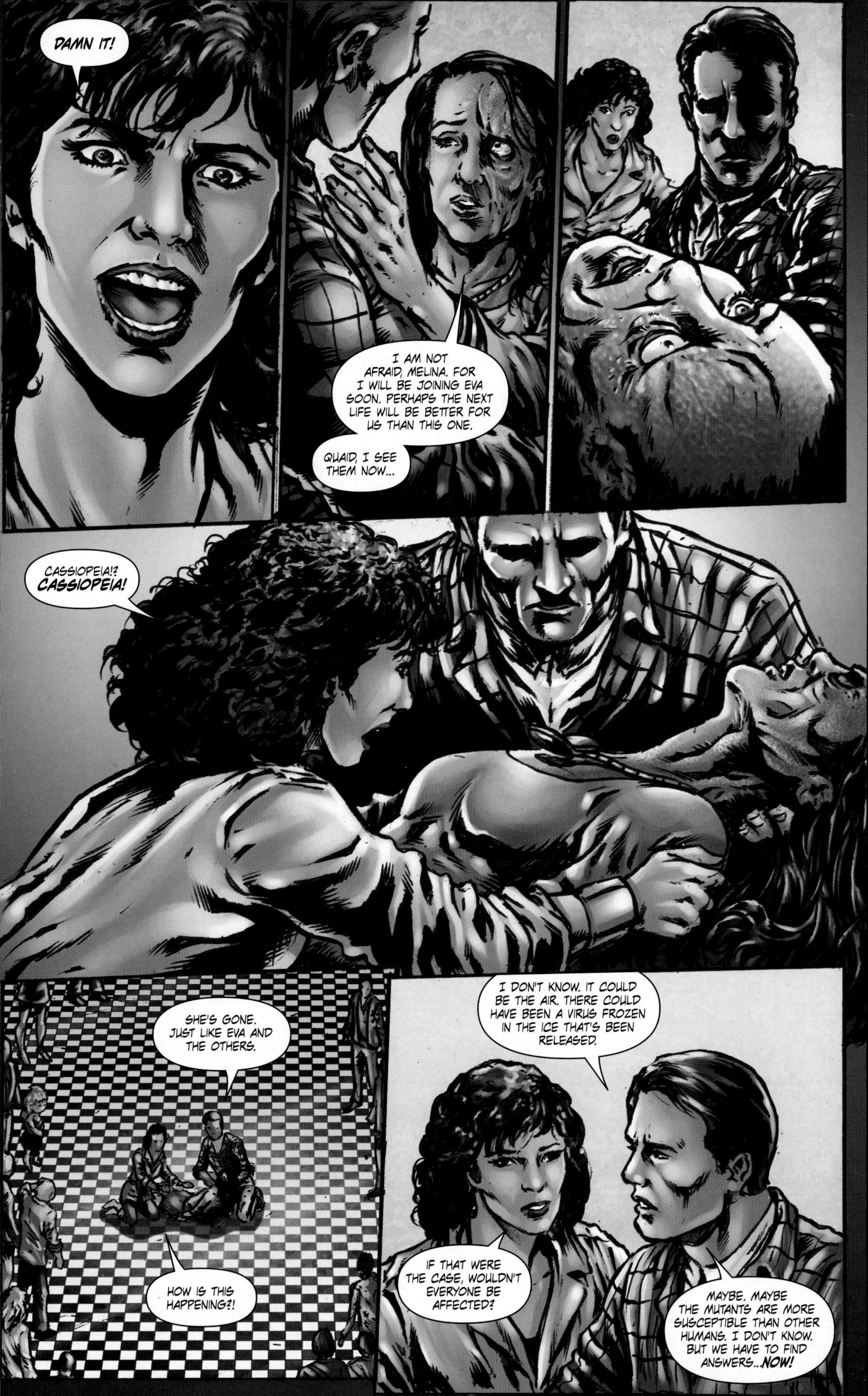
DAMN IT!
I AM NOT AFRAID, MELINA. FOR I WILL BE JOINING EVA SOON. PERHAPS THE NEXT LIFE WILL BE BETTER FOR US THAN THIS ONE.
QUAID, I SEE THEM NOW...
CASSIOPEIA!? CASSIOPEIA!
SHE'S GONE. JUST LIKE EVA AND THE OTHERS.
HOW IS THIS HAPPENING?!
I DON'T KNOW. IT COULD BE THE AIR. THERE COULD HAVE BEEN A VIRUS FROZEN IN THE ICE THAT'S BEEN RELEASED.
IF THAT WERE THE CASE, WOULDN'T EVERYONE BE AFFECTED?
MAYBE. MAYBE THE MUTANTS ARE MORE SUSCEPTIBLE THAN OTHER HUMANS. I DON'T KNOW. BUT WE HAVE TO FIND ANSWERS...NOW!

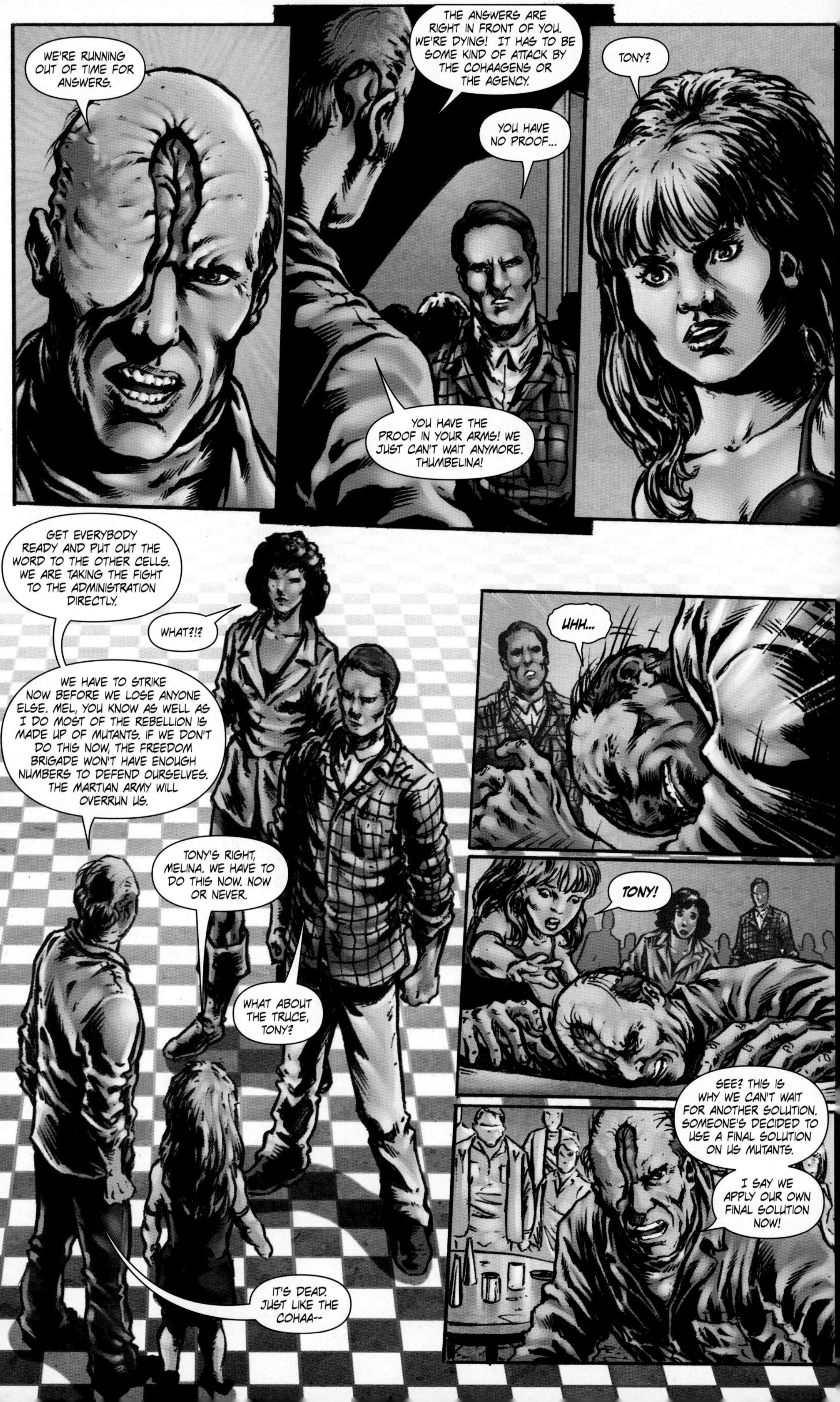
WE'RE RUNNING OUT OF TIME FOR ANSWERS.
THE ANSWERS ARE RIGHT IN FRONT OF YOU. WE'RE DYING! IT HAS TO BE SOME KIND OF ATTACK BY THE COHAAGENS OR THE AGENCY.
YOU HAVE NO PROOF...
YOU HAVE THE PROOF IN YOUR ARMS! WE JUST CAN'T WAIT ANYMORE. THUMBELINA!
TONY?
GET EVERYBODY READY AND PUT OUT THE WORD TO THE OTHER CELLS. WE ARE TAKING THE FIGHT TO THE ADMINISTRATION DIRECTLY.
WHAT?!?
WE HAVE TO STRIKE NOW BEFORE WE LOSE ANYONE ELSE. MEL, YOU KNOW AS WELL AS I DO MOST OF THE REBELLION IS MADE UP OF MUTANTS. IF WE DON'T DO THIS NOW, THE FREEDOM BRIGADE WON'T HAVE ENOUGH NUMBERS TO DEFEND OURSELVES. THE MARTIAN ARMY WILL OVERRUN US.
TONY'S RIGHT, MELINA. WE HAVE TO DO THIS NOW. NOW OR NEVER.
WHAT ABOUT THE TRUCE, TONY?
IT'S DEAD. JUST LIKE THE COHAA--
UHH...
TONY!
SEE? THIS IS WHY WE CAN'T WAIT FOR ANOTHER SOLUTION. SOMEONE'S DECIDED TO USE A FINAL SOLUTION ON US MUTANTS.
I SAY WE APPLY OUR OWN FINAL SOLUTION NOW!

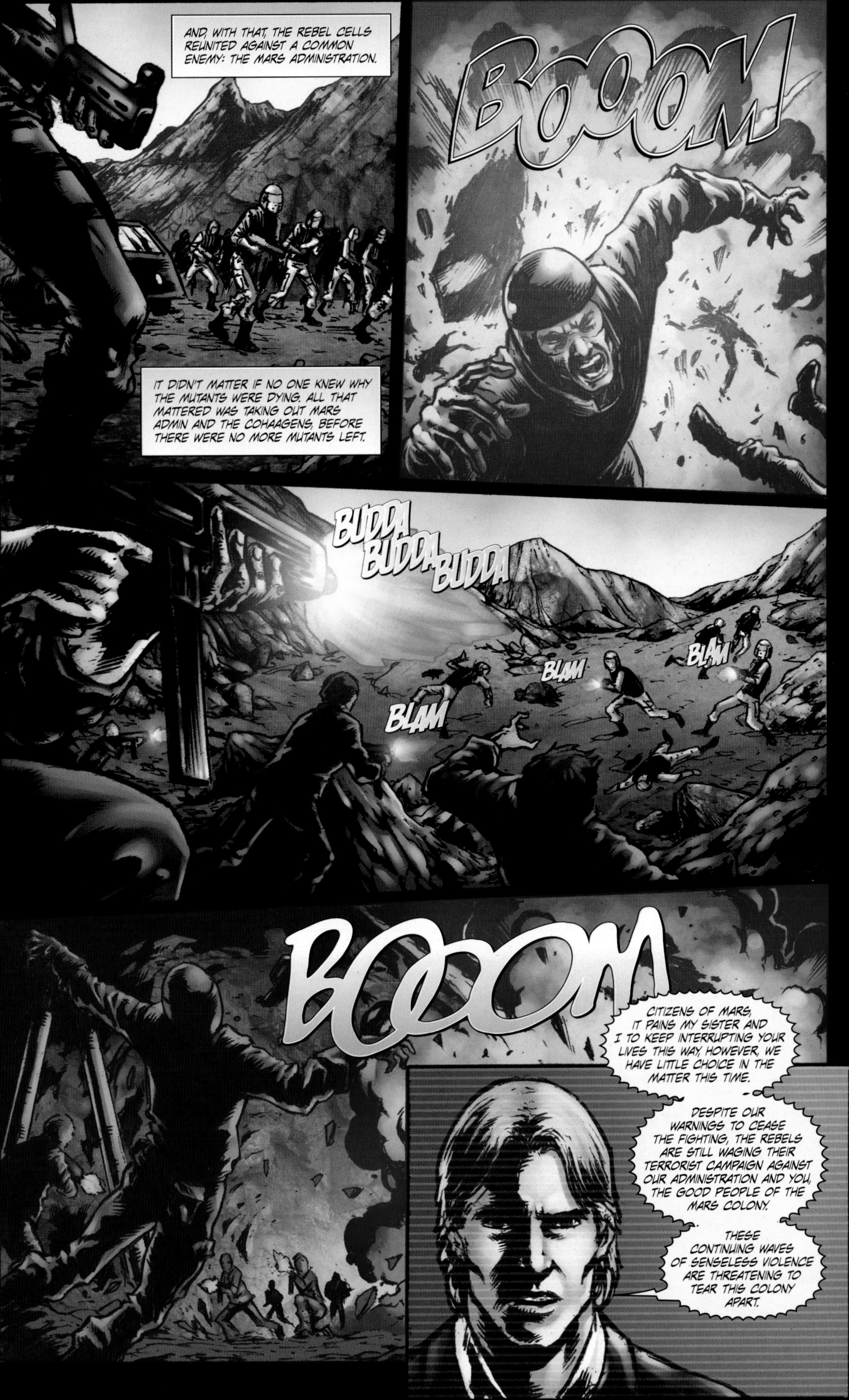
AND, WITH THAT, THE REBEL CELLS REUNITED AGAINST A COMMON ENEMY: THE MARS ADMINISTRATION.
IT DIDN'T MATTER IF NO ONE KNEW WHY THE MUTANTS WERE DYING. ALL THAT MATTERED WAS TAKING OUT MARS ADMIN AND THE COHAAGENS, BEFORE THERE WERE NO MORE MUTANTS LEFT.
BOOOM
BUDDA BUDDA BUDDA
BLAM
BLAM
BLAM
BOOOM
CITIZENS OF MARS, IT PAINS MY SISTER AND I TO KEEP INTERRUPTING YOUR LIVES THIS WAY. HOWEVER, WE HAVE LITTLE CHOICE IN THE MATTER THIS TIME.
DESPITE OUR WARNINGS TO CEASE THE FIGHTING, THE REBELS ARE STILL WAGING THEIR TERRORIST CAMPAIGN AGAINST OUR ADMINISTRATION AND YOU, THE GOOD PEOPLE OF THE MARS COLONY.
THESE CONTINUING WAVES OF SENSELESS VIOLENCE ARE THREATENING TO TEAR THIS COLONY APART.

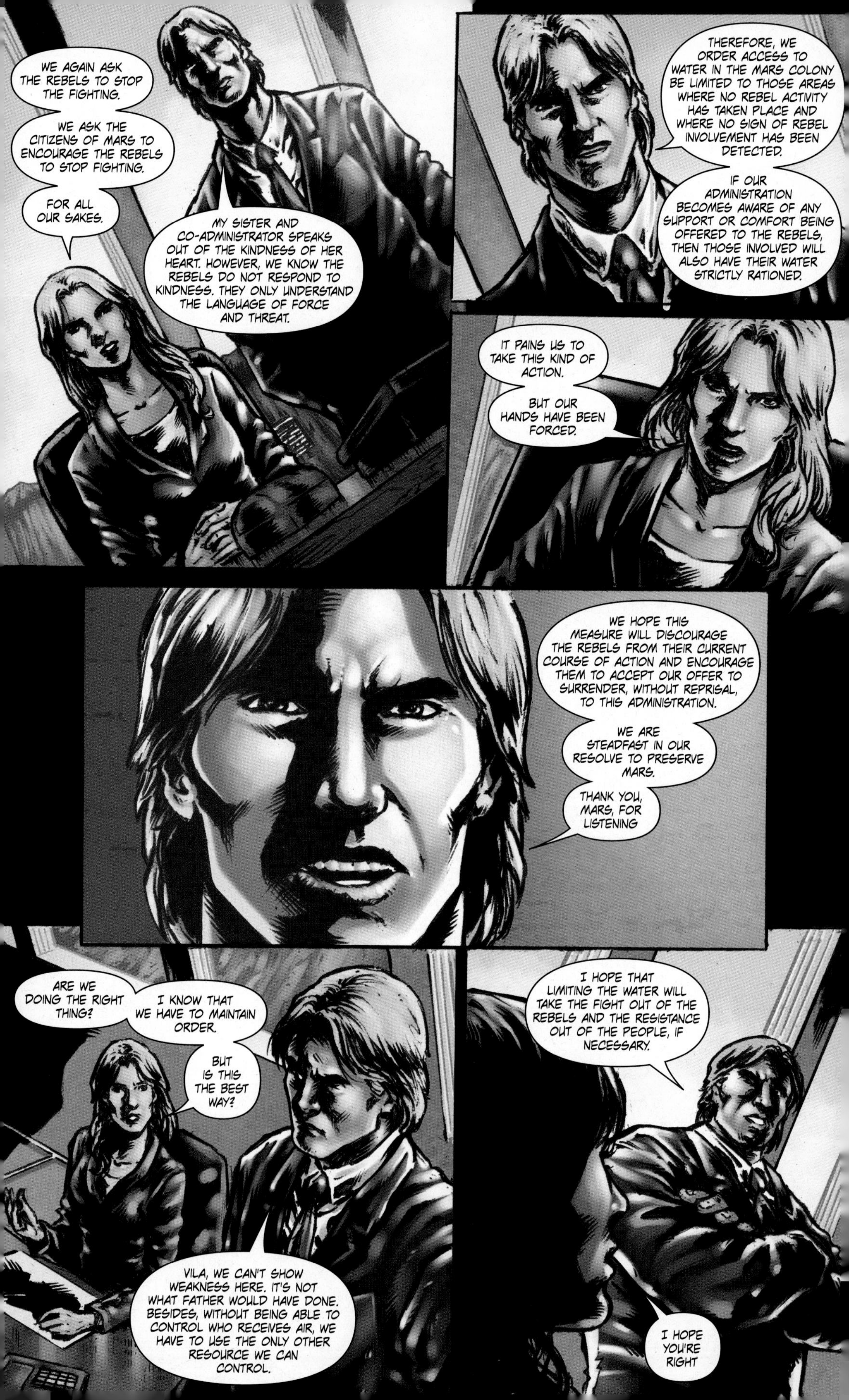
WE AGAIN ASK THE REBELS TO STOP THE FIGHTING.
WE ASK THE CITIZENS OF MARS TO ENCOURAGE THE REBELS TO STOP FIGHTING.
FOR ALL OUR SAKES.
MY SISTER AND CO-ADMINISTRATOR SPEAKS OUT OF THE KINDNESS OF HER HEART. HOWEVER, WE KNOW THE REBELS DO NOT RESPOND TO KINDNESS. THEY ONLY UNDERSTAND THE LANGUAGE OF FORCE AND THREAT.
THEREFORE, WE ORDER ACCESS TO WATER IN THE MARS COLONY BE LIMITED TO THOSE AREAS WHERE NO REBEL ACTIVITY HAS TAKEN PLACE AND WHERE NO SIGN OF REBEL INVOLVEMENT HAS BEEN DETECTED.
IF OUR ADMINISTRATION BECOMES AWARE OF ANY SUPPORT OR COMFORT BEING OFFERED TO THE REBELS, THEN THOSE INVOLVED WILL ALSO HAVE THEIR WATER STRICTLY RATIONED.
IT PAINS US TO TAKE THIS KIND OF ACTION.
BUT OUR HANDS HAVE BEEN FORCED.
WE HOPE THIS MEASURE WILL DISCOURAGE THE REBELS FROM THEIR CURRENT COURSE OF ACTION AND ENCOURAGE THEM TO ACCEPT OUR OFFER TO SURRENDER, WITHOUT REPRISAL, TO THIS ADMINISTRATION.
WE ARE STEADFAST IN OUR RESOLVE TO PRESERVE MARS.
THANK YOU, MARS, FOR LISTENING
ARE WE DOING THE RIGHT THING?
I KNOW THAT WE HAVE TO MAINTAIN ORDER.
BUT IS THIS THE BEST WAY?
VILA, WE CAN'T SHOW WEAKNESS HERE. IT'S NOT WHAT FATHER WOULD HAVE DONE. BESIDES, WITHOUT BEING ABLE TO CONTROL WHO RECEIVES AIR, WE HAVE TO USE THE ONLY OTHER RESOURCE WE CAN CONTROL.
I HOPE THAT LIMITING THE WATER WILL TAKE THE FIGHT OUT OF THE REBELS AND THE RESISTANCE OUT OF THE PEOPLE, IF NECESSARY.
I HOPE YOU'RE RIGHT

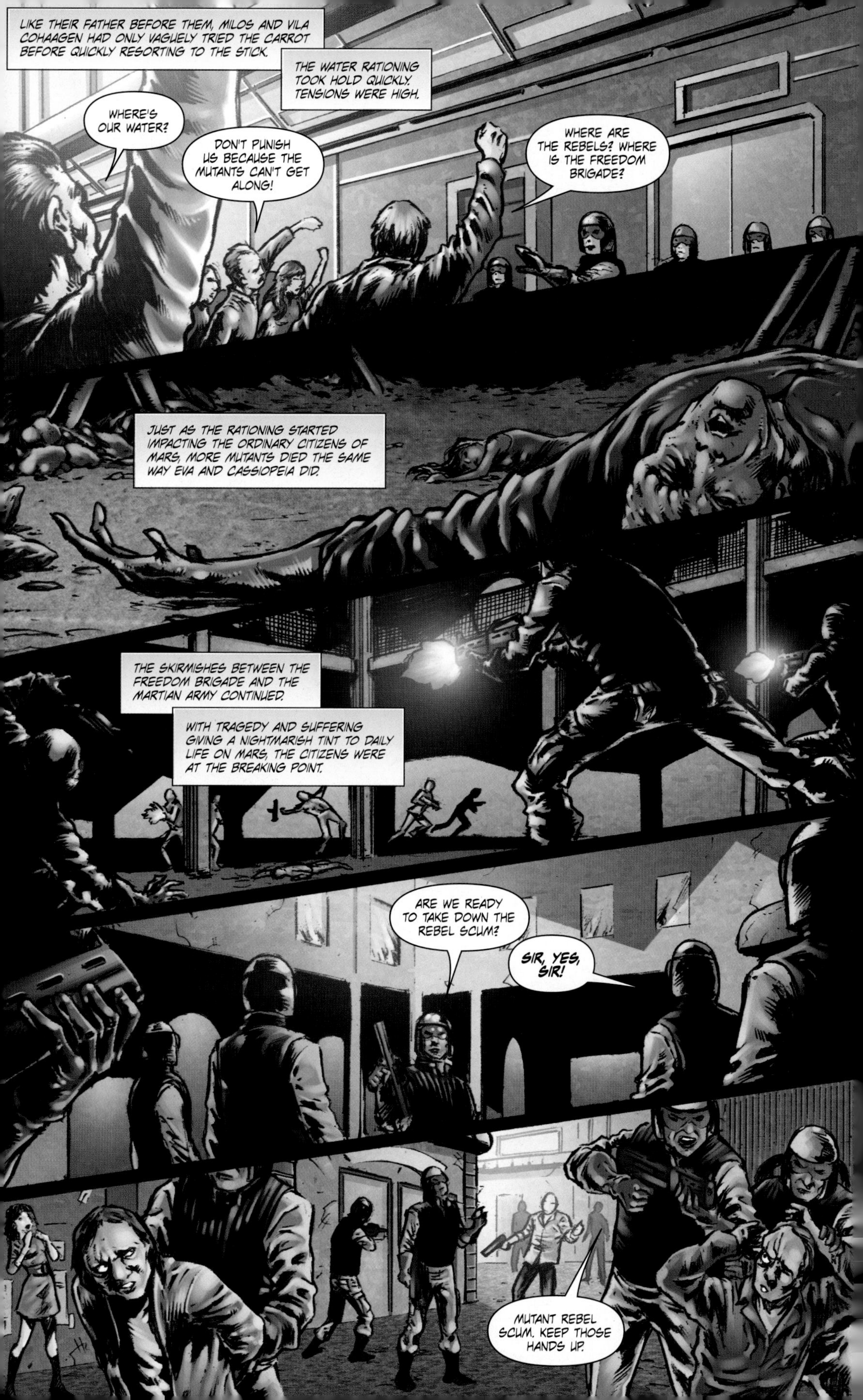
LIKE THEIR FATHER BEFORE THEM, MILOS AND VILA COHAAGEN HAD ONLY VAGUELY TRIED THE CARROT BEFORE QUICKLY RESORTING TO THE STICK.
THE WATER RATIONING TOOK HOLD QUICKLY. TENSIONS WERE HIGH.
WHERE'S OUR WATER?
DON'T PUNISH US BECAUSE THE MUTANTS CAN'T GET ALONG!
WHERE ARE THE REBELS? WHERE IS THE FREEDOM BRIGADE?
JUST AS THE RATIONING STARTED IMPACTING THE ORDINARY CITIZENS OF MARS, MORE MUTANTS DIED THE SAME WAY EVA AND CASSIOPEIA DID.
THE SKIRMISHES BETWEEN THE FREEDOM BRIGADE AND THE MARTIAN ARMY CONTINUED.
WITH TRAGEDY AND SUFFERING GIVING A NIGHTMARISH TINT TO DAILY LIFE ON MARS, THE CITIZENS WERE AT THE BREAKING POINT.
ARE WE READY TO TAKE DOWN THE REBEL SCUM?
SIR, YES, SIR!
MUTANT REBEL SCUM. KEEP THOSE HANDS UP.

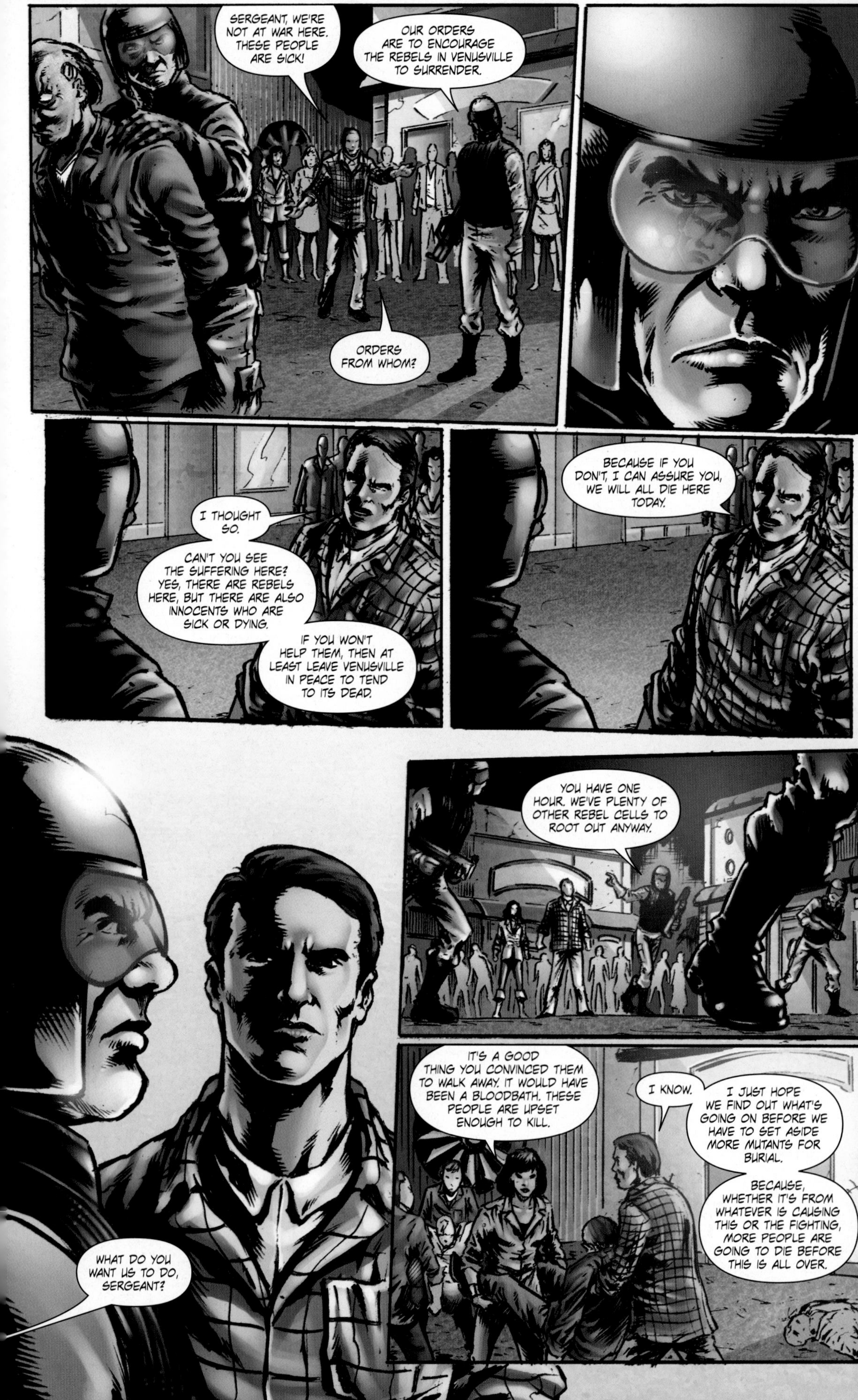

SERGEANT, WE'RE NOT AT WAR HERE. THESE PEOPLE ARE SICK!
OUR ORDERS ARE TO ENCOURAGE THE REBELS IN VENUSVILLE TO SURRENDER.
ORDERS FROM WHOM?
I THOUGHT SO.
CAN'T YOU SEE THE SUFFERING HERE? YES, THERE ARE REBELS HERE, BUT THERE ARE ALSO INNOCENTS WHO ARE SICK OR DYING.
IF YOU WON'T HELP THEM, THEN AT LEAST LEAVE VENUSVILLE IN PEACE TO TEND TO ITS DEAD.
BECAUSE IF YOU DON'T, I CAN ASSURE YOU, WE WILL ALL DIE HERE TODAY.
WHAT DO YOU WANT US TO DO, SERGEANT?
YOU HAVE ONE HOUR. WE'VE PLENTY OF OTHER REBEL CELLS TO ROOT OUT ANYWAY.
IT'S A GOOD THING YOU CONVINCED THEM TO WALK AWAY. IT WOULD HAVE BEEN A BLOODBATH. THESE PEOPLE ARE UPSET ENOUGH TO KILL.
I KNOW.
I JUST HOPE WE FIND OUT WHAT'S GOING ON BEFORE WE HAVE TO SET ASIDE MORE MUTANTS FOR BURIAL.
BECAUSE, WHETHER IT'S FROM WHATEVER IS CAUSING THIS OR THE FIGHTING, MORE PEOPLE ARE GOING TO DIE BEFORE THIS IS ALL OVER.

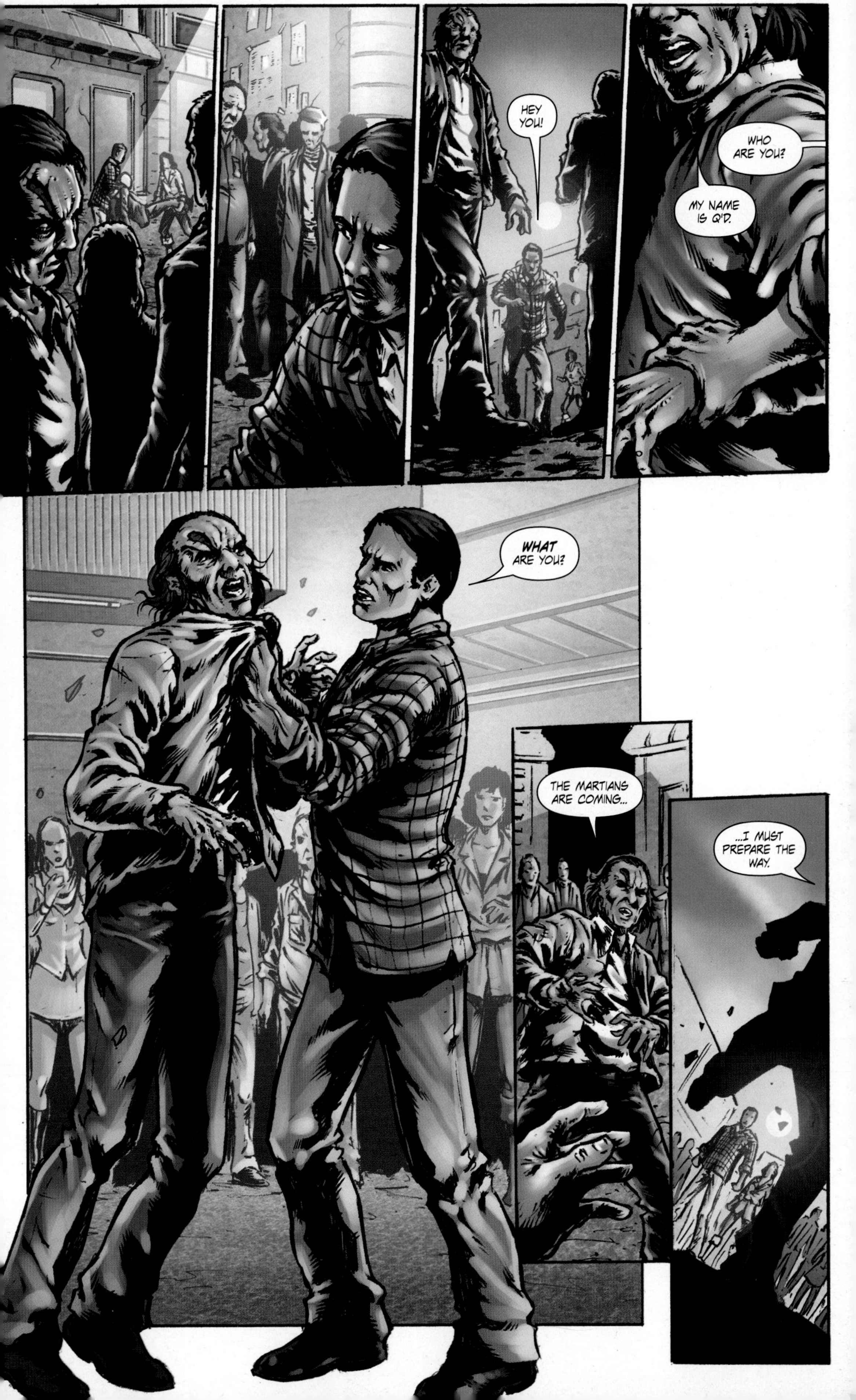
HEY YOU!
WHO ARE YOU?
MY NAME IS Q'D.
WHAT ARE YOU?
THE MARTIANS ARE COMING...
...I MUST PREPARE THE WAY.

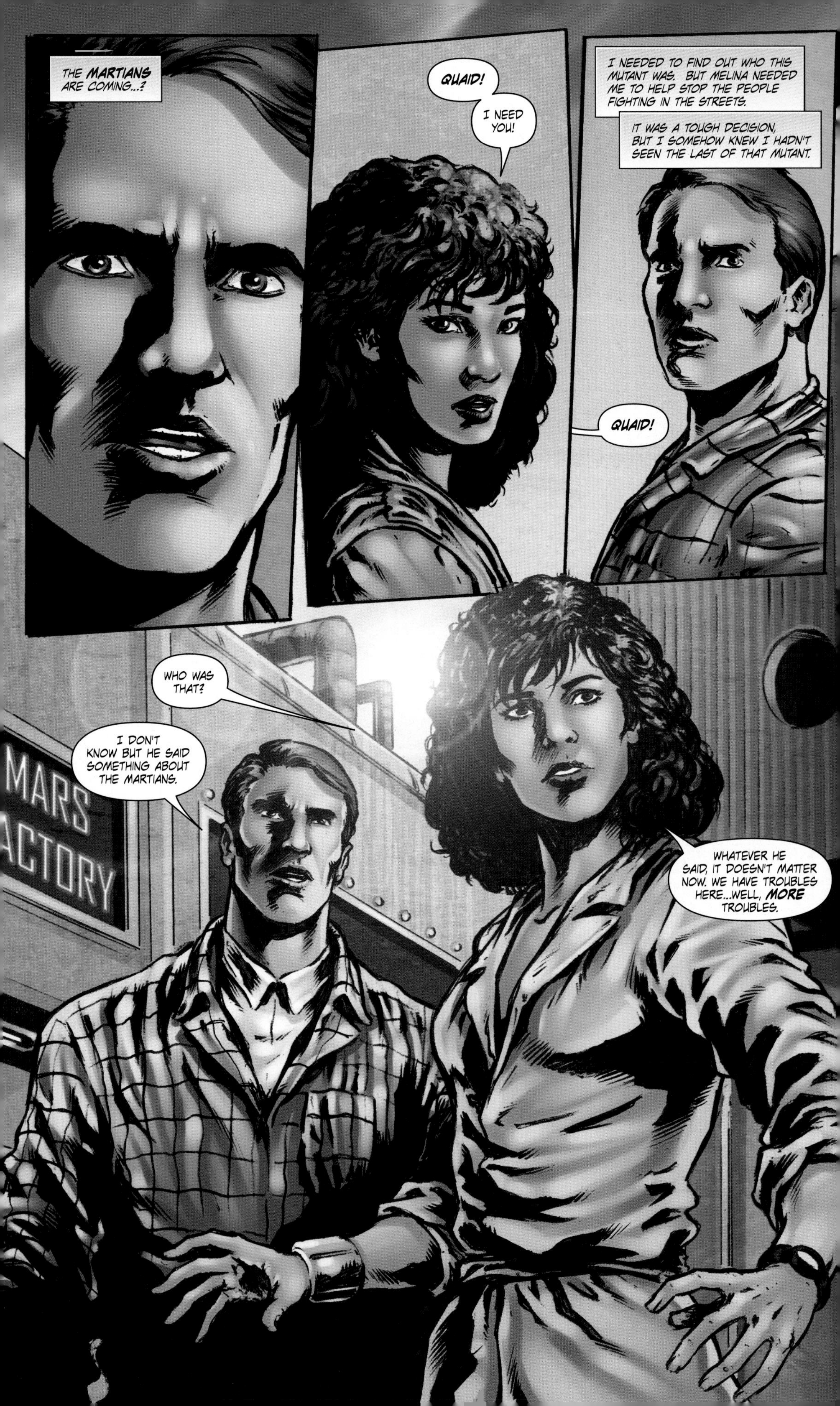
THE MARTIANS ARE COMING...?
QUAID!
I NEED YOU!
I NEEDED TO FIND OUT WHO THIS MUTANT WAS. BUT MELINA NEEDED ME TO HELP STOP THE PEOPLE FIGHTING IN THE STREETS.
IT WAS A TOUGH DECISION, BUT I SOMEHOW KNEW I HADN'T SEEN THE LAST OF THAT MUTANT.
QUAID!
WHO WAS THAT?
I DON'T KNOW BUT HE SAID SOMETHING ABOUT THE MARTIANS.
MARS
ACTORY
WHATEVER HE SAID, IT DOESN'T MATTER NOW. WE HAVE TROUBLES HERE...WELL, MORE TROUBLES.

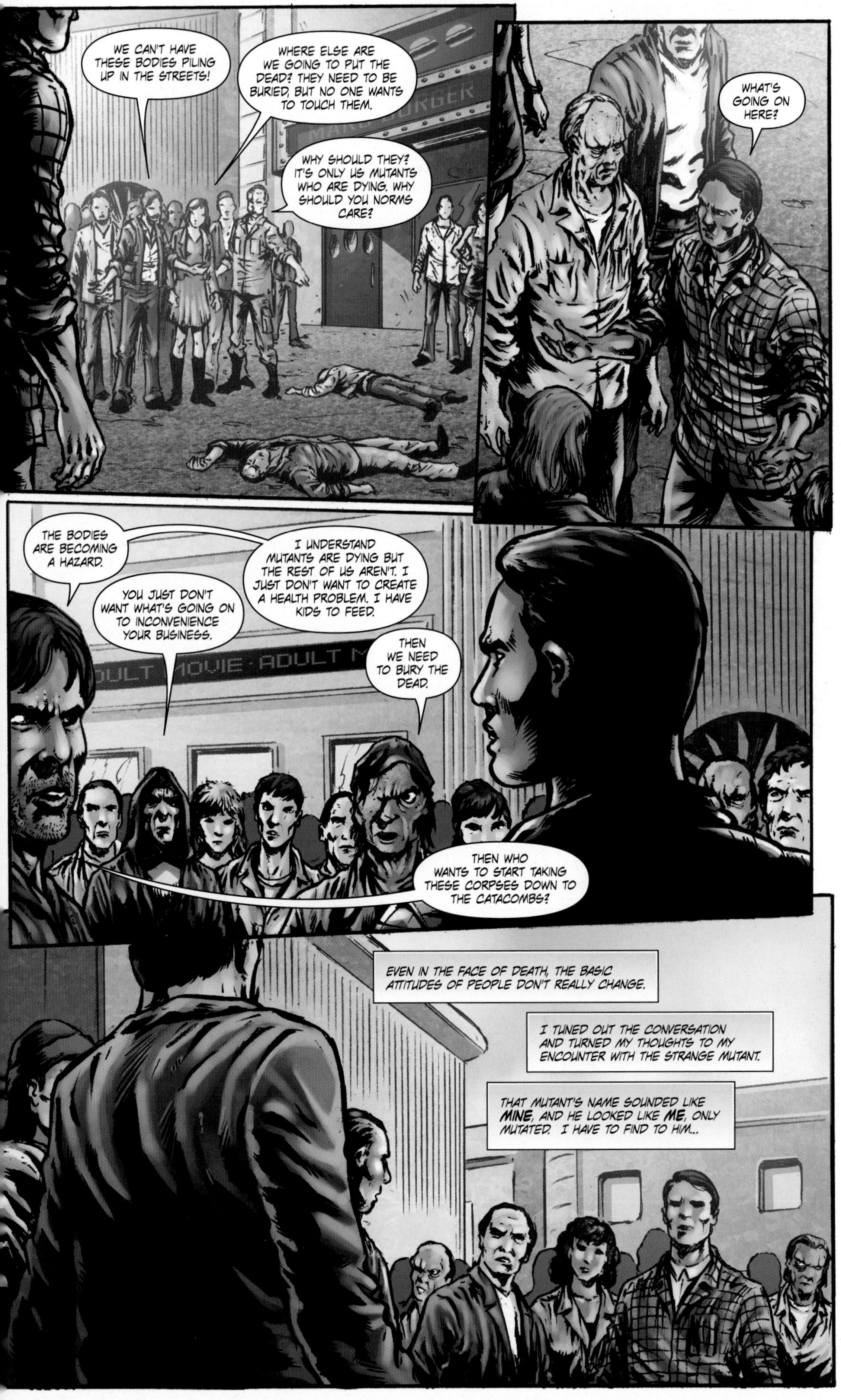
WE CAN'T HAVE THESE BODIES PILING UP IN THE STREETS!
WHERE ELSE ARE WE GOING TO PUT THE DEAD? THEY NEED TO BE BURIED, BUT NO ONE WANTS TO TOUCH THEM.
WHY SHOULD THEY? IT'S ONLY US MUTANTS WHO ARE DYING. WHY SHOULD YOU NORMS CARE?
WHAT'S GOING ON HERE?
THE BODIES ARE BECOMING A HAZARD.
I UNDERSTAND MUTANTS ARE DYING BUT THE REST OF US AREN'T. I JUST DON'T WANT TO CREATE A HEALTH PROBLEM. I HAVE KIDS TO FEED.
YOU JUST DON'T WANT WHAT'S GOING ON TO INCONVENIENCE YOUR BUSINESS.
ADULT MOVIE · ADULT M
THEN WE NEED TO BURY THE DEAD.
THEN WHO WANTS TO START TAKING THESE CORPSES DOWN TO THE CATACOMBS?
EVEN IN THE FACE OF DEATH, THE BASIC ATTITUDES OF PEOPLE DON'T REALLY CHANGE.
I TUNED OUT THE CONVERSATION AND TURNED MY THOUGHTS TO MY ENCOUNTER WITH THE STRANGE MUTANT.
THAT MUTANT'S NAME SOUNDED LIKE MINE, AND HE LOOKED LIKE ME, ONLY MUTATED. I HAVE TO FIND TO HIM...

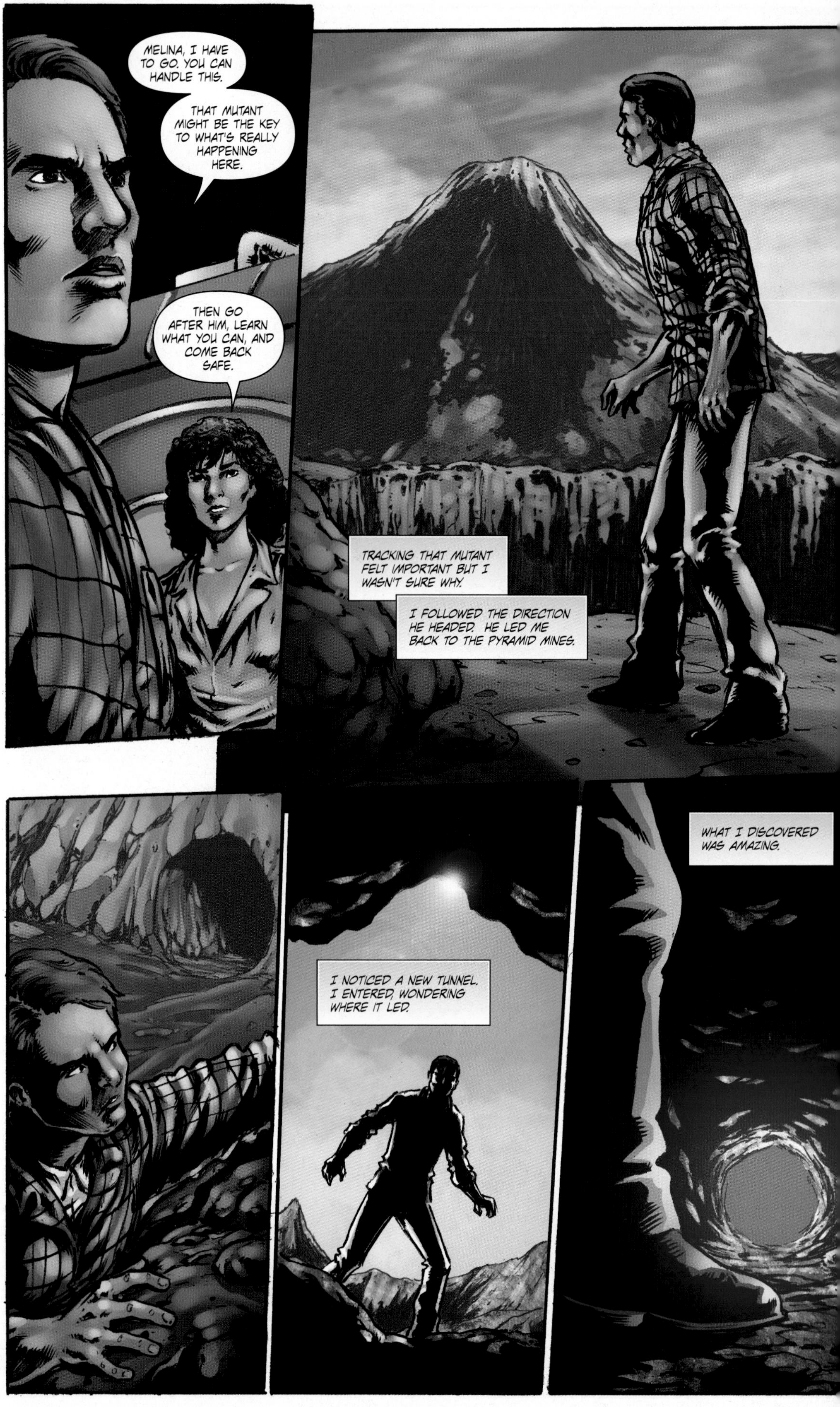

MELINA, I HAVE TO GO. YOU CAN HANDLE THIS.
THAT MUTANT MIGHT BE THE KEY TO WHAT'S REALLY HAPPENING HERE.
THEN GO AFTER HIM, LEARN WHAT YOU CAN, AND COME BACK SAFE.
TRACKING THAT MUTANT FELT IMPORTANT BUT I WASN'T SURE WHY.
I FOLLOWED THE DIRECTION HE HEADED. HE LED ME BACK TO THE PYRAMID MINES.
I NOTICED A NEW TUNNEL. I ENTERED, WONDERING WHERE IT LED.
WHAT I DISCOVERED WAS AMAZING.

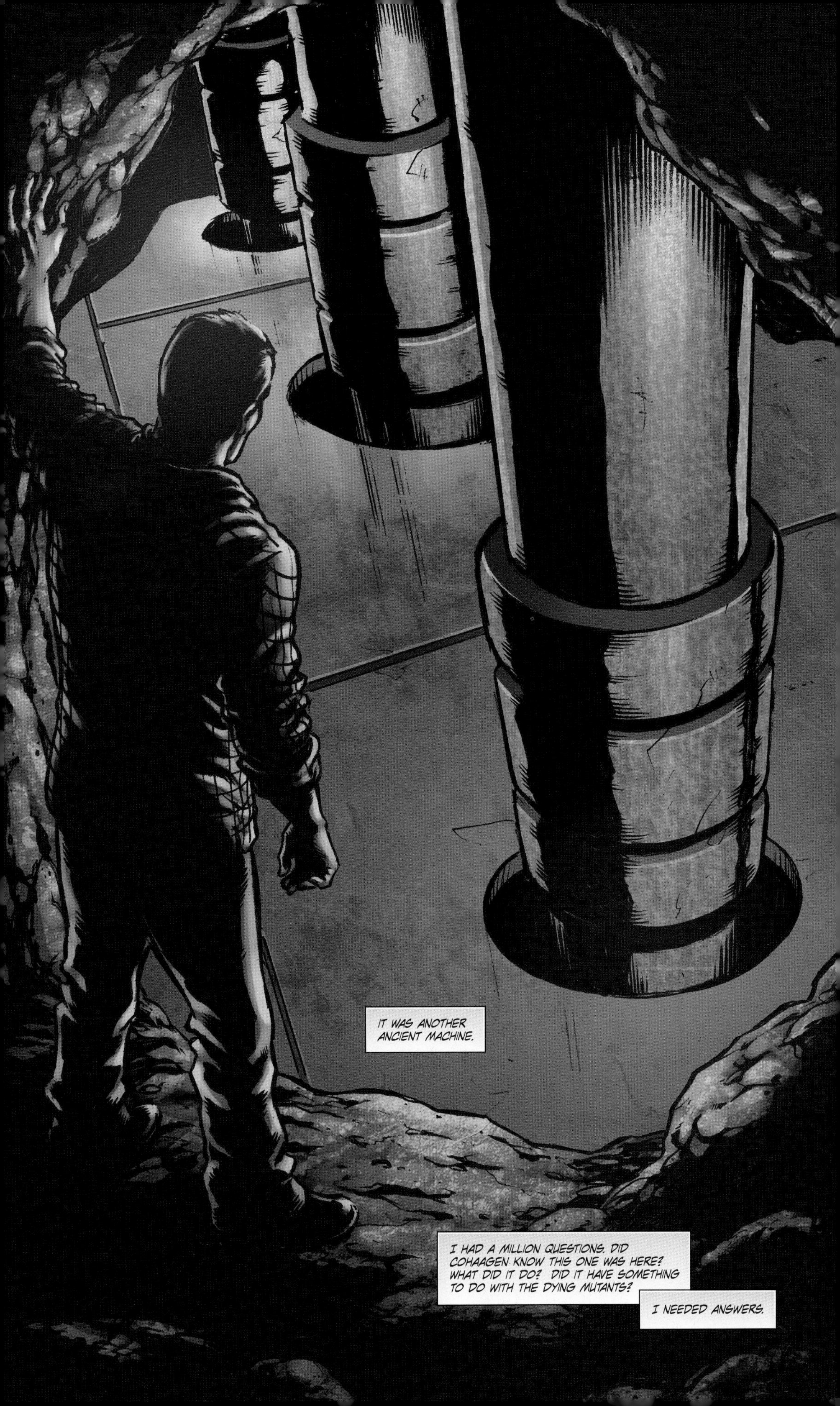

IT WAS ANOTHER ANCIENT MACHINE.
I HAD A MILLION QUESTIONS. DID COHAAGEN KNOW THIS ONE WAS HERE? WHAT DID IT DO? DID IT HAVE SOMETHING TO DO WITH THE DYING MUTANTS?
I NEEDED ANSWERS.

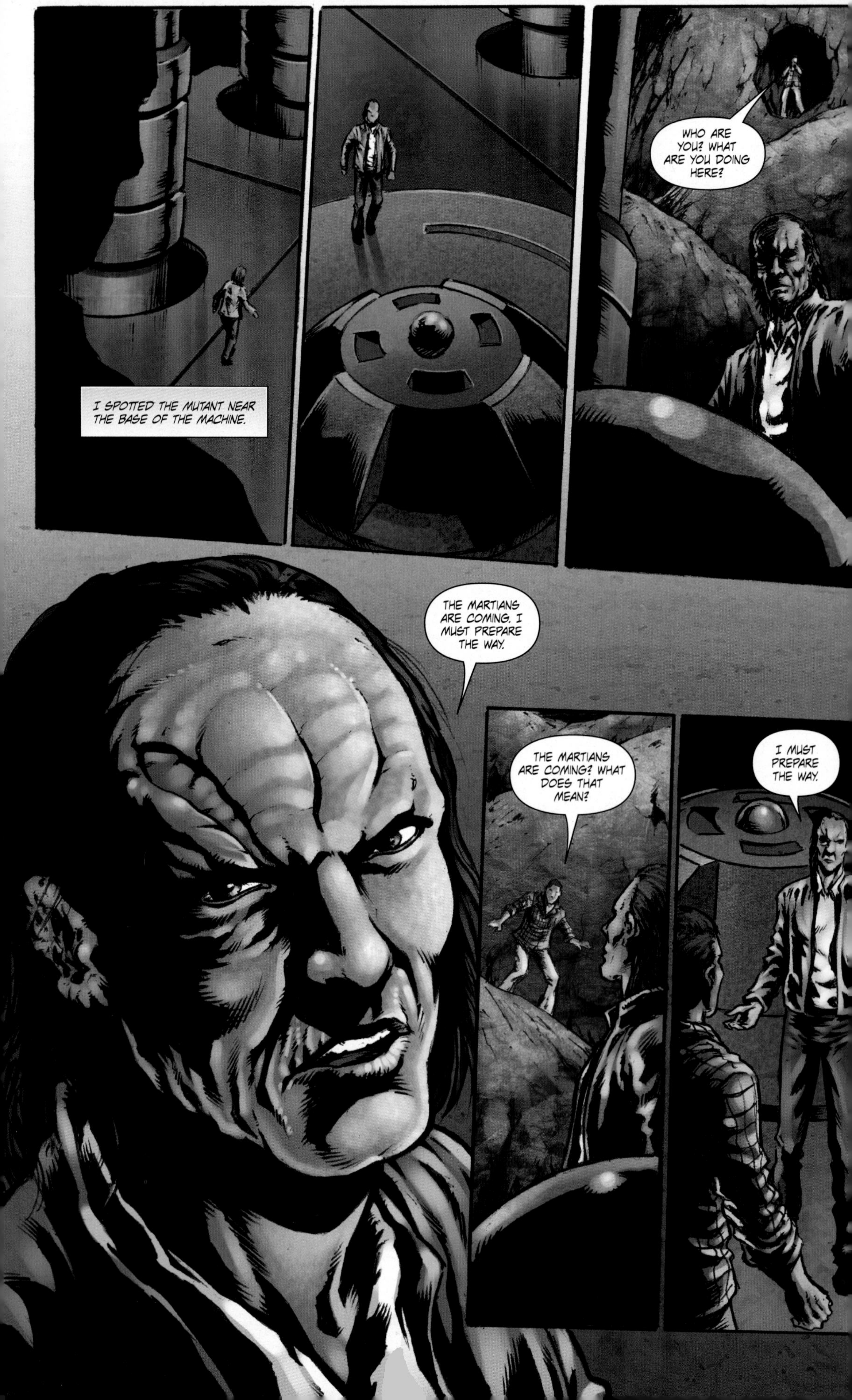
I SPOTTED THE MUTANT NEAR THE BASE OF THE MACHINE.
WHO ARE YOU? WHAT ARE YOU DOING HERE?
THE MARTIANS ARE COMING. I MUST PREPARE THE WAY.
THE MARTIANS ARE COMING? WHAT DOES THAT MEAN?
I MUST PREPARE THE WAY.

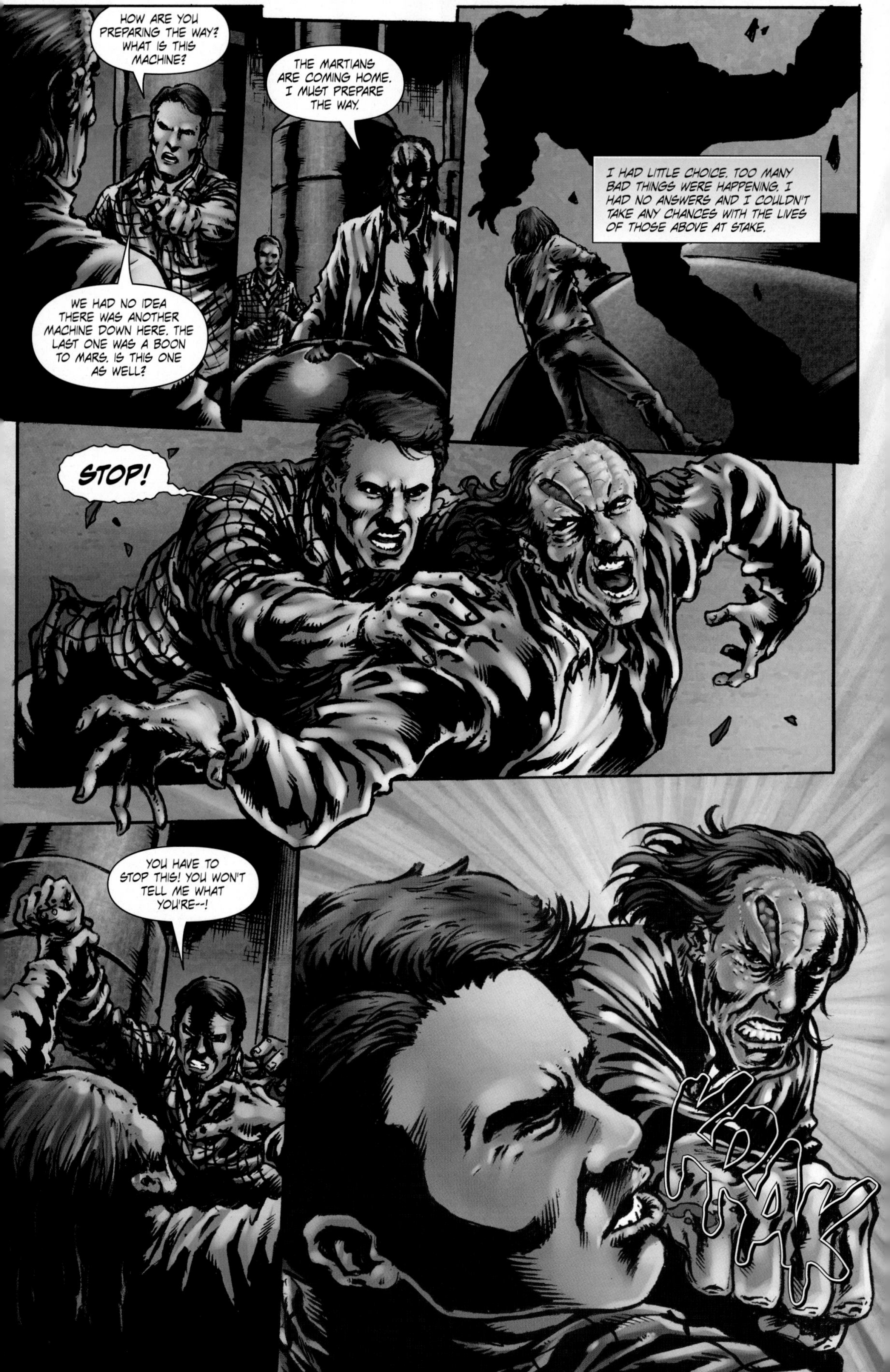
HOW ARE YOU PREPARING THE WAY? WHAT IS THIS MACHINE?
WE HAD NO IDEA THERE WAS ANOTHER MACHINE DOWN HERE. THE LAST ONE WAS A BOON TO MARS. IS THIS ONE AS WELL?
THE MARTIANS ARE COMING HOME. I MUST PREPARE THE WAY.
I HAD LITTLE CHOICE. TOO MANY BAD THINGS WERE HAPPENING. I HAD NO ANSWERS AND I COULDN'T TAKE ANY CHANCES WITH THE LIVES OF THOSE ABOVE AT STAKE.
STOP!
YOU HAVE TO STOP THIS! YOU WON'T TELL ME WHAT YOU'RE--!

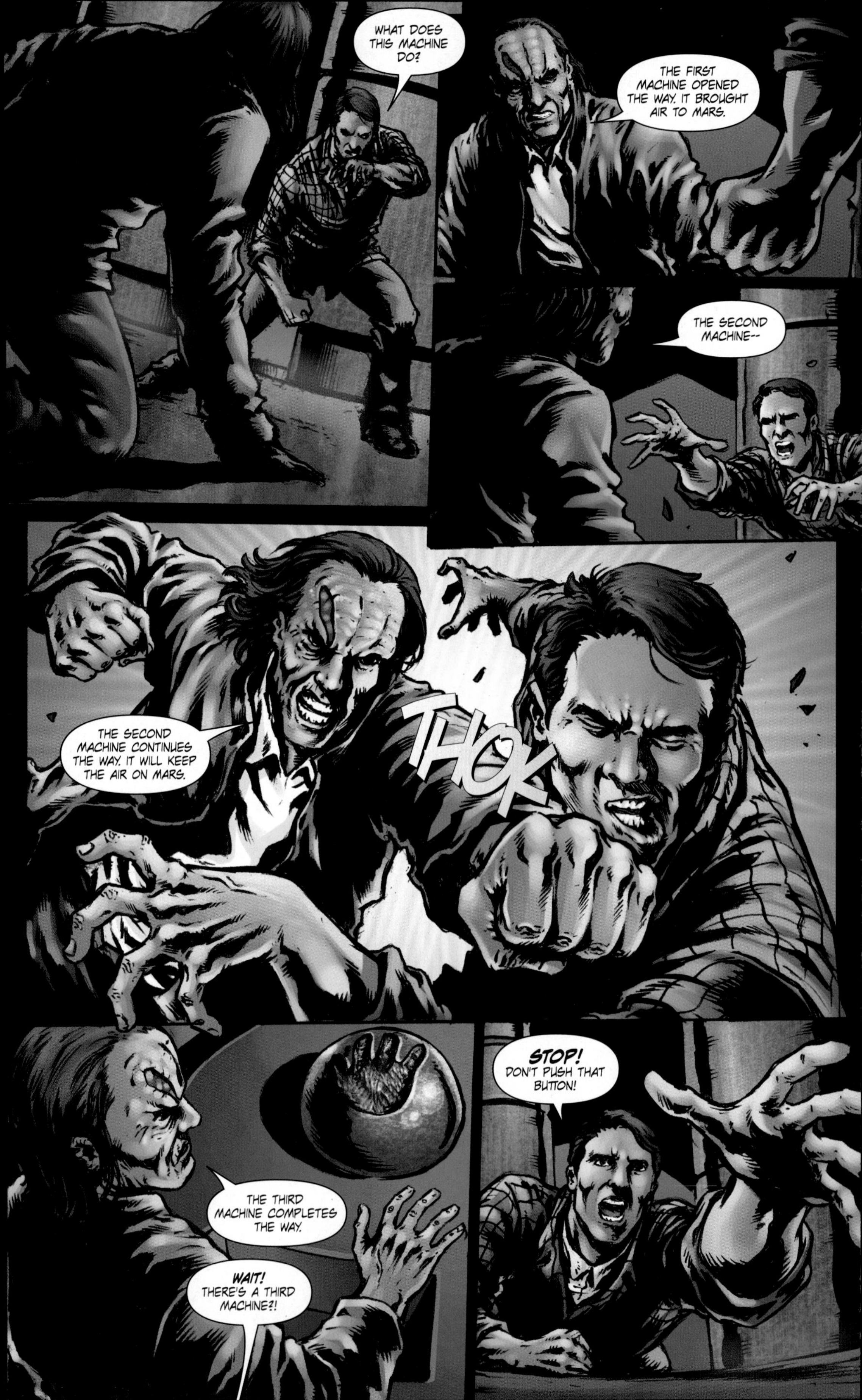
WHAT DOES THIS MACHINE DO?
THE FIRST MACHINE OPENED THE WAY. IT BROUGHT AIR TO MARS.
THE SECOND MACHINE--
THE SECOND MACHINE CONTINUES THE WAY. IT WILL KEEP THE AIR ON MARS.
THOK
THE THIRD MACHINE COMPLETES THE WAY.
WAIT! THERE'S A THIRD MACHINE?!
STOP! DON'T PUSH THAT BUTTON!

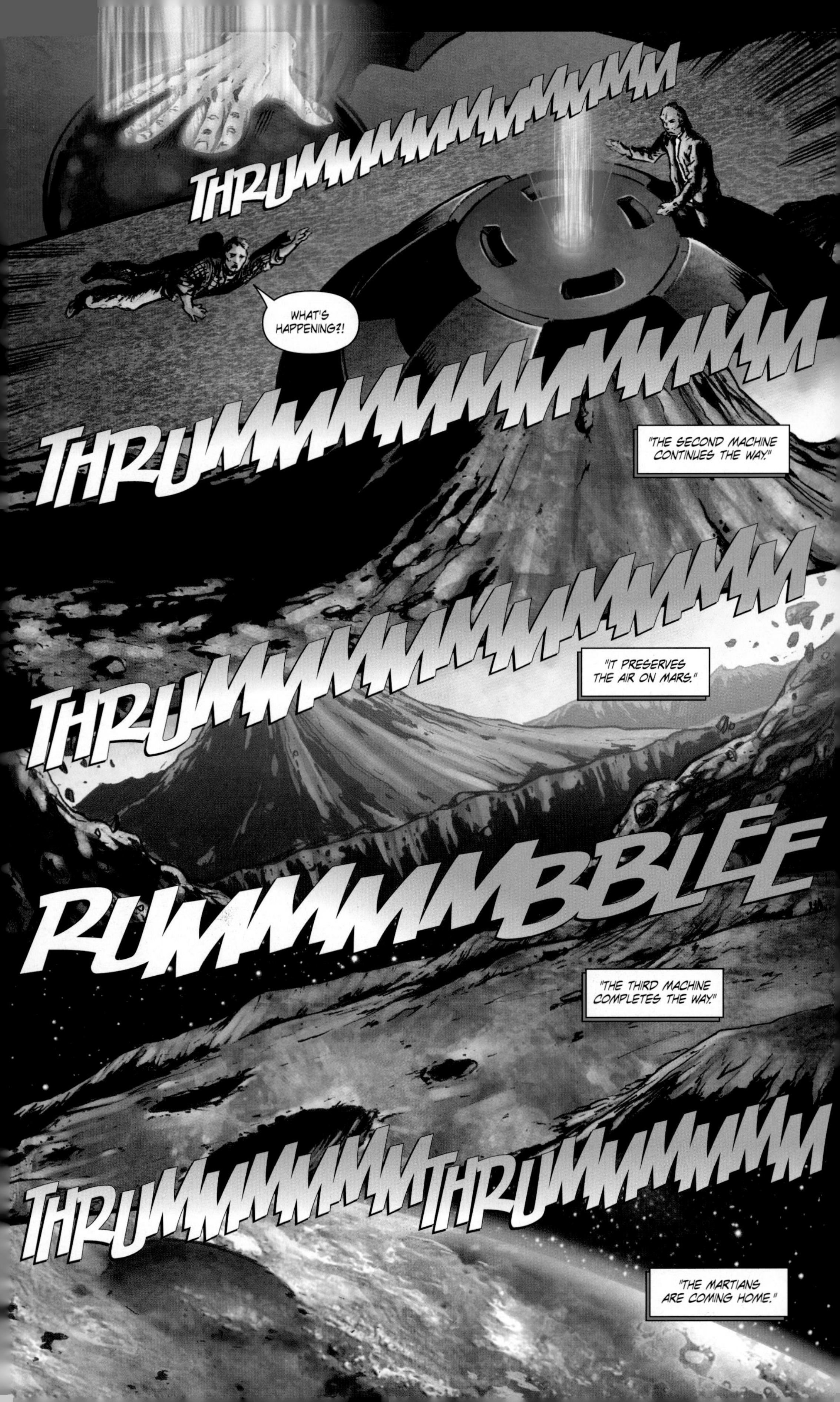
THRUMMMMMMMMMMM
WHAT'S HAPPENING?!
THRUMMMMMMMMMMMMM
"THE SECOND MACHINE CONTINUES THE WAY."
THRUMMMMMMMMMMMMMM
"IT PRESERVES THE AIR ON MARS."
RUMMMMBBLEE
"THE THIRD MACHINE COMPLETES THE WAY."
THRUMMMMMMMTHRUMMMMMMM
"THE MARTIANS ARE COMING HOME."

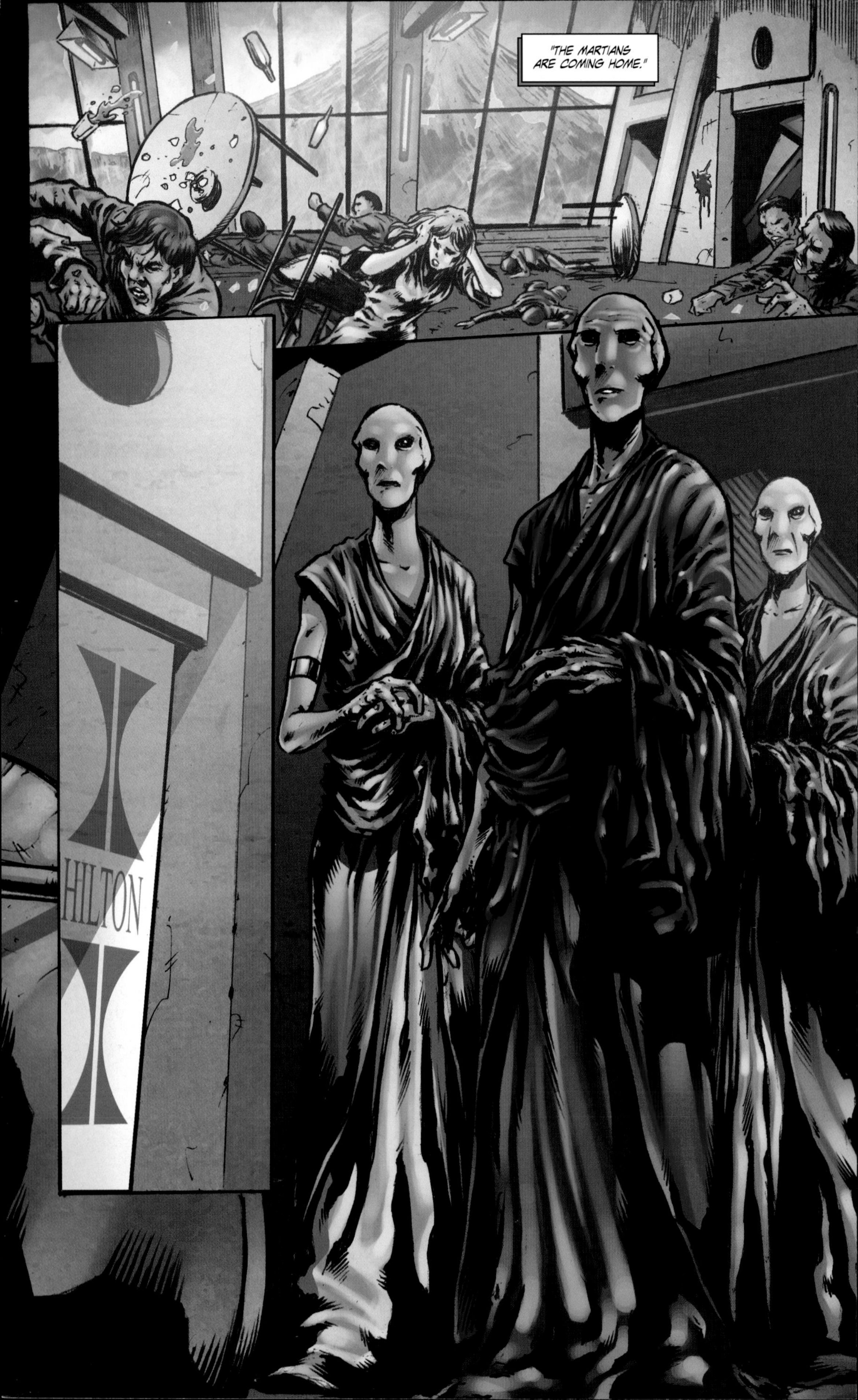
"THE MARTIANS ARE COMING HOME."
HILTON

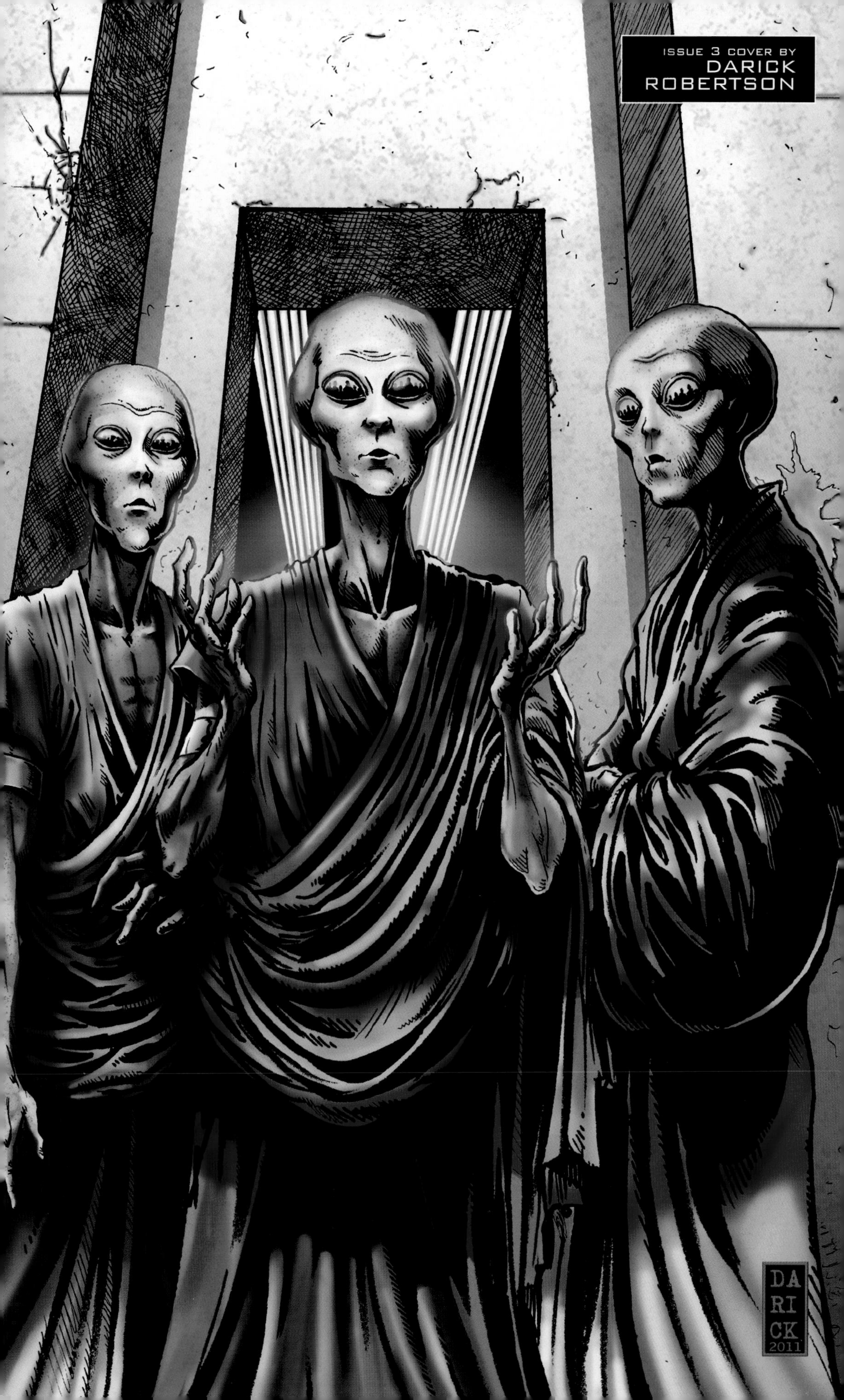
DA
RI
CK
2011
ISSUE 3 COVER BY
DARICK
ROBERTSON

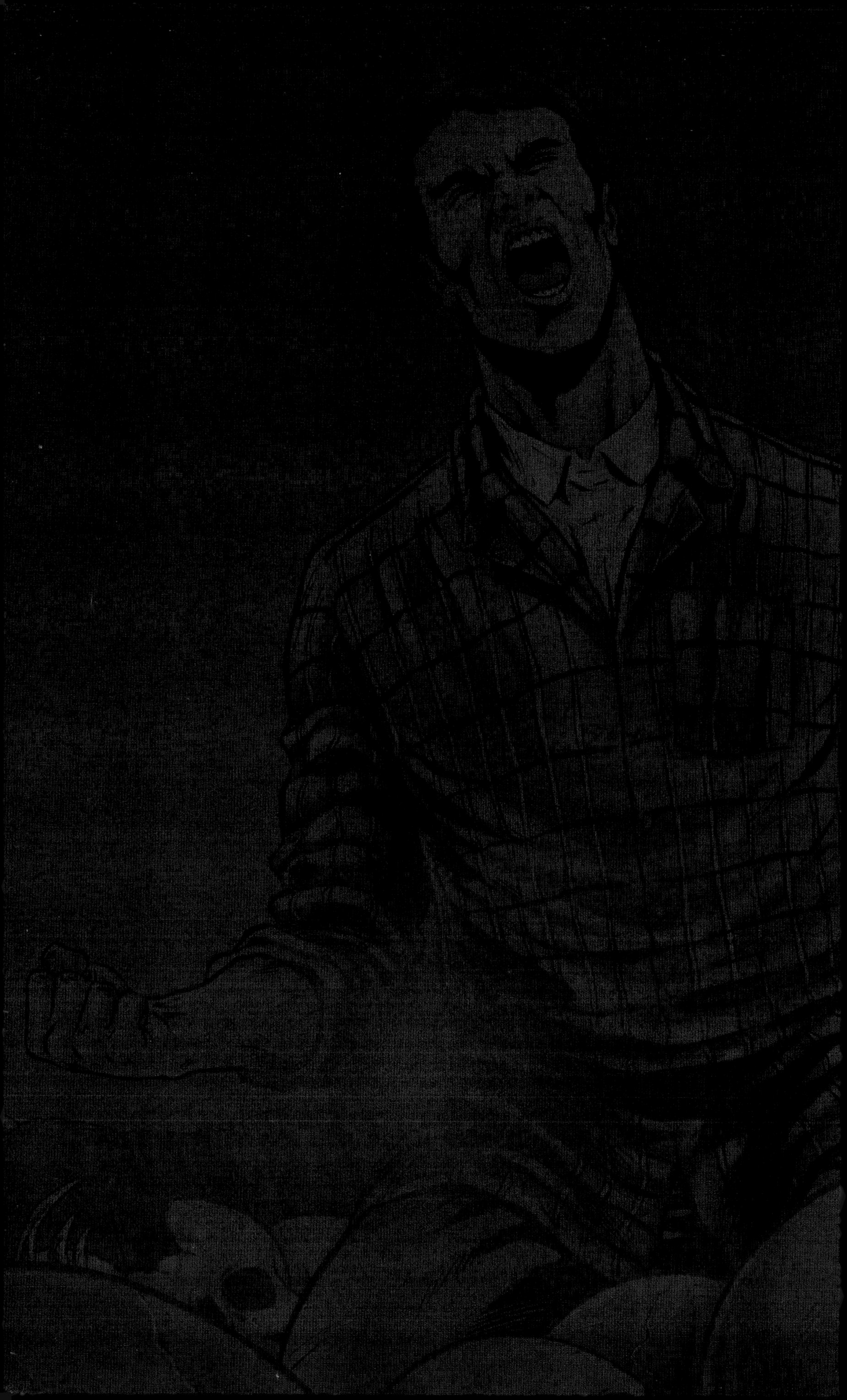

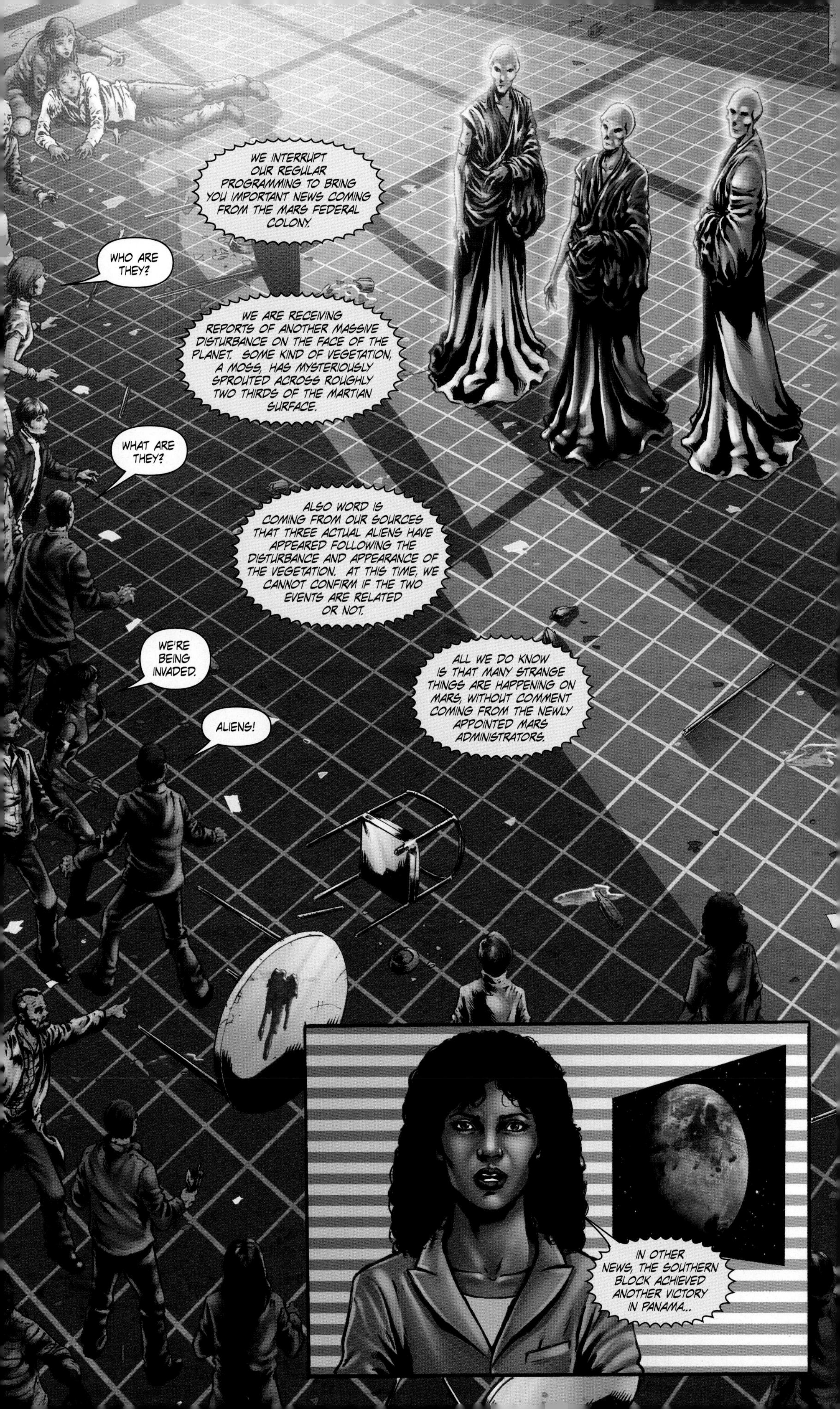
WE INTERRUPT OUR REGULAR PROGRAMMING TO BRING YOU IMPORTANT NEWS COMING FROM THE MARS FEDERAL COLONY.
WHO ARE THEY?
WE ARE RECEIVING REPORTS OF ANOTHER MASSIVE DISTURBANCE ON THE FACE OF THE PLANET. SOME KIND OF VEGETATION, A MOSS, HAS MYSTERIOUSLY SPROUTED ACROSS ROUGHLY TWO THIRDS OF THE MARTIAN SURFACE.
WHAT ARE THEY?
ALSO WORD IS COMING FROM OUR SOURCES THAT THREE ACTUAL ALIENS HAVE APPEARED FOLLOWING THE DISTURBANCE AND APPEARANCE OF THE VEGETATION. AT THIS TIME, WE CANNOT CONFIRM IF THE TWO EVENTS ARE RELATED OR NOT.
WE'RE BEING INVADED.
ALL WE DO KNOW IS THAT MANY STRANGE THINGS ARE HAPPENING ON MARS, WITHOUT COMMENT COMING FROM THE NEWLY APPOINTED MARS ADMINISTRATORS.
ALIENS!
IN OTHER NEWS, THE SOUTHERN BLOCK ACHIEVED ANOTHER VICTORY IN PANAMA...

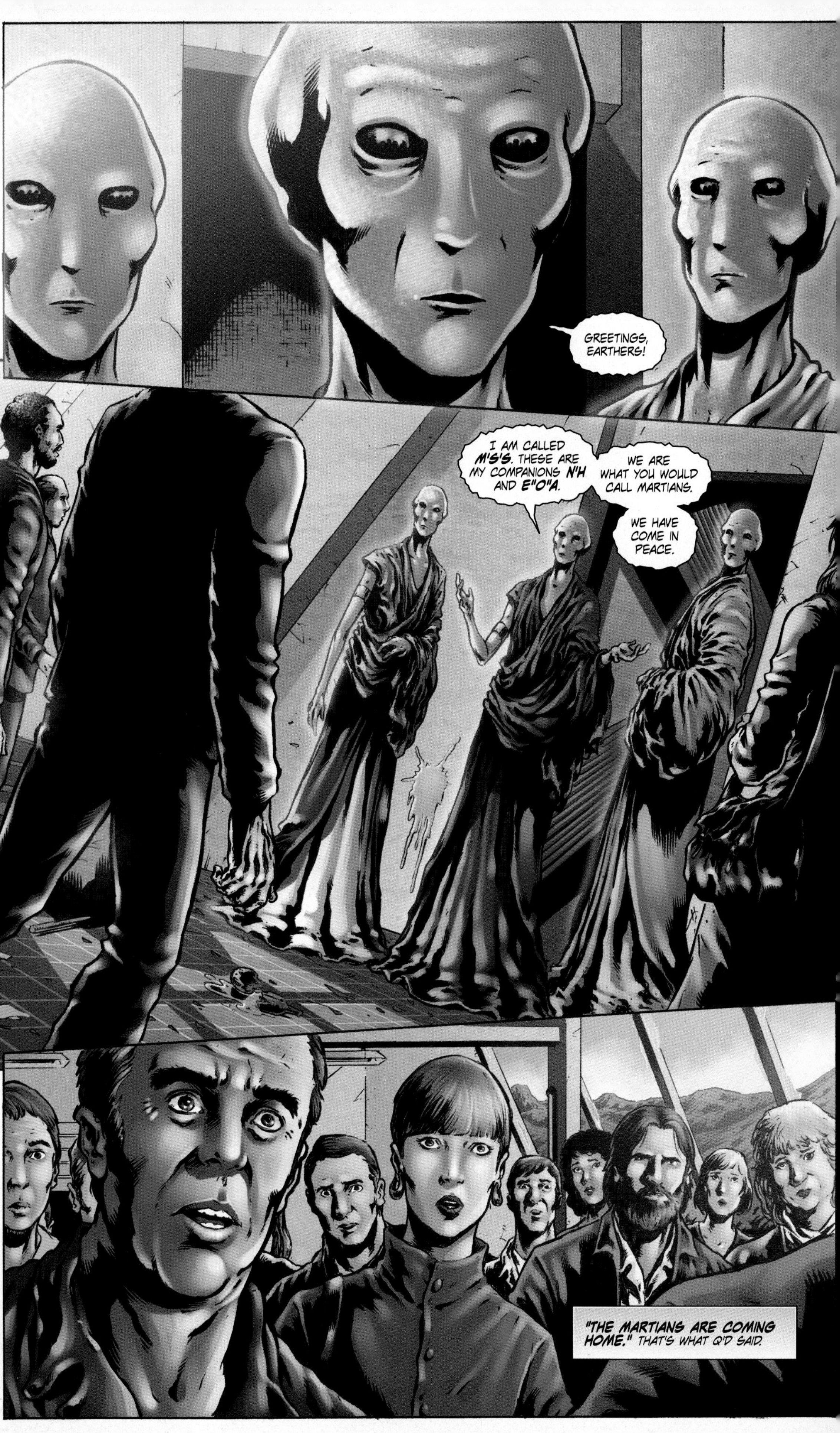
GREETINGS, EARTHERS!
I AM CALLED M'S'S. THESE ARE MY COMPANIONS N'H AND E"O"A.
WE ARE WHAT YOU WOULD CALL MARTIANS.
WE HAVE COME IN PEACE.
"THE MARTIANS ARE COMING HOME." THAT'S WHAT Q'D SAID.

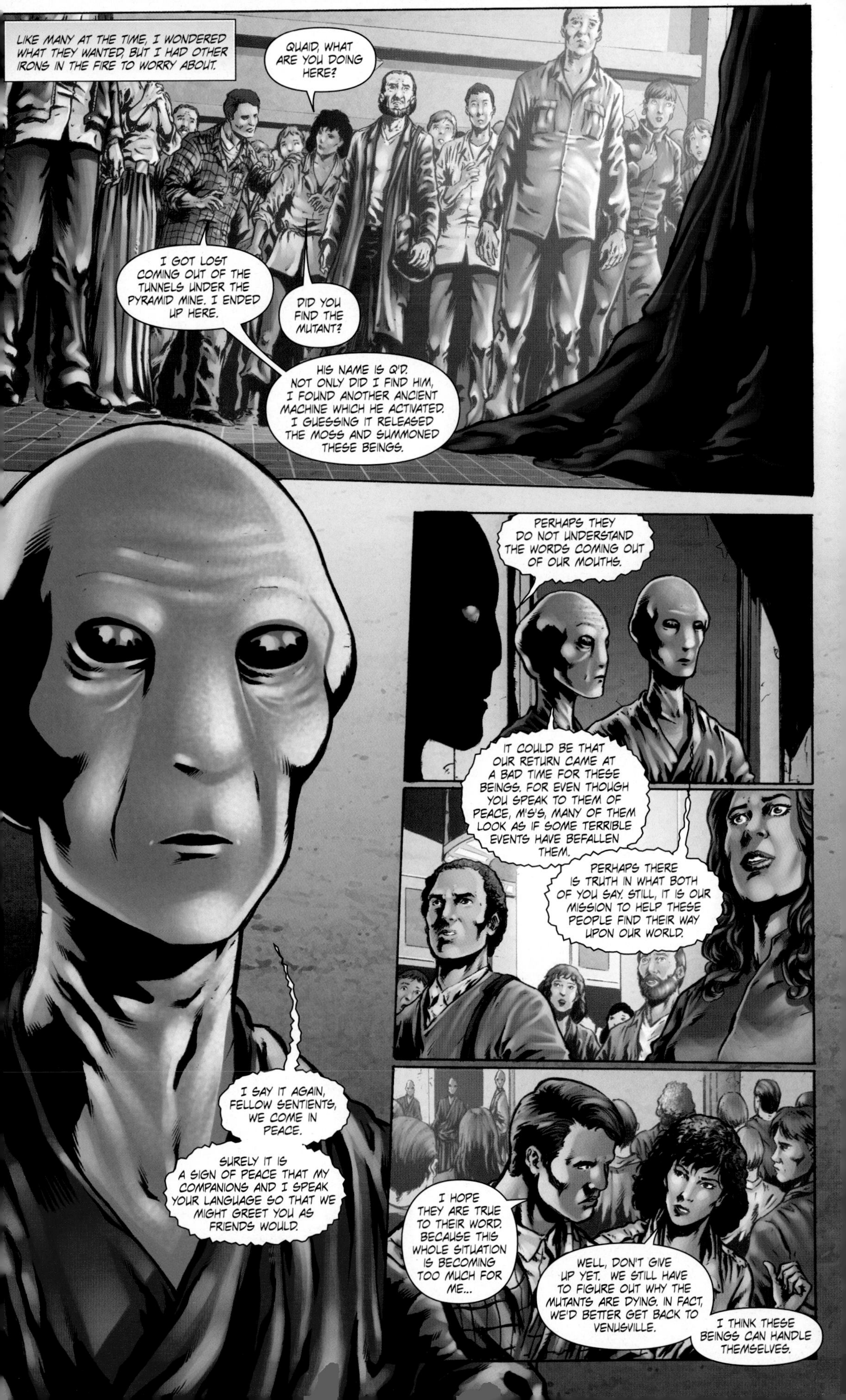

LIKE MANY AT THE TIME, I WONDERED WHAT THEY WANTED, BUT I HAD OTHER IRONS IN THE FIRE TO WORRY ABOUT.
QUAID, WHAT ARE YOU DOING HERE?
I GOT LOST COMING OUT OF THE TUNNELS UNDER THE PYRAMID MINE. I ENDED UP HERE.
DID YOU FIND THE MUTANT?
HIS NAME IS Q'D. NOT ONLY DID I FIND HIM, I FOUND ANOTHER ANCIENT MACHINE WHICH HE ACTIVATED. I GUESSING IT RELEASED THE MOSS AND SUMMONED THESE BEINGS.
I SAY IT AGAIN, FELLOW SENTIENTS, WE COME IN PEACE.
SURELY IT IS A SIGN OF PEACE THAT MY COMPANIONS AND I SPEAK YOUR LANGUAGE SO THAT WE MIGHT GREET YOU AS FRIENDS WOULD.
PERHAPS THEY DO NOT UNDERSTAND THE WORDS COMING OUT OF OUR MOUTHS.
IT COULD BE THAT OUR RETURN CAME AT A BAD TIME FOR THESE BEINGS. FOR EVEN THOUGH YOU SPEAK TO THEM OF PEACE, M'S'S, MANY OF THEM LOOK AS IF SOME TERRIBLE EVENTS HAVE BEFALLEN THEM.
PERHAPS THERE IS TRUTH IN WHAT BOTH OF YOU SAY. STILL, IT IS OUR MISSION TO HELP THESE PEOPLE FIND THEIR WAY UPON OUR WORLD.
I HOPE THEY ARE TRUE TO THEIR WORD. BECAUSE THIS WHOLE SITUATION IS BECOMING TOO MUCH FOR ME...
WELL, DON'T GIVE UP YET. WE STILL HAVE TO FIGURE OUT WHY THE MUTANTS ARE DYING. IN FACT, WE'D BETTER GET BACK TO VENUSVILLE.
I THINK THESE BEINGS CAN HANDLE THEMSELVES.

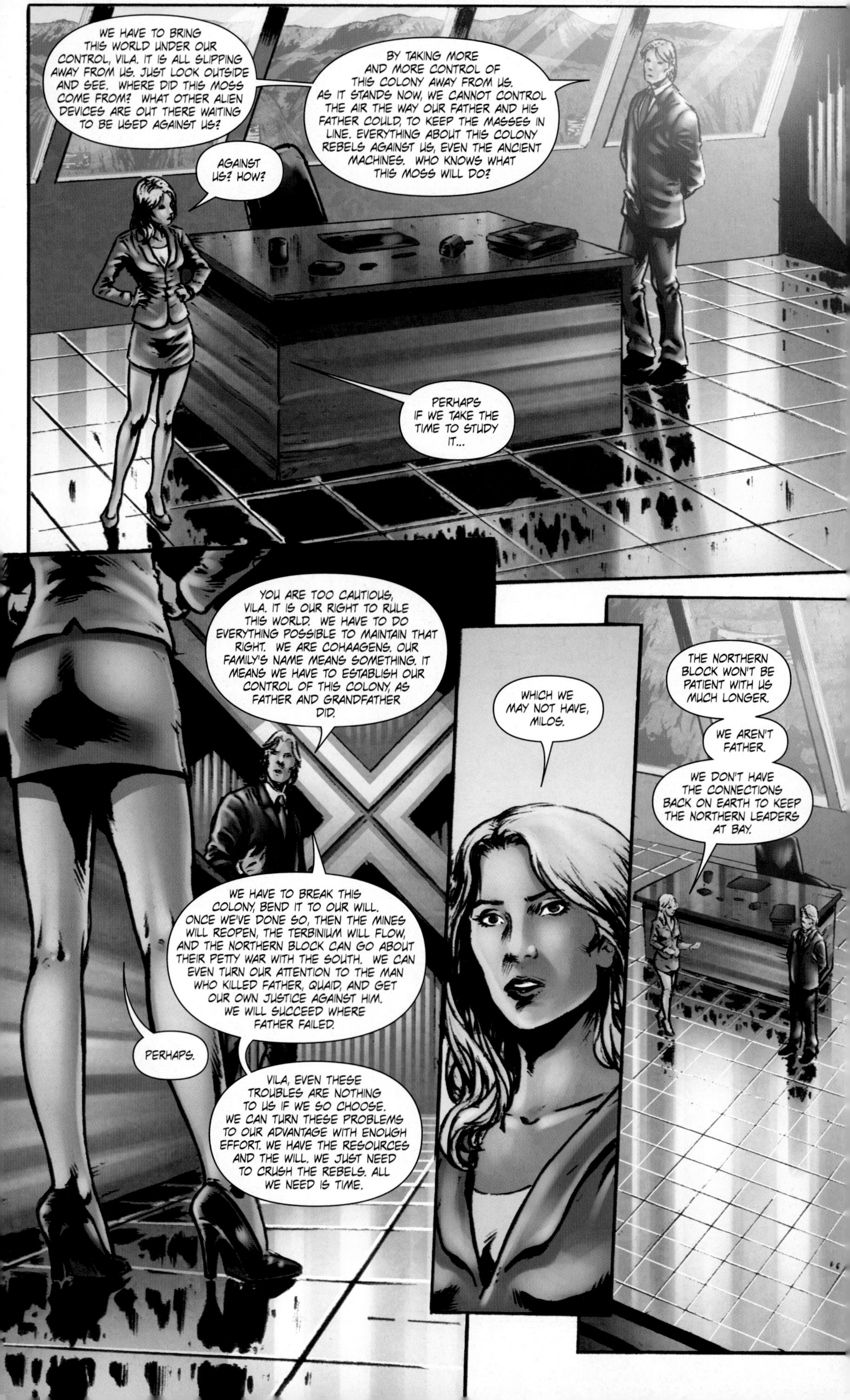
WE HAVE TO BRING THIS WORLD UNDER OUR CONTROL, VILA. IT IS ALL SLIPPING AWAY FROM US. JUST LOOK OUTSIDE AND SEE. WHERE DID THIS MOSS COME FROM? WHAT OTHER ALIEN DEVICES ARE OUT THERE WAITING TO BE USED AGAINST US?
AGAINST US? HOW?
BY TAKING MORE AND MORE CONTROL OF THIS COLONY AWAY FROM US. AS IT STANDS NOW, WE CANNOT CONTROL THE AIR THE WAY OUR FATHER AND HIS FATHER COULD, TO KEEP THE MASSES IN LINE. EVERYTHING ABOUT THIS COLONY REBELS AGAINST US, EVEN THE ANCIENT MACHINES. WHO KNOWS WHAT THIS MOSS WILL DO?
PERHAPS IF WE TAKE THE TIME TO STUDY IT...
YOU ARE TOO CAUTIOUS, VILA. IT IS OUR RIGHT TO RULE THIS WORLD. WE HAVE TO DO EVERYTHING POSSIBLE TO MAINTAIN THAT RIGHT. WE ARE COHAAGENS. OUR FAMILY'S NAME MEANS SOMETHING. IT MEANS WE HAVE TO ESTABLISH OUR CONTROL OF THIS COLONY, AS FATHER AND GRANDFATHER DID.
WE HAVE TO BREAK THIS COLONY, BEND IT TO OUR WILL. ONCE WE'VE DONE SO, THEN THE MINES WILL REOPEN, THE TERBINIUM WILL FLOW, AND THE NORTHERN BLOCK CAN GO ABOUT THEIR PETTY WAR WITH THE SOUTH. WE CAN EVEN TURN OUR ATTENTION TO THE MAN WHO KILLED FATHER, QUAID, AND GET OUR OWN JUSTICE AGAINST HIM. WE WILL SUCCEED WHERE FATHER FAILED.
PERHAPS.
VILA, EVEN THESE TROUBLES ARE NOTHING TO US IF WE SO CHOOSE. WE CAN TURN THESE PROBLEMS TO OUR ADVANTAGE WITH ENOUGH EFFORT. WE HAVE THE RESOURCES AND THE WILL. WE JUST NEED TO CRUSH THE REBELS. ALL WE NEED IS TIME.
WHICH WE MAY NOT HAVE, MILOS.
THE NORTHERN BLOCK WON'T BE PATIENT WITH US MUCH LONGER.
WE AREN'T FATHER.
WE DON'T HAVE THE CONNECTIONS BACK ON EARTH TO KEEP THE NORTHERN LEADERS AT BAY.

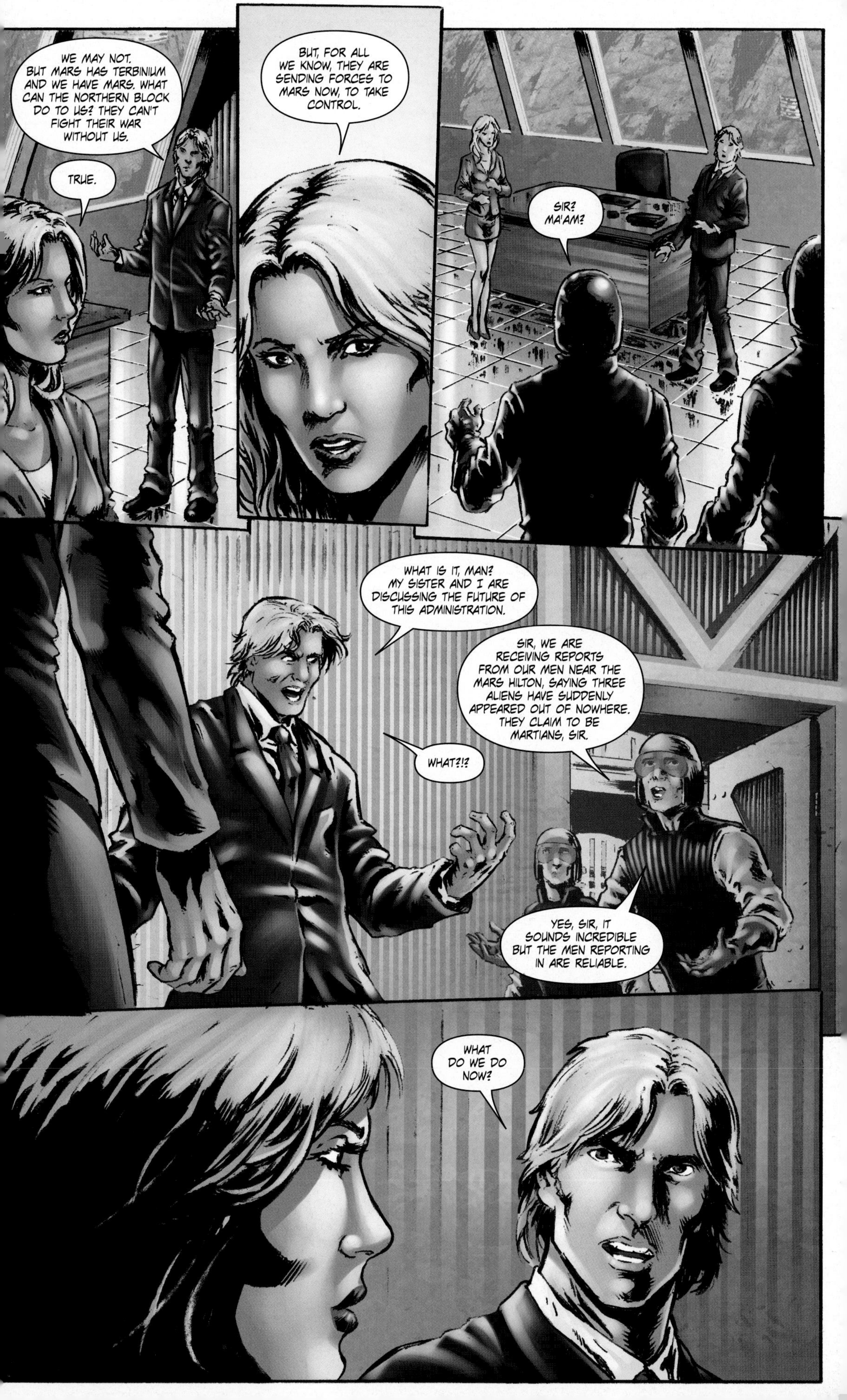
WE MAY NOT. BUT MARS HAS TERBINIUM AND WE HAVE MARS. WHAT CAN THE NORTHERN BLOCK DO TO US? THEY CAN'T FIGHT THEIR WAR WITHOUT US.
TRUE.
BUT, FOR ALL WE KNOW, THEY ARE SENDING FORCES TO MARS NOW, TO TAKE CONTROL.
SIR? MA'AM?
WHAT IS IT, MAN? MY SISTER AND I ARE DISCUSSING THE FUTURE OF THIS ADMINISTRATION.
SIR, WE ARE RECEIVING REPORTS FROM OUR MEN NEAR THE MARS HILTON, SAYING THREE ALIENS HAVE SUDDENLY APPEARED OUT OF NOWHERE. THEY CLAIM TO BE MARTIANS, SIR.
WHAT?!?
YES, SIR, IT SOUNDS INCREDIBLE BUT THE MEN REPORTING IN ARE RELIABLE.
WHAT DO WE DO NOW?

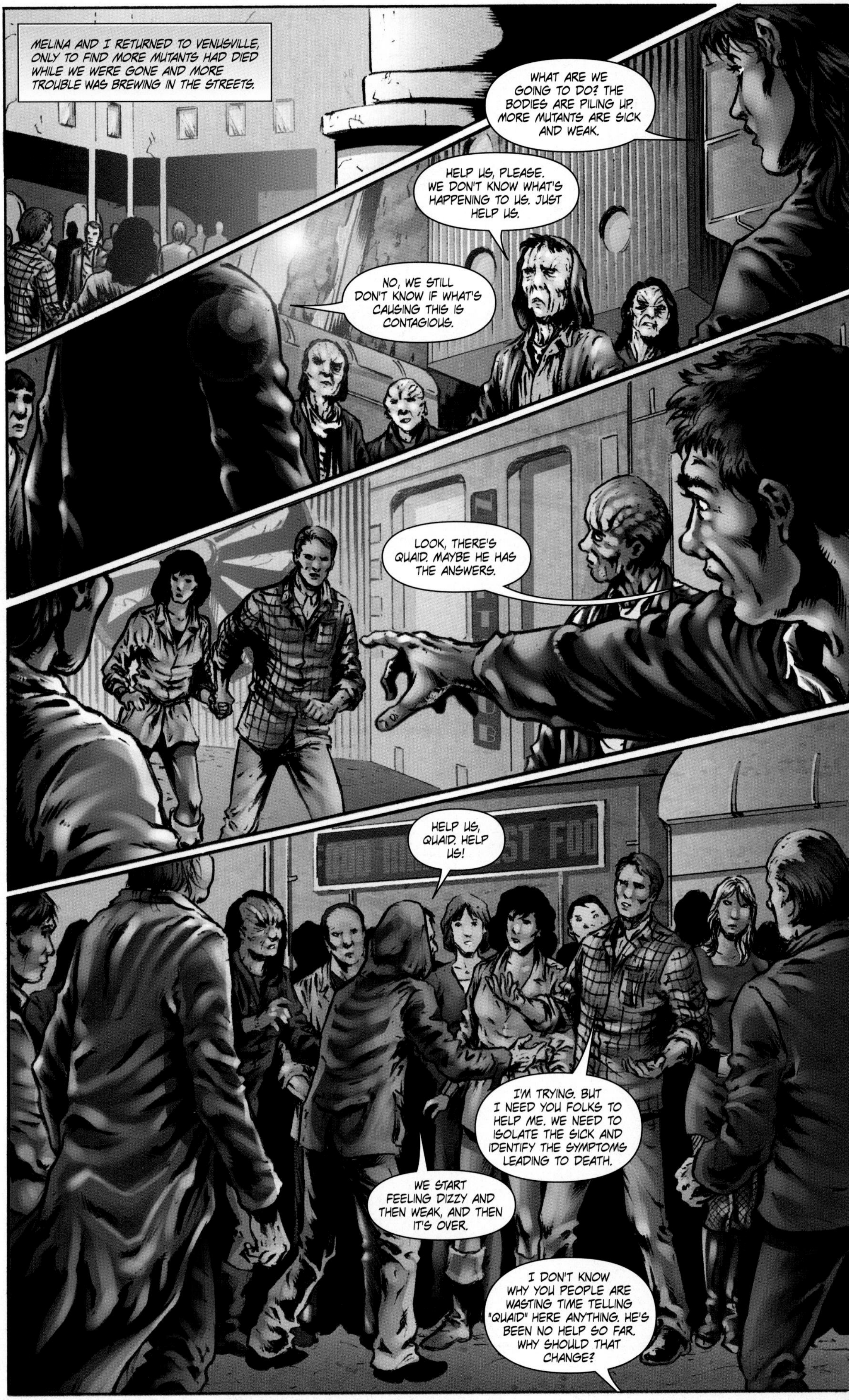
MELINA AND I RETURNED TO VENUSVILLE, ONLY TO FIND MORE MUTANTS HAD DIED WHILE WE WERE GONE AND MORE TROUBLE WAS BREWING IN THE STREETS.
WHAT ARE WE GOING TO DO? THE BODIES ARE PILING UP. MORE MUTANTS ARE SICK AND WEAK.
HELP US, PLEASE. WE DON'T KNOW WHAT'S HAPPENING TO US. JUST HELP US.
NO, WE STILL DON'T KNOW IF WHAT'S CAUSING THIS IS CONTAGIOUS.
LOOK, THERE'S QUAID. MAYBE HE HAS THE ANSWERS.
HELP US, QUAID. HELP US!
I'M TRYING. BUT I NEED YOU FOLKS TO HELP ME. WE NEED TO ISOLATE THE SICK AND IDENTIFY THE SYMPTOMS LEADING TO DEATH.
WE START FEELING DIZZY AND THEN WEAK, AND THEN IT'S OVER.
I DON'T KNOW WHY YOU PEOPLE ARE WASTING TIME TELLING "QUAID" HERE ANYTHING. HE'S BEEN NO HELP SO FAR. WHY SHOULD THAT CHANGE?

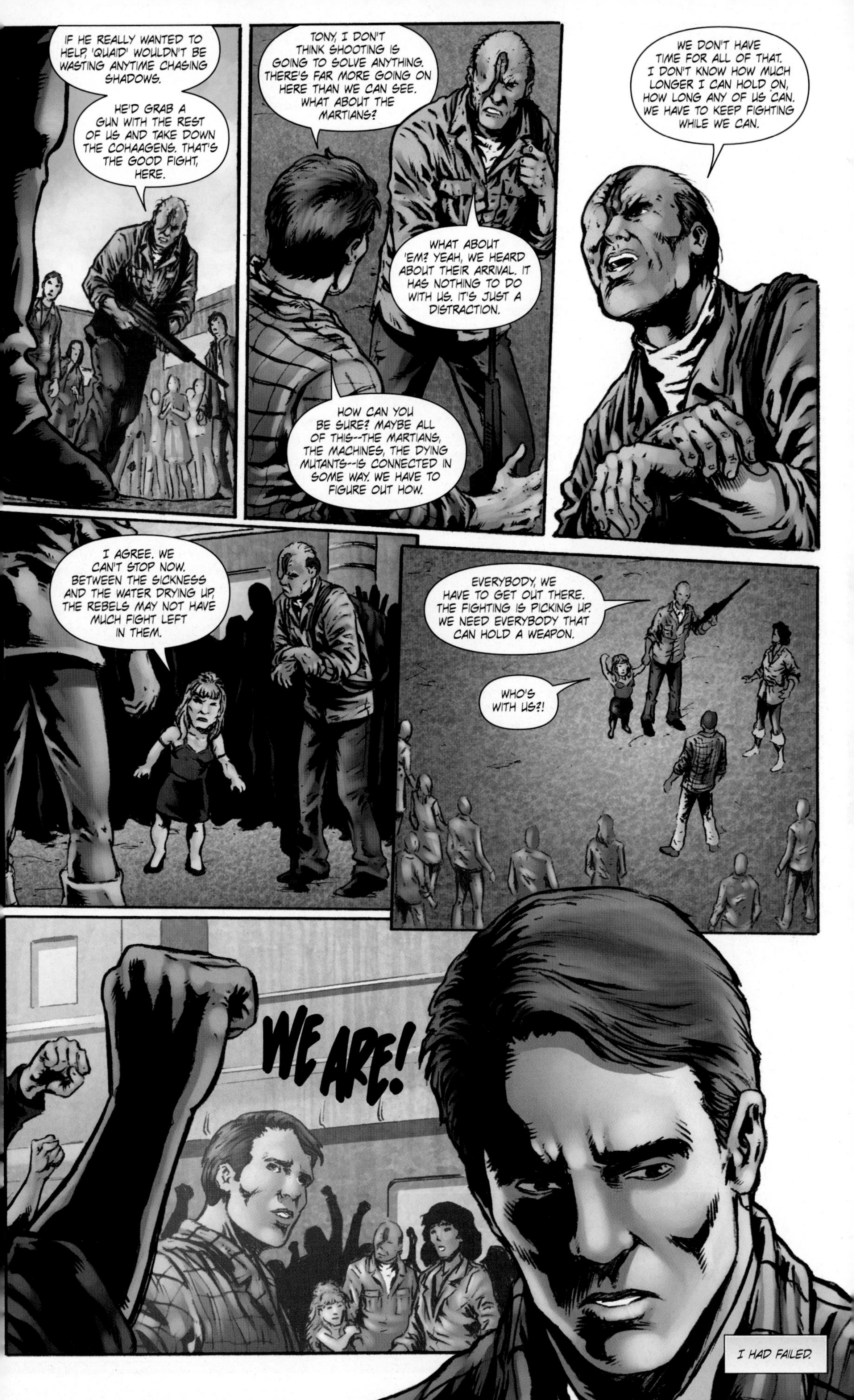
IF HE REALLY WANTED TO HELP, 'QUAID' WOULDN'T BE WASTING ANYTIME CHASING SHADOWS.
HE'D GRAB A GUN WITH THE REST OF US AND TAKE DOWN THE COHAAGENS. THAT'S THE GOOD FIGHT, HERE.
TONY, I DON'T THINK SHOOTING IS GOING TO SOLVE ANYTHING. THERE'S FAR MORE GOING ON HERE THAN WE CAN SEE. WHAT ABOUT THE MARTIANS?
WHAT ABOUT 'EM? YEAH, WE HEARD ABOUT THEIR ARRIVAL. IT HAS NOTHING TO DO WITH US. IT'S JUST A DISTRACTION.
HOW CAN YOU BE SURE? MAYBE ALL OF THIS--THE MARTIANS, THE MACHINES, THE DYING MUTANTS--IS CONNECTED IN SOME WAY. WE HAVE TO FIGURE OUT HOW.
WE DON'T HAVE TIME FOR ALL OF THAT. I DON'T KNOW HOW MUCH LONGER I CAN HOLD ON, HOW LONG ANY OF US CAN. WE HAVE TO KEEP FIGHTING WHILE WE CAN.
I AGREE. WE CAN'T STOP NOW. BETWEEN THE SICKNESS AND THE WATER DRYING UP, THE REBELS MAY NOT HAVE MUCH FIGHT LEFT IN THEM.
EVERYBODY, WE HAVE TO GET OUT THERE. THE FIGHTING IS PICKING UP. WE NEED EVERYBODY THAT CAN HOLD A WEAPON.
WHO'S WITH US?!
WE ARE!
I HAD FAILED.

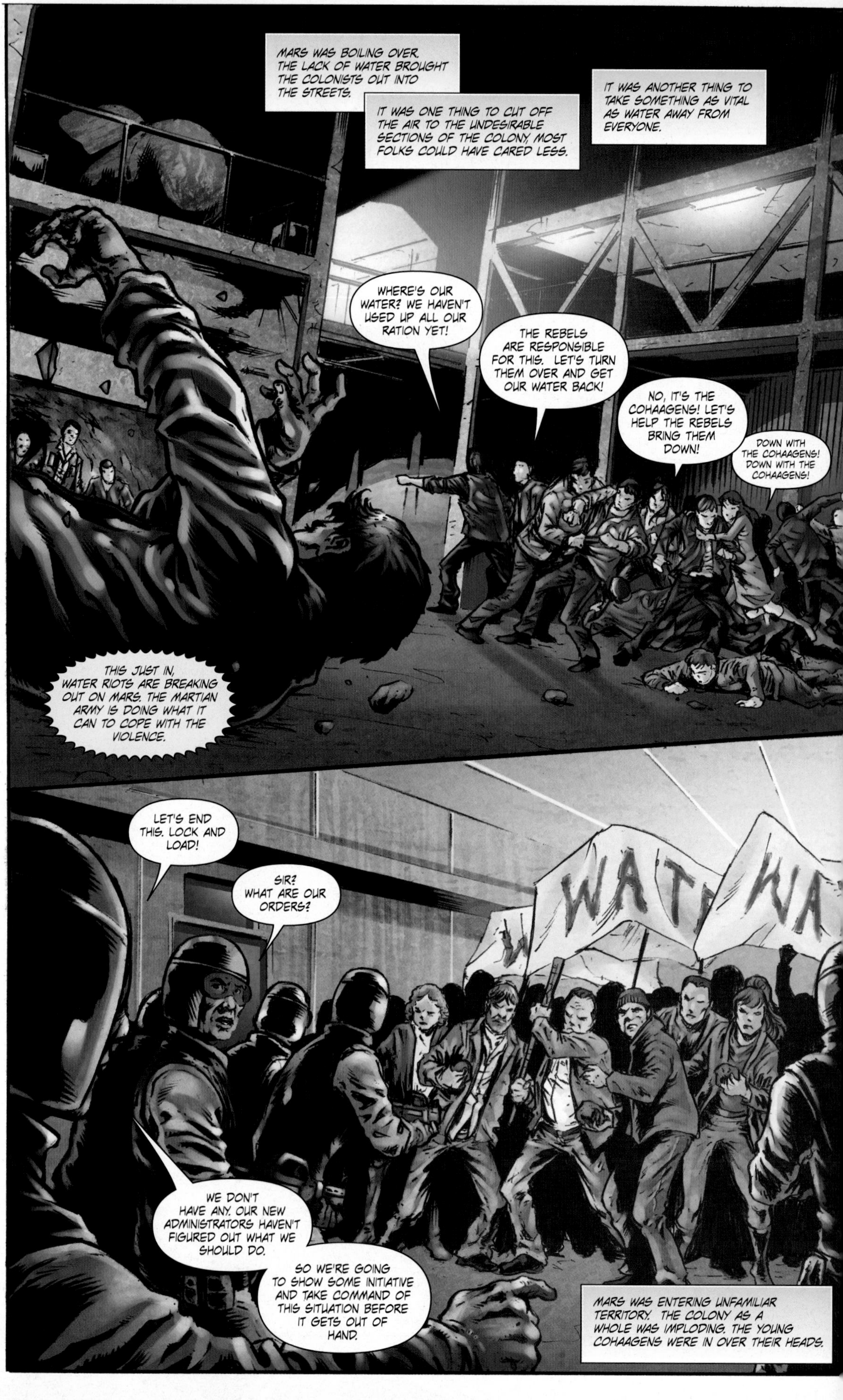
MARS WAS BOILING OVER. THE LACK OF WATER BROUGHT THE COLONISTS OUT INTO THE STREETS.
IT WAS ONE THING TO CUT OFF THE AIR TO THE UNDESIRABLE SECTIONS OF THE COLONY, MOST FOLKS COULD HAVE CARED LESS.
IT WAS ANOTHER THING TO TAKE SOMETHING AS VITAL AS WATER AWAY FROM EVERYONE.
WHERE'S OUR WATER? WE HAVEN'T USED UP ALL OUR RATION YET!
THE REBELS ARE RESPONSIBLE FOR THIS. LET'S TURN THEM OVER AND GET OUR WATER BACK!
NO, IT'S THE COHAAGENS! LET'S HELP THE REBELS BRING THEM DOWN!
DOWN WITH THE COHAAGENS! DOWN WITH THE COHAAGENS!
THIS JUST IN, WATER RIOTS ARE BREAKING OUT ON MARS. THE MARTIAN ARMY IS DOING WHAT IT CAN TO COPE WITH THE VIOLENCE.
LET'S END THIS. LOCK AND LOAD!
SIR? WHAT ARE OUR ORDERS?
WE DON'T HAVE ANY. OUR NEW ADMINISTRATORS HAVEN'T FIGURED OUT WHAT WE SHOULD DO.
SO WE'RE GOING TO SHOW SOME INITIATIVE AND TAKE COMMAND OF THIS SITUATION BEFORE IT GETS OUT OF HAND.
MARS WAS ENTERING UNFAMILIAR TERRITORY. THE COLONY AS A WHOLE WAS IMPLODING. THE YOUNG COHAAGENS WERE IN OVER THEIR HEADS.

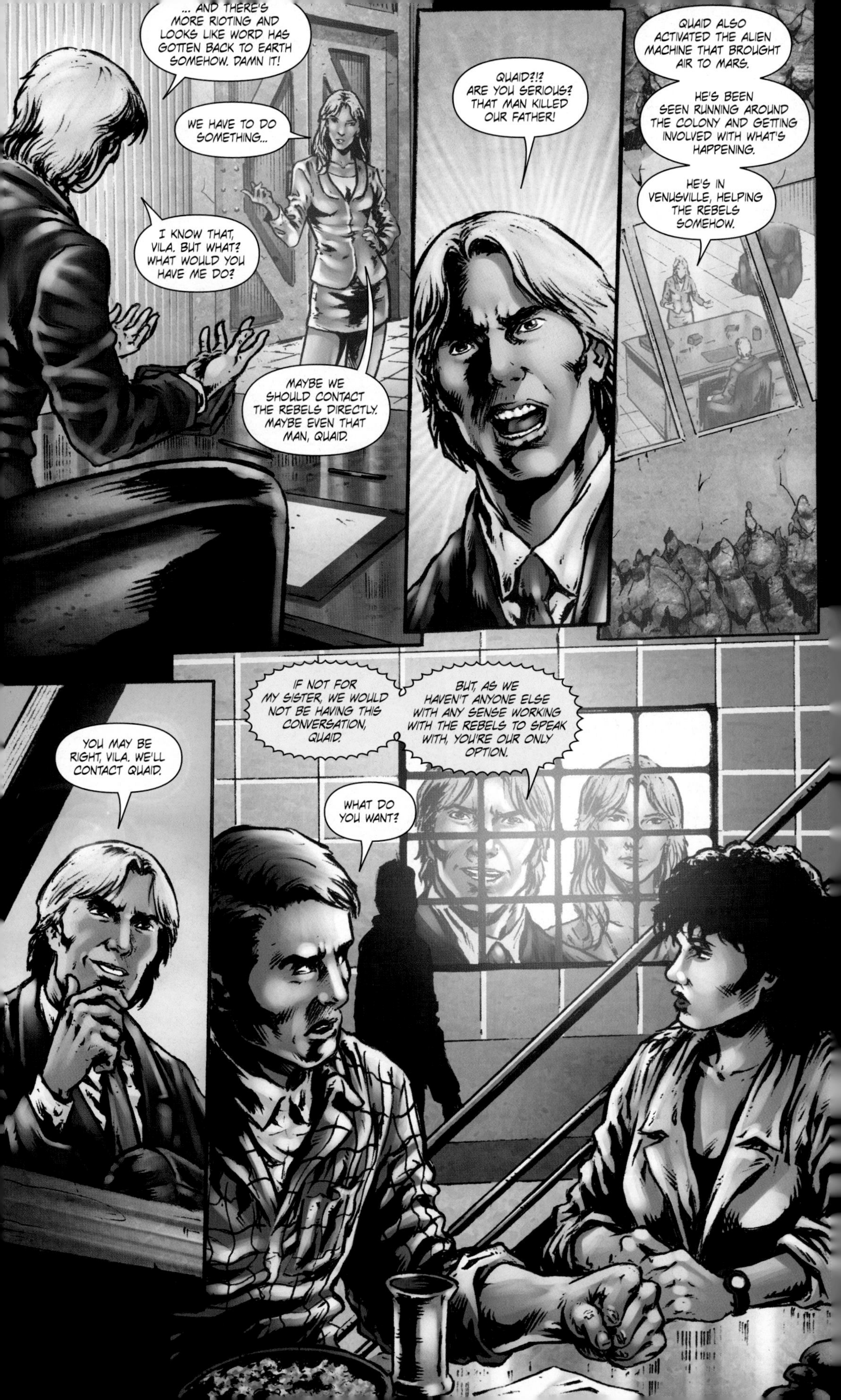
... AND THERE'S MORE RIOTING AND LOOKS LIKE WORD HAS GOTTEN BACK TO EARTH SOMEHOW. DAMN IT!
WE HAVE TO DO SOMETHING...
I KNOW THAT, VILA. BUT WHAT? WHAT WOULD YOU HAVE ME DO?
MAYBE WE SHOULD CONTACT THE REBELS DIRECTLY. MAYBE EVEN THAT MAN, QUAID.
QUAID?!? ARE YOU SERIOUS? THAT MAN KILLED OUR FATHER!
QUAID ALSO ACTIVATED THE ALIEN MACHINE THAT BROUGHT AIR TO MARS.
HE'S BEEN SEEN RUNNING AROUND THE COLONY AND GETTING INVOLVED WITH WHAT'S HAPPENING.
HE'S IN VENUSVILLE, HELPING THE REBELS SOMEHOW.
YOU MAY BE RIGHT, VILA. WE'LL CONTACT QUAID.
IF NOT FOR MY SISTER, WE WOULD NOT BE HAVING THIS CONVERSATION, QUAID.
BUT, AS WE HAVEN'T ANYONE ELSE WITH ANY SENSE WORKING WITH THE REBELS TO SPEAK WITH, YOU'RE OUR ONLY OPTION.
WHAT DO YOU WANT?

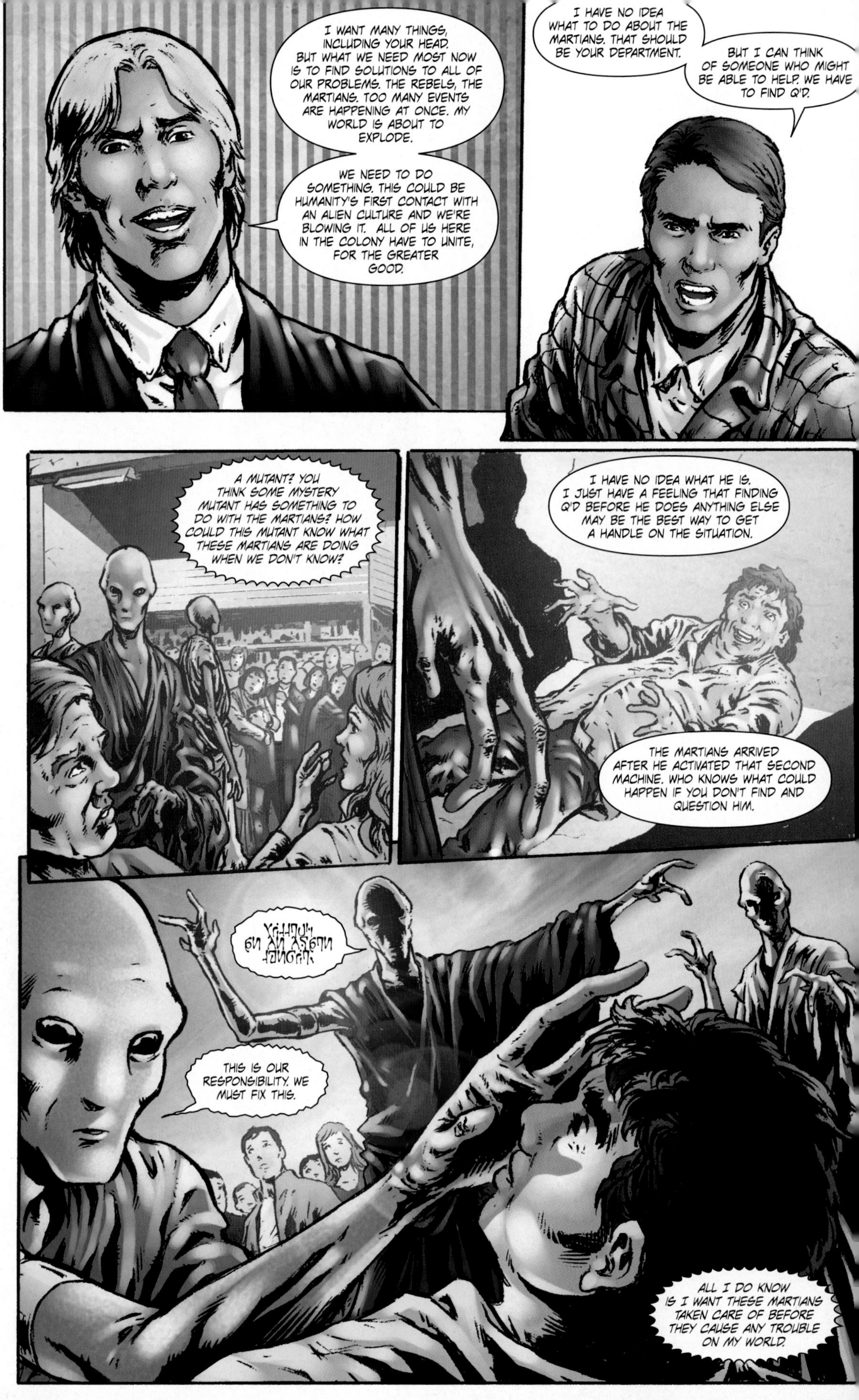
I WANT MANY THINGS, INCLUDING YOUR HEAD. BUT WHAT WE NEED MOST NOW IS TO FIND SOLUTIONS TO ALL OF OUR PROBLEMS. THE REBELS, THE MARTIANS. TOO MANY EVENTS ARE HAPPENING AT ONCE. MY WORLD IS ABOUT TO EXPLODE.
WE NEED TO DO SOMETHING. THIS COULD BE HUMANITY'S FIRST CONTACT WITH AN ALIEN CULTURE AND WE'RE BLOWING IT. ALL OF US HERE IN THE COLONY HAVE TO UNITE, FOR THE GREATER GOOD.
I HAVE NO IDEA WHAT TO DO ABOUT THE MARTIANS. THAT SHOULD BE YOUR DEPARTMENT.
BUT I CAN THINK OF SOMEONE WHO MIGHT BE ABLE TO HELP. WE HAVE TO FIND Q'D.
A MUTANT? YOU THINK SOME MYSTERY MUTANT HAS SOMETHING TO DO WITH THE MARTIANS? HOW COULD THIS MUTANT KNOW WHAT THESE MARTIANS ARE DOING WHEN WE DON'T KNOW?
I HAVE NO IDEA WHAT HE IS. I JUST HAVE A FEELING THAT FINDING Q'D BEFORE HE DOES ANYTHING ELSE MAY BE THE BEST WAY TO GET A HANDLE ON THE SITUATION.
THE MARTIANS ARRIVED AFTER HE ACTIVATED THAT SECOND MACHINE. WHO KNOWS WHAT COULD HAPPEN IF YOU DON'T FIND AND QUESTION HIM.
THIS IS OUR RESPONSIBILITY. WE MUST FIX THIS.
ALL I DO KNOW IS I WANT THESE MARTIANS TAKEN CARE OF BEFORE THEY CAUSE ANY TROUBLE ON MY WORLD.

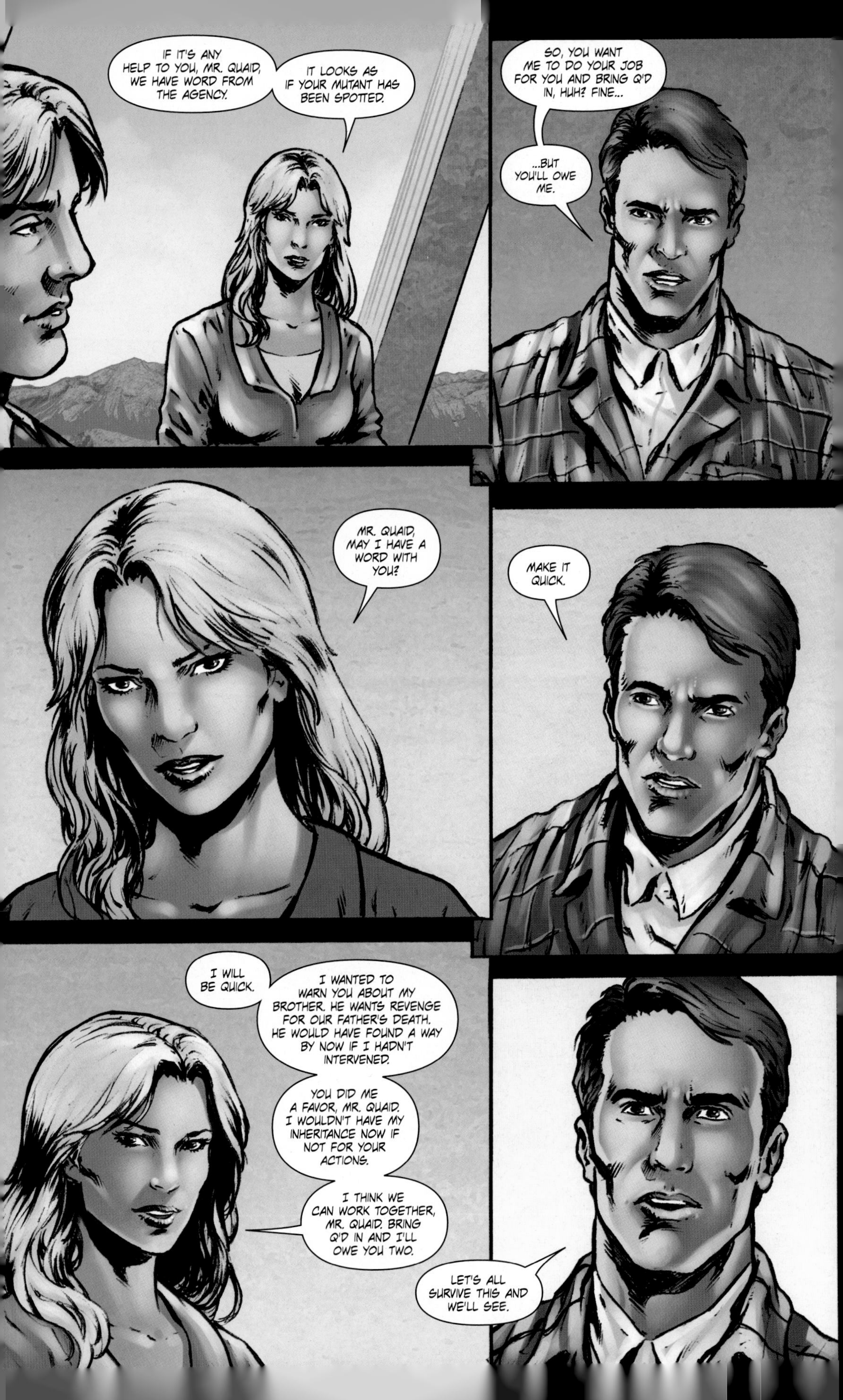
IF IT'S ANY HELP TO YOU, MR. QUAID, WE HAVE WORD FROM THE AGENCY.
IT LOOKS AS IF YOUR MUTANT HAS BEEN SPOTTED.
SO, YOU WANT ME TO DO YOUR JOB FOR YOU AND BRING Q'D IN, HUH? FINE...
...BUT YOU'LL OWE ME.
MR. QUAID, MAY I HAVE A WORD WITH YOU?
MAKE IT QUICK.
I WILL BE QUICK.
I WANTED TO WARN YOU ABOUT MY BROTHER. HE WANTS REVENGE FOR OUR FATHER'S DEATH. HE WOULD HAVE FOUND A WAY BY NOW IF I HADN'T INTERVENED.
YOU DID ME A FAVOR, MR. QUAID. I WOULDN'T HAVE MY INHERITANCE NOW IF NOT FOR YOUR ACTIONS.
I THINK WE CAN WORK TOGETHER, MR. QUAID. BRING Q'D IN AND I'LL OWE YOU TWO.
LET'S ALL SURVIVE THIS AND WE'LL SEE.

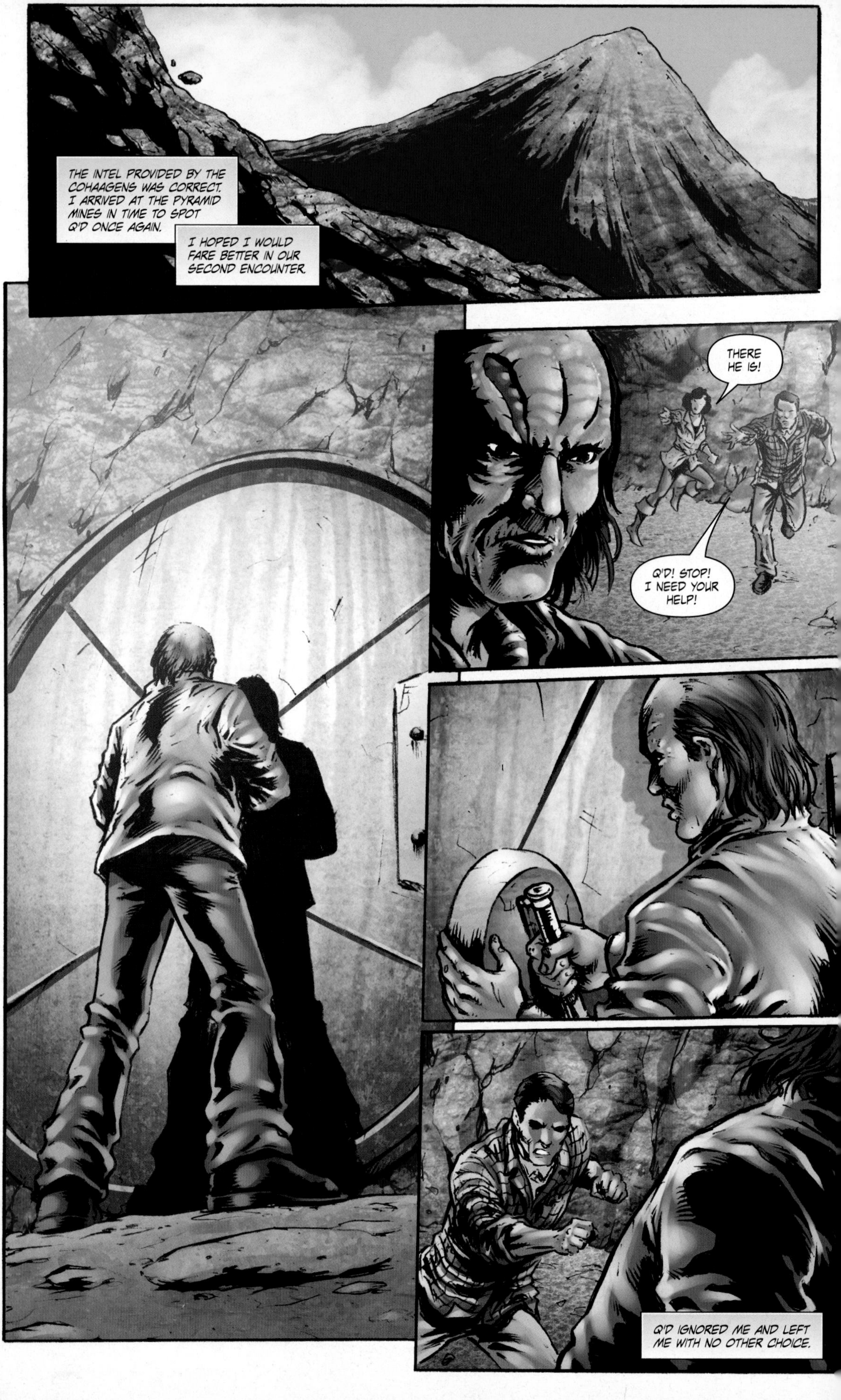

THE INTEL PROVIDED BY THE COHAAGENS WAS CORRECT. I ARRIVED AT THE PYRAMID MINES IN TIME TO SPOT Q'D ONCE AGAIN.
I HOPED I WOULD FARE BETTER IN OUR SECOND ENCOUNTER.
THERE HE IS!
Q'D! STOP! I NEED YOUR HELP!
Q'D IGNORED ME AND LEFT ME WITH NO OTHER CHOICE.

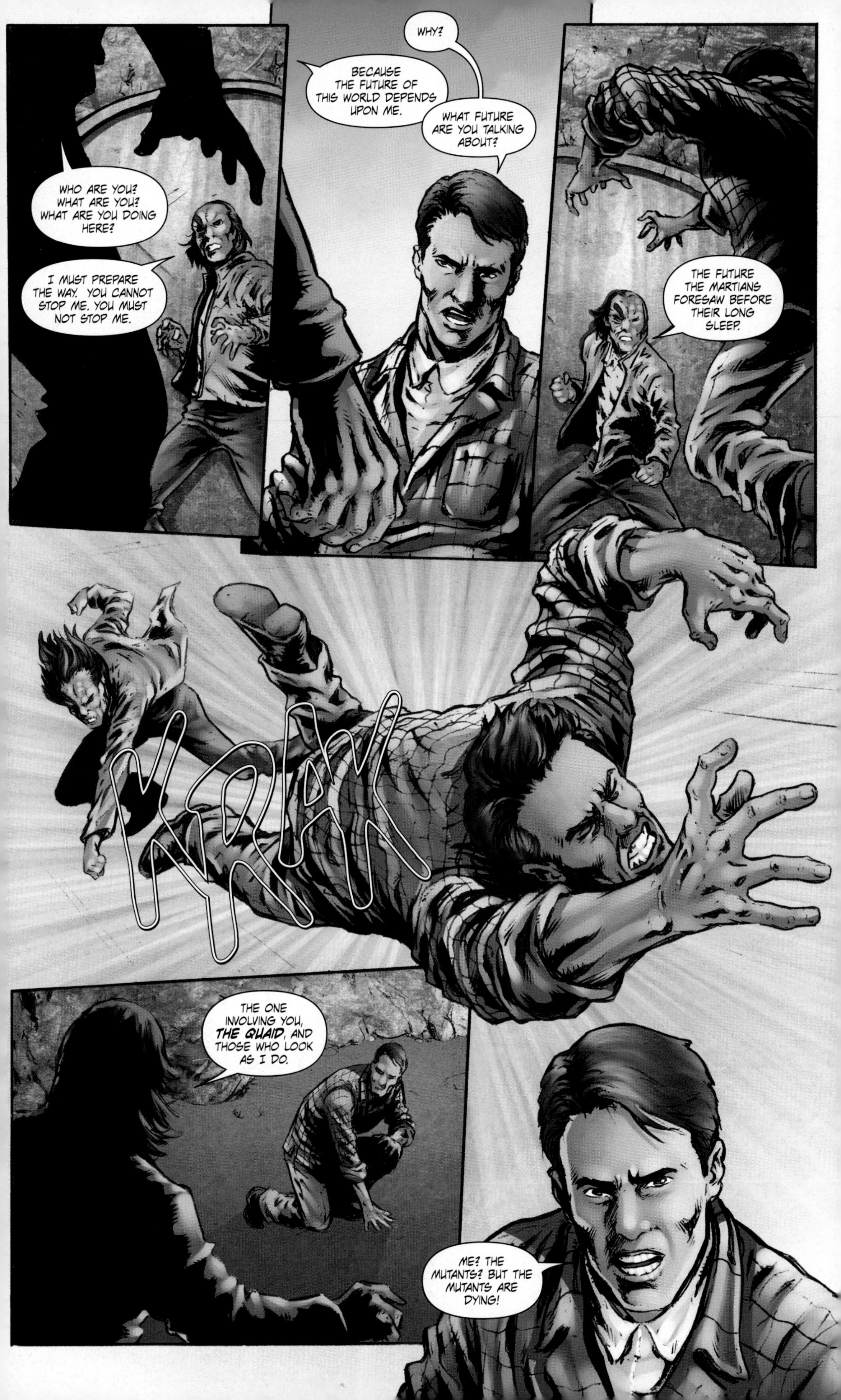

WHO ARE YOU? WHAT ARE YOU? WHAT ARE YOU DOING HERE?
I MUST PREPARE THE WAY. YOU CANNOT STOP ME. YOU MUST NOT STOP ME.
WHY?
BECAUSE THE FUTURE OF THIS WORLD DEPENDS UPON ME.
WHAT FUTURE ARE YOU TALKING ABOUT?
THE FUTURE THE MARTIANS FORESAW BEFORE THEIR LONG SLEEP.
KRAK
THE ONE INVOLVING YOU, **THE QUAID**, AND THOSE WHO LOOK AS I DO.
ME? THE MUTANTS? BUT THE MUTANTS ARE DYING!

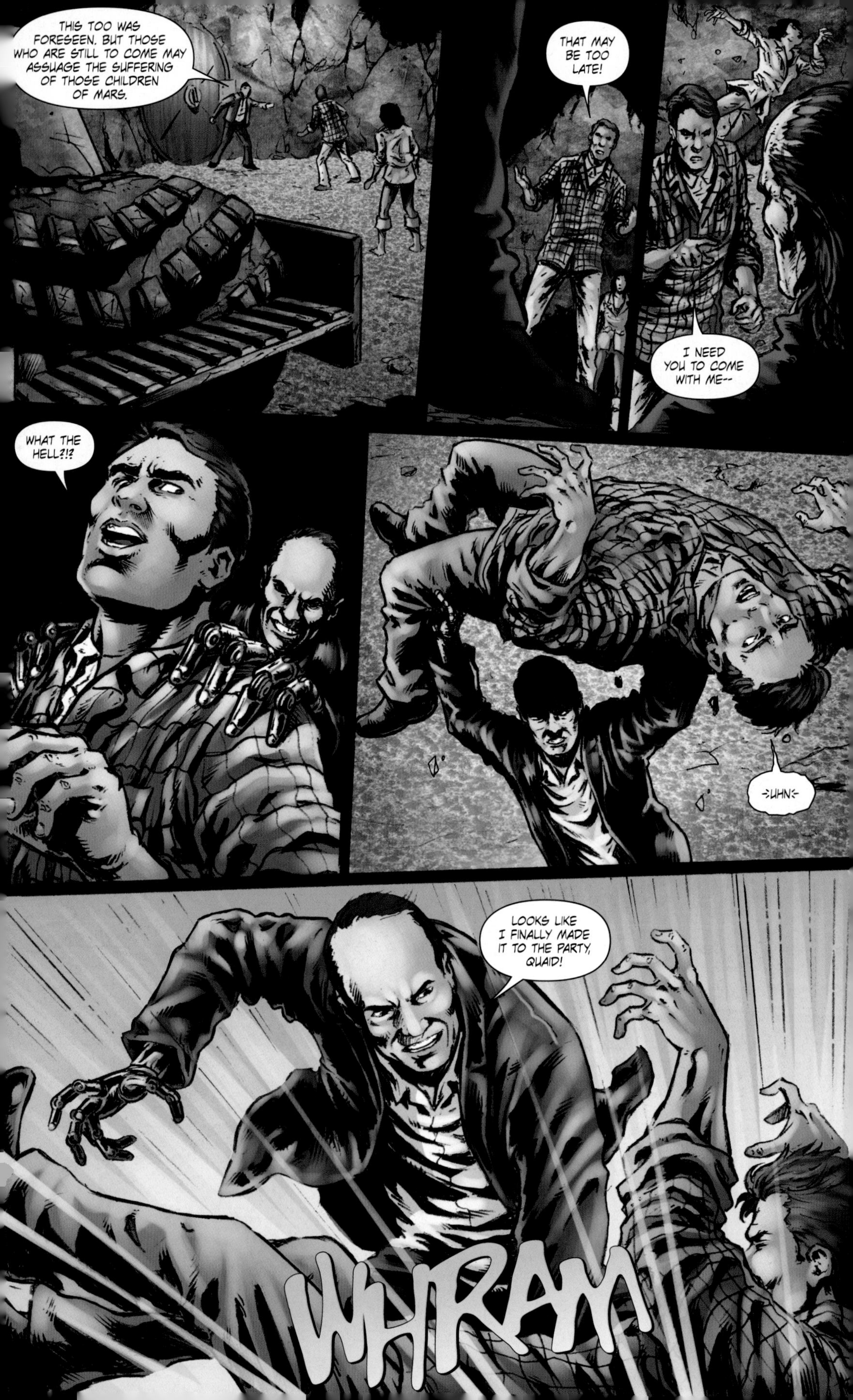
THIS TOO WAS FORESEEN. BUT THOSE WHO ARE STILL TO COME MAY ASSUAGE THE SUFFERING OF THOSE CHILDREN OF MARS.
THAT MAY BE TOO LATE!
I NEED YOU TO COME WITH ME--
WHAT THE HELL?!?
-UHN-
LOOKS LIKE I FINALLY MADE IT TO THE PARTY, QUAID!
WHRAM

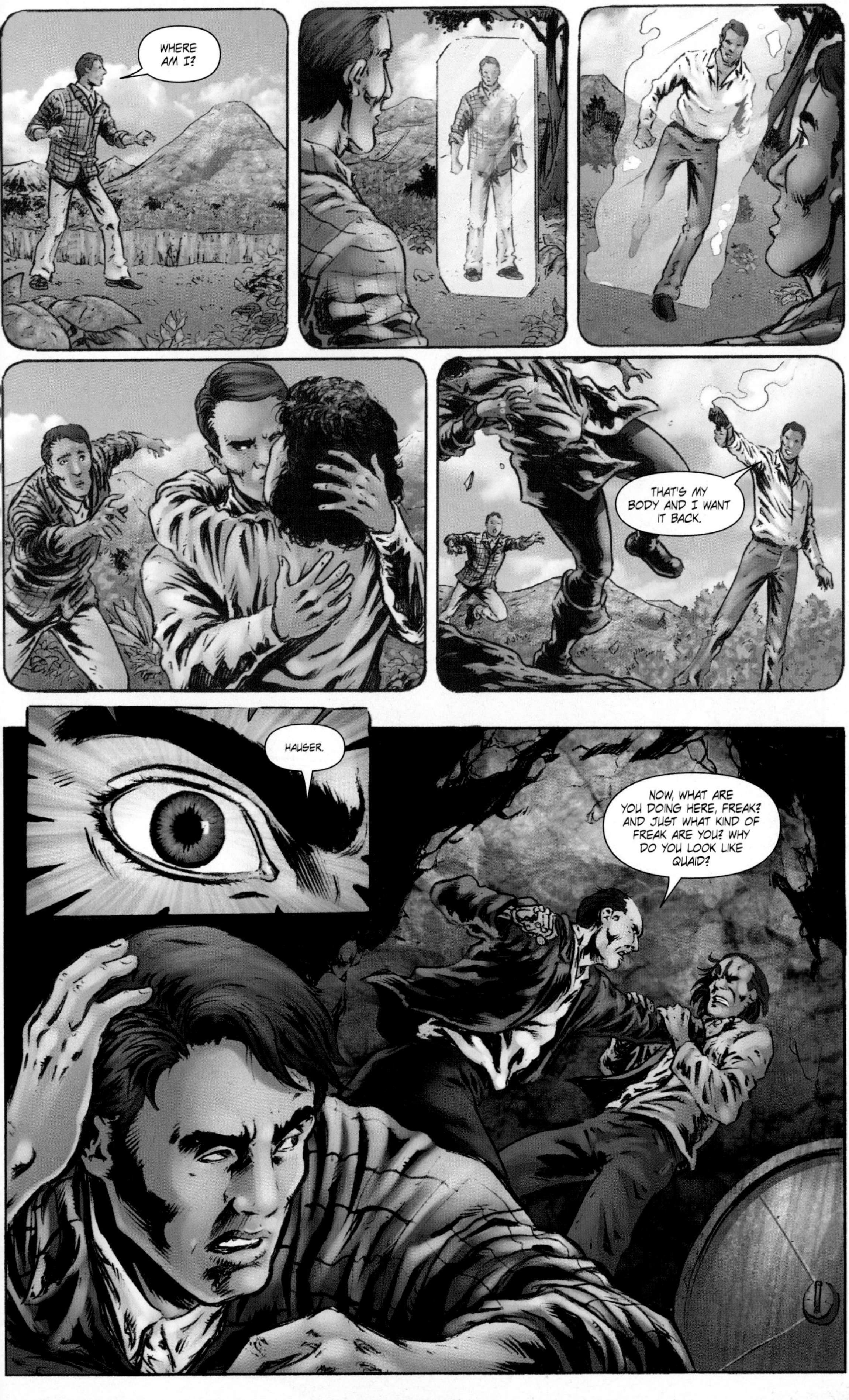
WHERE AM I?
THAT'S MY BODY AND I WANT IT BACK.
HAUSER.
NOW, WHAT ARE YOU DOING HERE, FREAK? AND JUST WHAT KIND OF FREAK ARE YOU? WHY DO YOU LOOK LIKE QUAID?

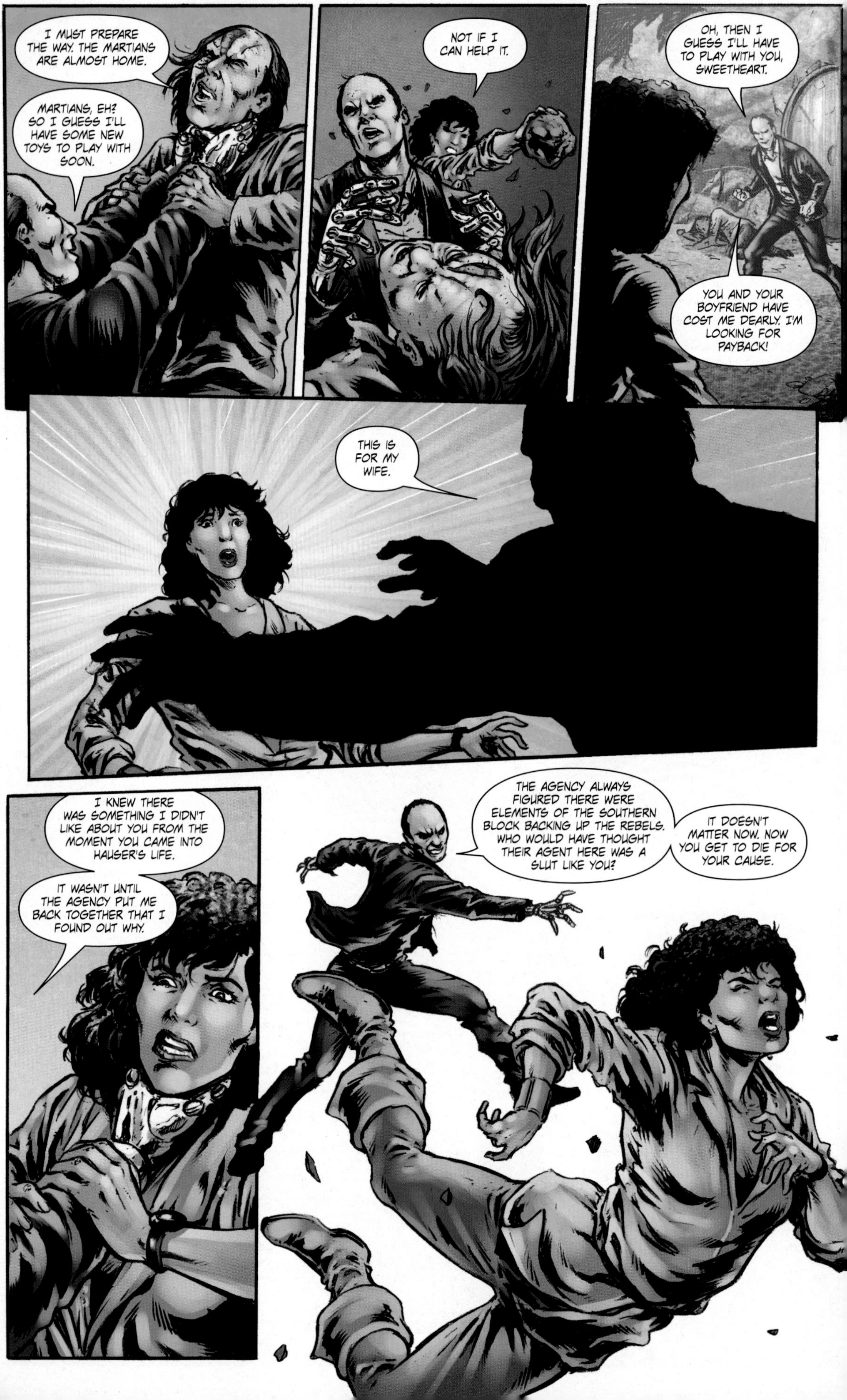
I MUST PREPARE THE WAY. THE MARTIANS ARE ALMOST HOME.
MARTIANS, EH? SO I GUESS I'LL HAVE SOME NEW TOYS TO PLAY WITH SOON.
NOT IF I CAN HELP IT.
OH, THEN I GUESS I'LL HAVE TO PLAY WITH YOU, SWEETHEART.
YOU AND YOUR BOYFRIEND HAVE COST ME DEARLY. I'M LOOKING FOR PAYBACK!
THIS IS FOR MY WIFE.
I KNEW THERE WAS SOMETHING I DIDN'T LIKE ABOUT YOU FROM THE MOMENT YOU CAME INTO HAUSER'S LIFE.
IT WASN'T UNTIL THE AGENCY PUT ME BACK TOGETHER THAT I FOUND OUT WHY.
THE AGENCY ALWAYS FIGURED THERE WERE ELEMENTS OF THE SOUTHERN BLOCK BACKING UP THE REBELS. WHO WOULD HAVE THOUGHT THEIR AGENT HERE WAS A SLUT LIKE YOU?
IT DOESN'T MATTER NOW. NOW YOU GET TO DIE FOR YOUR CAUSE.

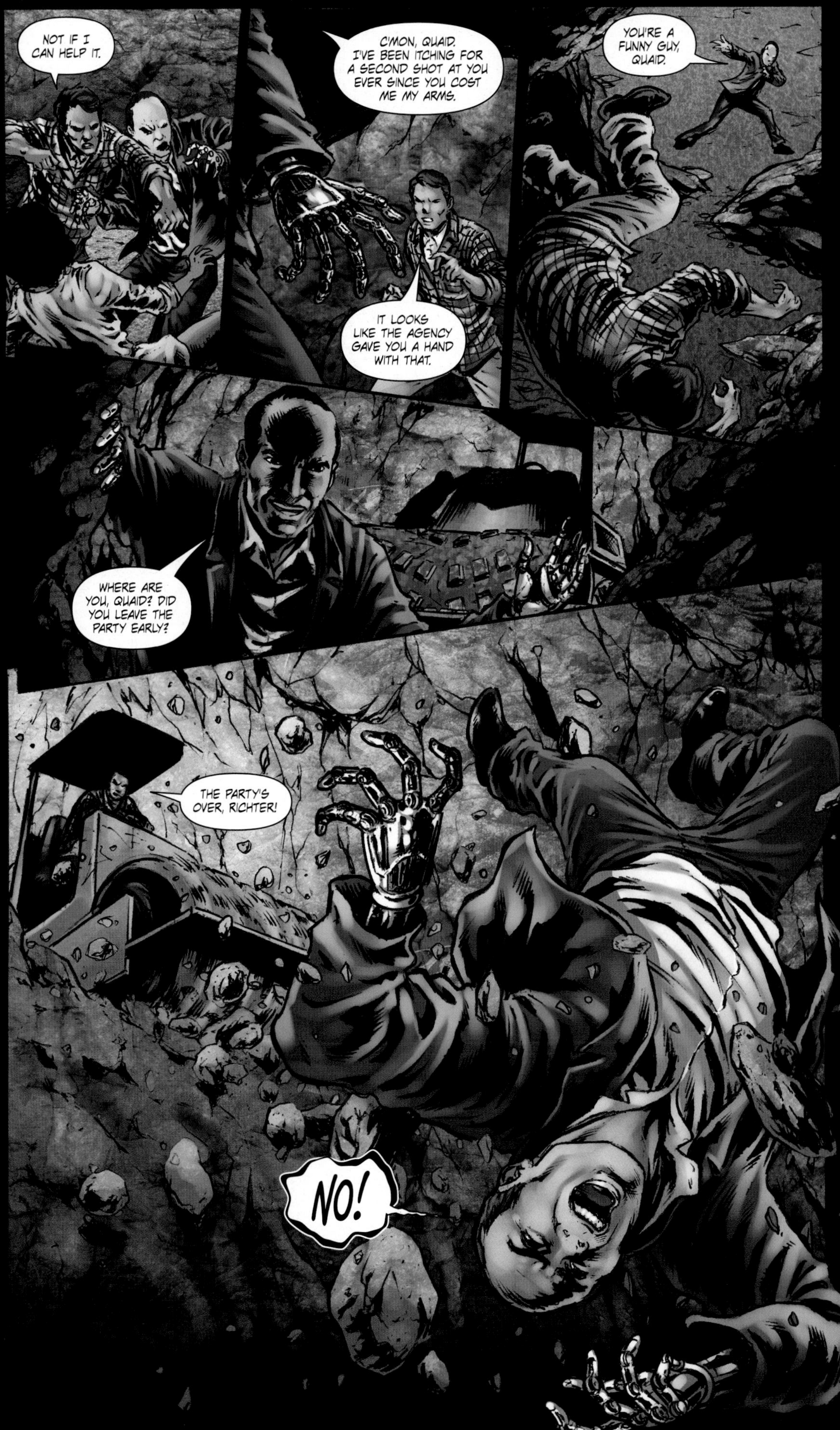
NOT IF I CAN HELP IT.
C'MON, QUAID. I'VE BEEN ITCHING FOR A SECOND SHOT AT YOU EVER SINCE YOU COST ME MY ARMS.
IT LOOKS LIKE THE AGENCY GAVE YOU A HAND WITH THAT.
YOU'RE A FUNNY GUY, QUAID.
WHERE ARE YOU, QUAID? DID YOU LEAVE THE PARTY EARLY?
THE PARTY'S OVER, RICHTER!
NO!

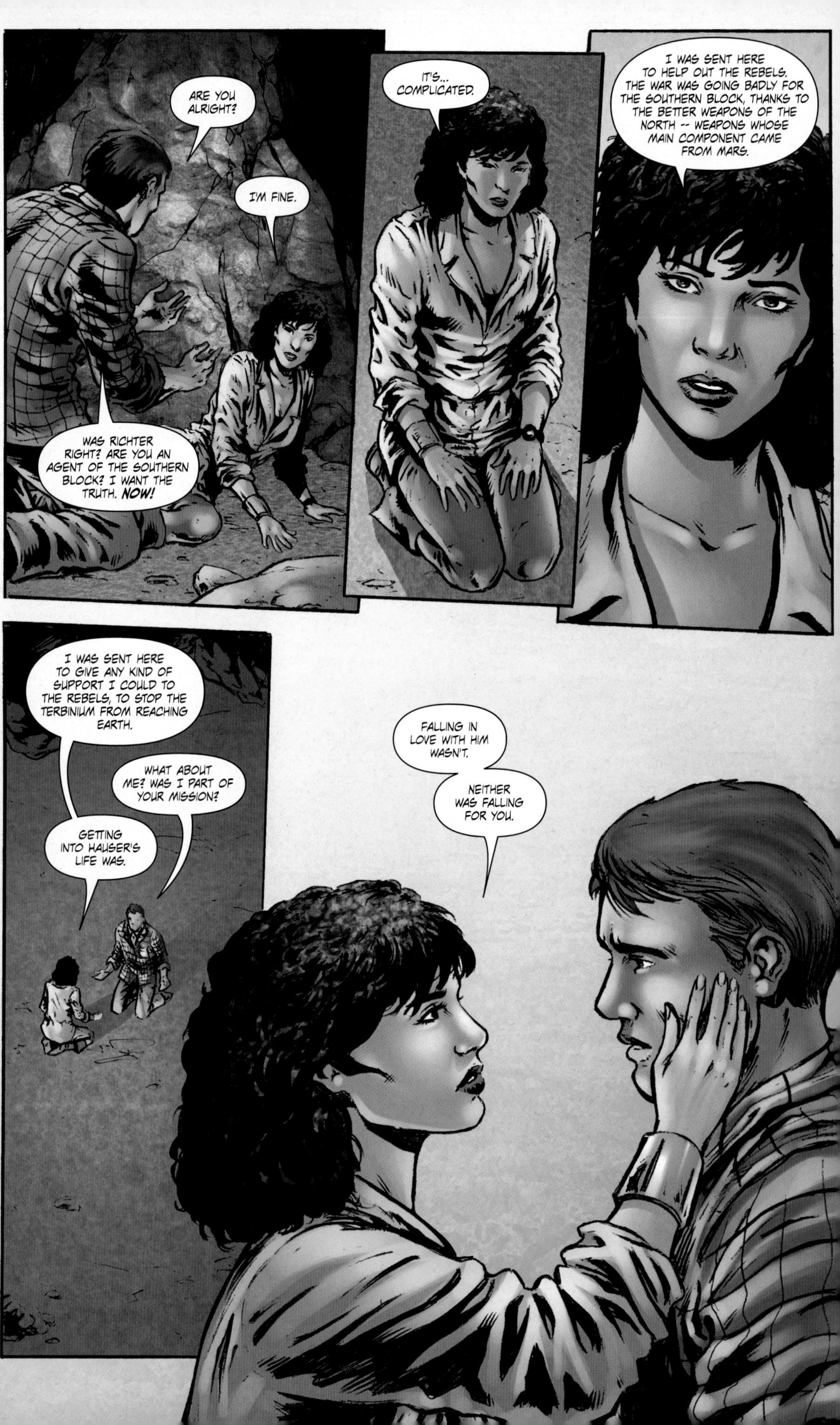
ARE YOU ALRIGHT?
I'M FINE.
WAS RICHTER RIGHT? ARE YOU AN AGENT OF THE SOUTHERN BLOCK? I WANT THE TRUTH. NOW!
IT'S... COMPLICATED.
I WAS SENT HERE TO HELP OUT THE REBELS. THE WAR WAS GOING BADLY FOR THE SOUTHERN BLOCK, THANKS TO THE BETTER WEAPONS OF THE NORTH -- WEAPONS WHOSE MAIN COMPONENT CAME FROM MARS.
I WAS SENT HERE TO GIVE ANY KIND OF SUPPORT I COULD TO THE REBELS, TO STOP THE TERBINIUM FROM REACHING EARTH.
WHAT ABOUT ME? WAS I PART OF YOUR MISSION?
GETTING INTO HAUSER'S LIFE WAS.
FALLING IN LOVE WITH HIM WASN'T.
NEITHER WAS FALLING FOR YOU.

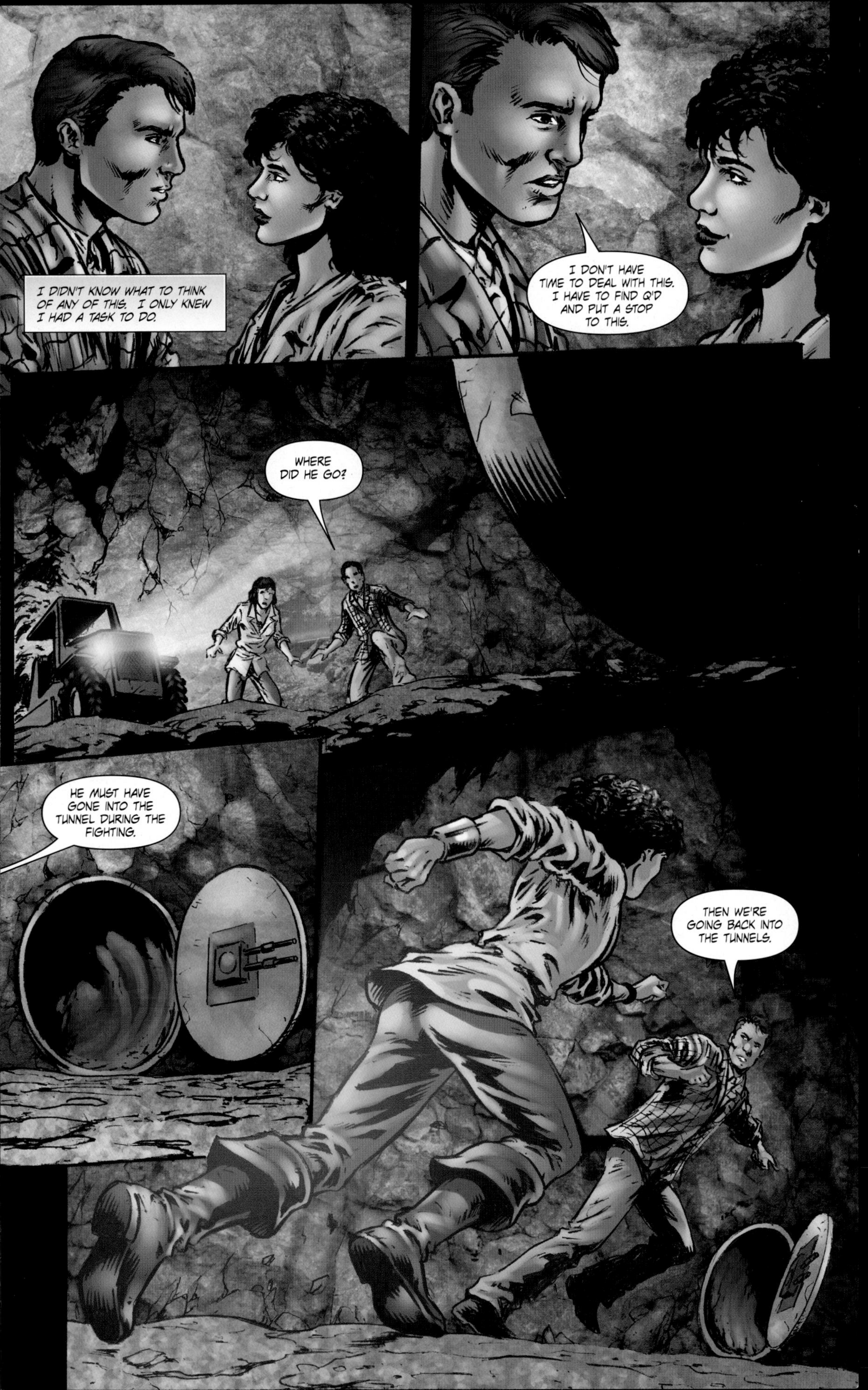
I DIDN'T KNOW WHAT TO THINK OF ANY OF THIS. I ONLY KNEW I HAD A TASK TO DO.
I DON'T HAVE TIME TO DEAL WITH THIS. I HAVE TO FIND Q'D AND PUT A STOP TO THIS.
WHERE DID HE GO?
HE MUST HAVE GONE INTO THE TUNNEL DURING THE FIGHTING.
THEN WE'RE GOING BACK INTO THE TUNNELS.

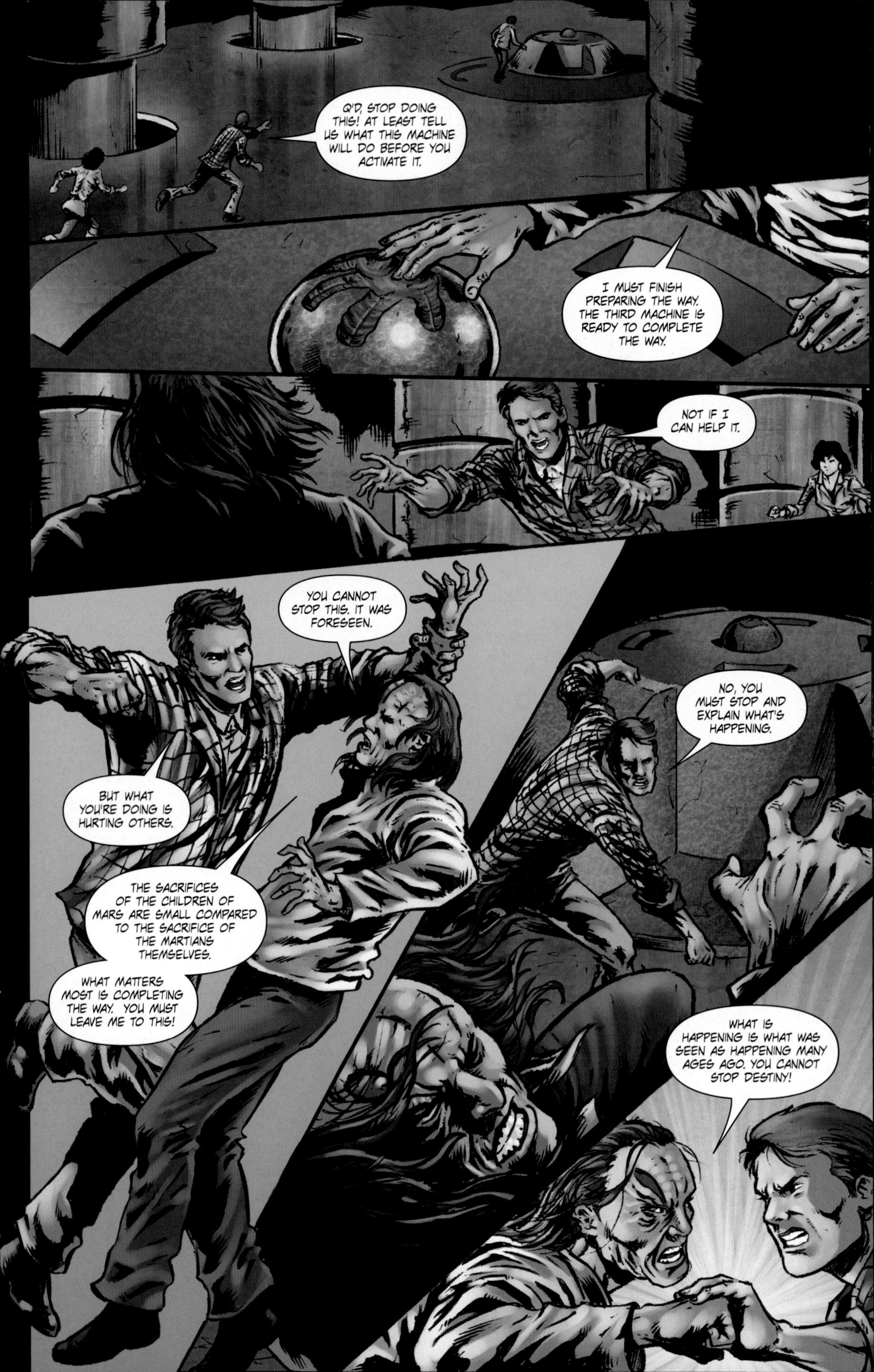
Q'D, STOP DOING THIS! AT LEAST TELL US WHAT THIS MACHINE WILL DO BEFORE YOU ACTIVATE IT.
I MUST FINISH PREPARING THE WAY. THE THIRD MACHINE IS READY TO COMPLETE THE WAY.
NOT IF I CAN HELP IT.
YOU CANNOT STOP THIS. IT WAS FORESEEN.
BUT WHAT YOU'RE DOING IS HURTING OTHERS.
THE SACRIFICES OF THE CHILDREN OF MARS ARE SMALL COMPARED TO THE SACRIFICE OF THE MARTIANS THEMSELVES.
WHAT MATTERS MOST IS COMPLETING THE WAY. YOU MUST LEAVE ME TO THIS!
NO, YOU MUST STOP AND EXPLAIN WHAT'S HAPPENING.
WHAT IS HAPPENING IS WHAT WAS SEEN AS HAPPENING MANY AGES AGO. YOU CANNOT STOP DESTINY!

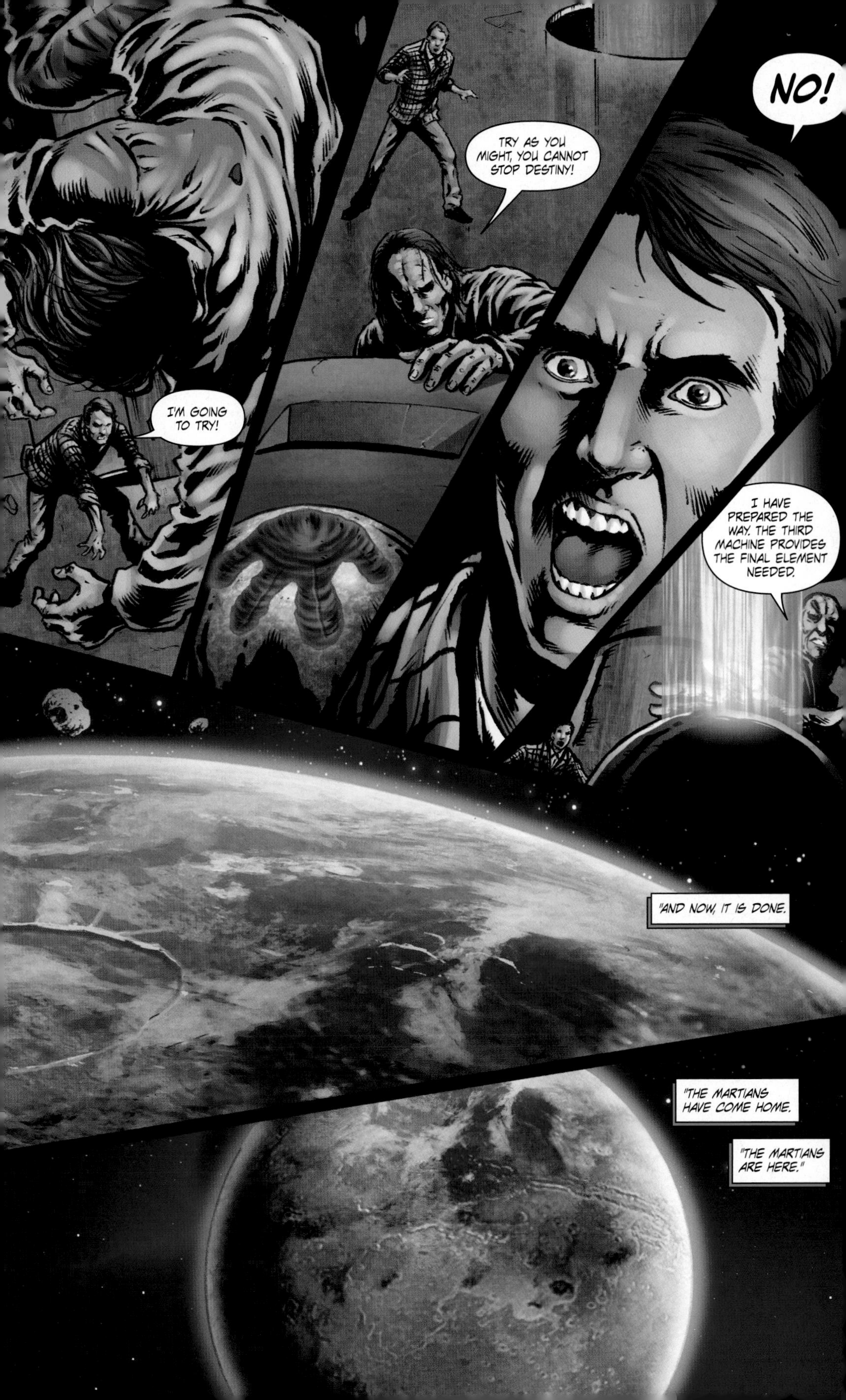
I'M GOING TO TRY!
TRY AS YOU MIGHT, YOU CANNOT STOP DESTINY!
NO!
I HAVE PREPARED THE WAY. THE THIRD MACHINE PROVIDES THE FINAL ELEMENT NEEDED.
"AND NOW, IT IS DONE.
"THE MARTIANS HAVE COME HOME.
"THE MARTIANS ARE HERE."

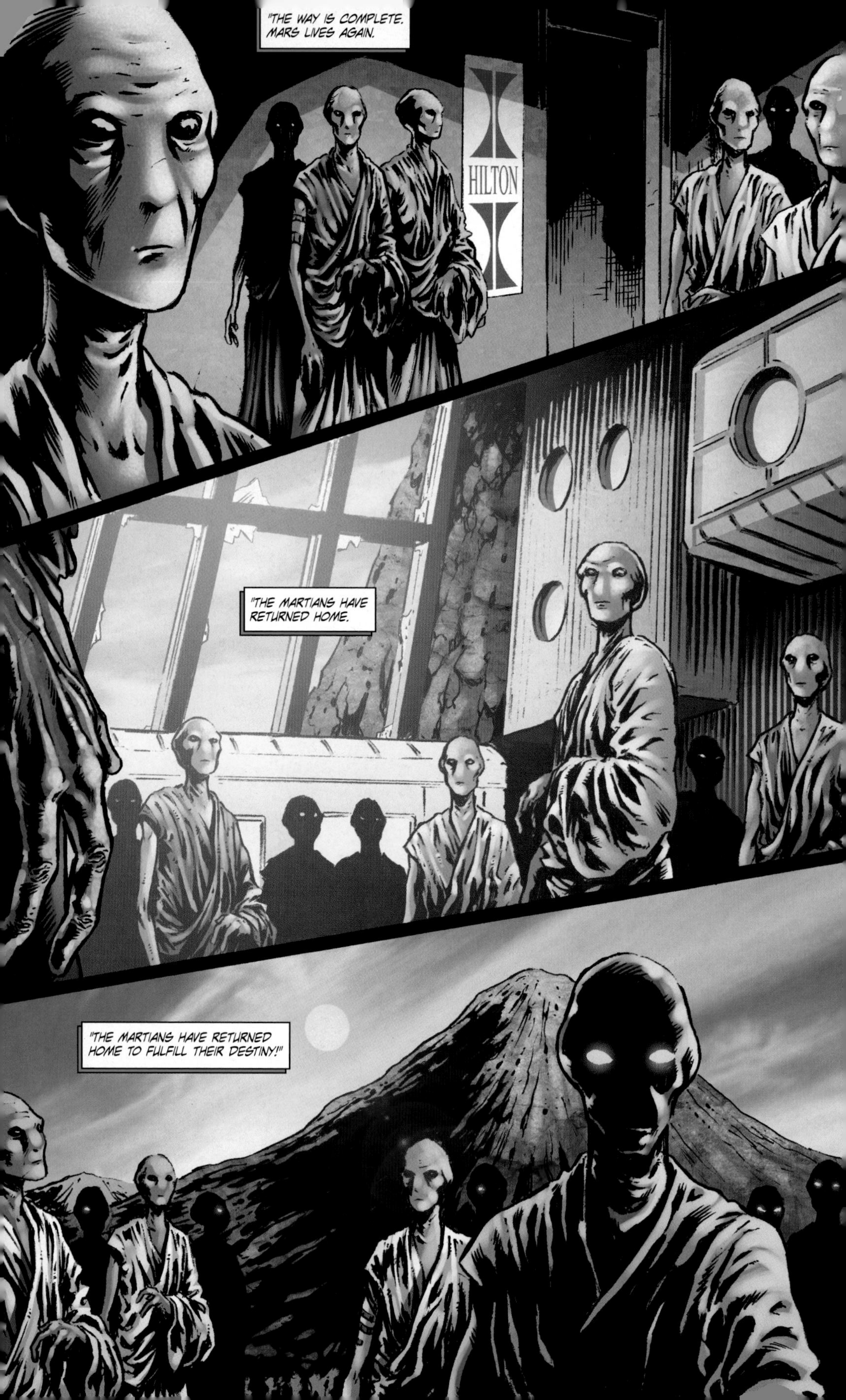
"THE WAY IS COMPLETE. MARS LIVES AGAIN.
HILTON
"THE MARTIANS HAVE RETURNED HOME.
"THE MARTIANS HAVE RETURNED HOME TO FULFILL THEIR DESTINY!"

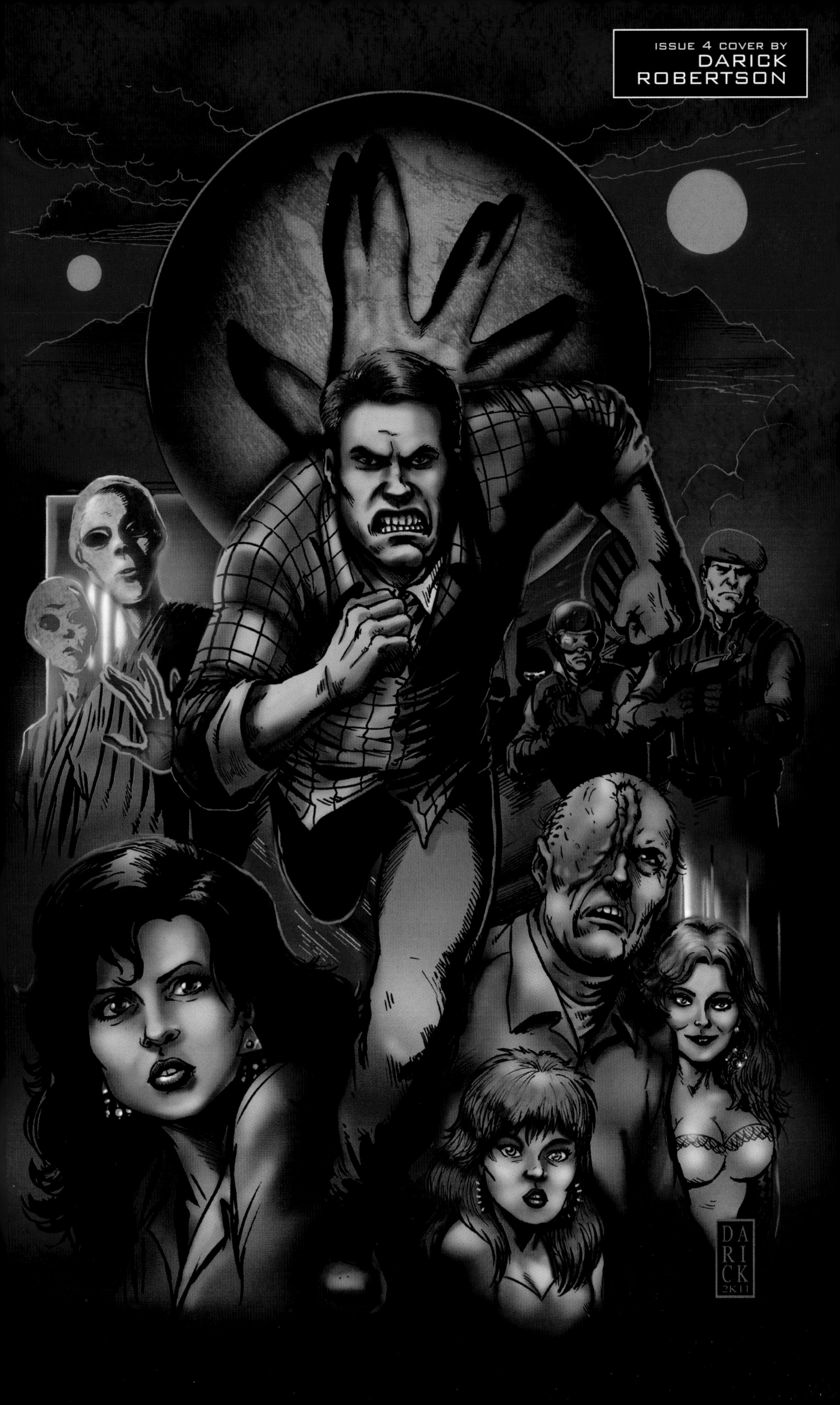
DA
RI
CK
2K11

ISSUE 4 COVER BY
DARICK
ROBERTSON

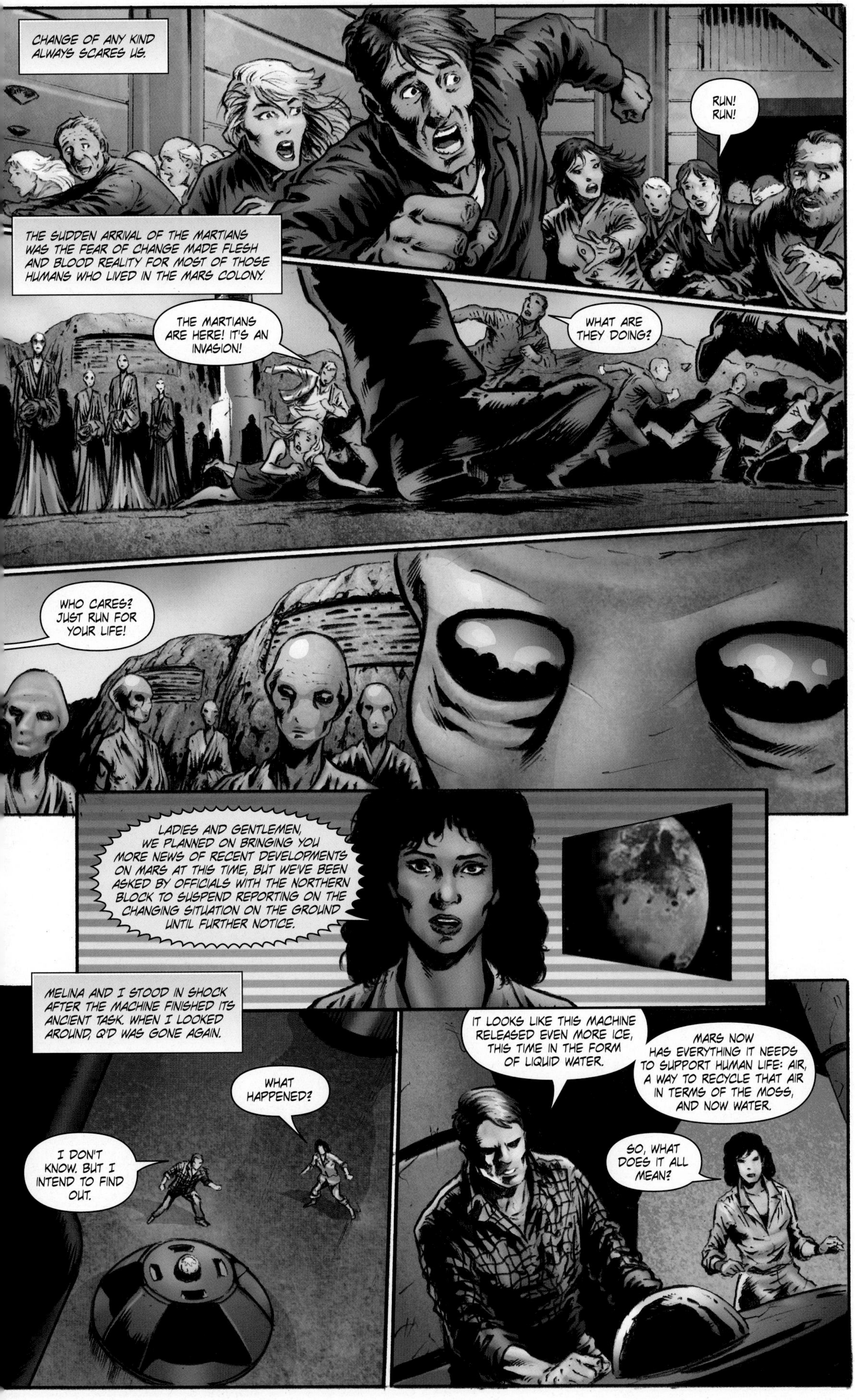

CHANGE OF ANY KIND ALWAYS SCARES US.
RUN! RUN!
THE SUDDEN ARRIVAL OF THE MARTIANS WAS THE FEAR OF CHANGE MADE FLESH AND BLOOD REALITY FOR MOST OF THOSE HUMANS WHO LIVED IN THE MARS COLONY.
THE MARTIANS ARE HERE! IT'S AN INVASION!
WHAT ARE THEY DOING?
WHO CARES? JUST RUN FOR YOUR LIFE!
LADIES AND GENTLEMEN, WE PLANNED ON BRINGING YOU MORE NEWS OF RECENT DEVELOPMENTS ON MARS AT THIS TIME, BUT WE'VE BEEN ASKED BY OFFICIALS WITH THE NORTHERN BLOCK TO SUSPEND REPORTING ON THE CHANGING SITUATION ON THE GROUND UNTIL FURTHER NOTICE.
MELINA AND I STOOD IN SHOCK AFTER THE MACHINE FINISHED ITS ANCIENT TASK. WHEN I LOOKED AROUND, Q'D WAS GONE AGAIN.
WHAT HAPPENED?
I DON'T KNOW. BUT I INTEND TO FIND OUT.
IT LOOKS LIKE THIS MACHINE RELEASED EVEN MORE ICE, THIS TIME IN THE FORM OF LIQUID WATER.
MARS NOW HAS EVERYTHING IT NEEDS TO SUPPORT HUMAN LIFE: AIR, A WAY TO RECYCLE THAT AIR IN TERMS OF THE MOSS, AND NOW WATER.
SO, WHAT DOES IT ALL MEAN?

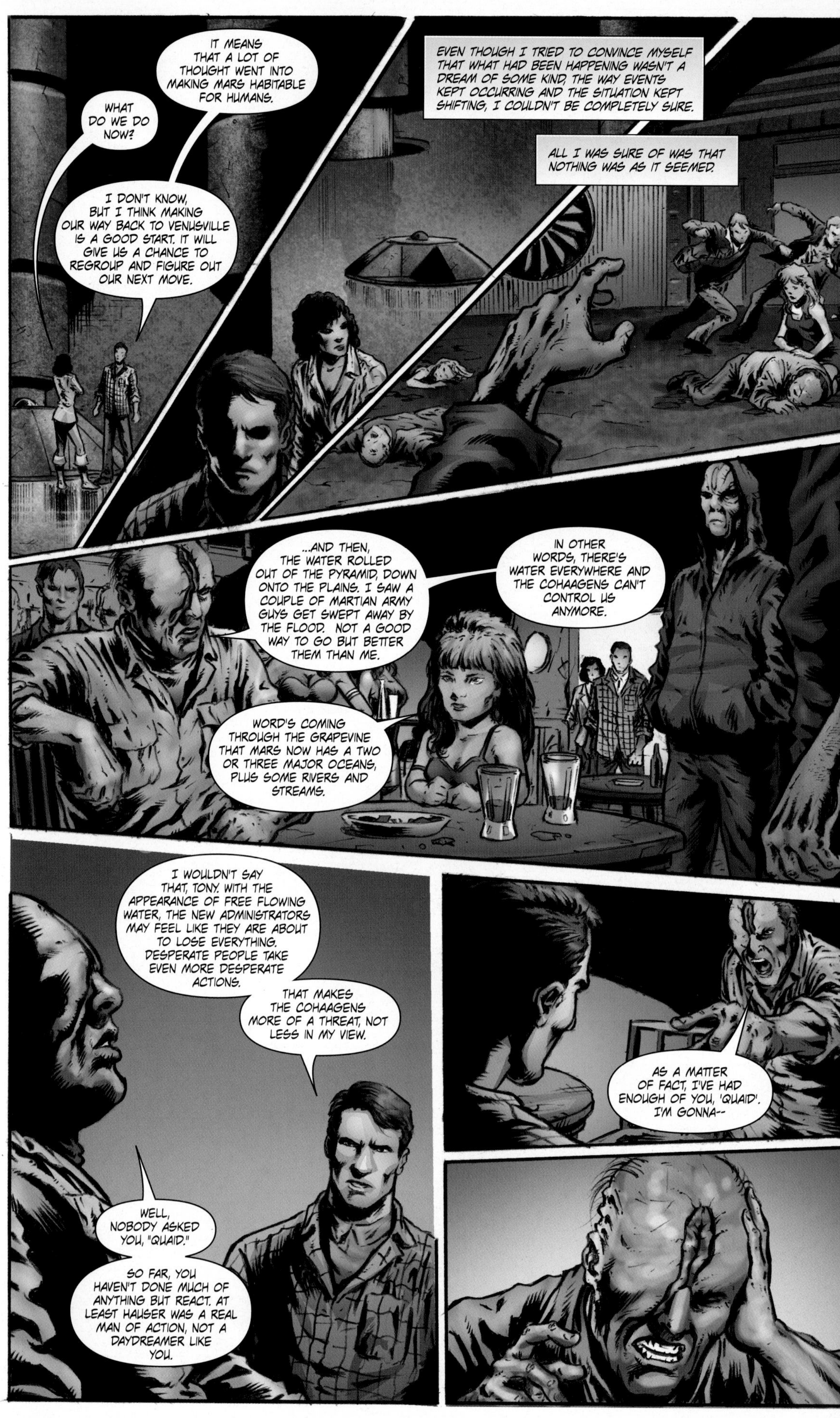
WHAT DO WE DO NOW?
IT MEANS THAT A LOT OF THOUGHT WENT INTO MAKING MARS HABITABLE FOR HUMANS.
I DON'T KNOW, BUT I THINK MAKING OUR WAY BACK TO VENUSVILLE IS A GOOD START. IT WILL GIVE US A CHANCE TO REGROUP AND FIGURE OUT OUR NEXT MOVE.
EVEN THOUGH I TRIED TO CONVINCE MYSELF THAT WHAT HAD BEEN HAPPENING WASN'T A DREAM OF SOME KIND, THE WAY EVENTS KEPT OCCURRING AND THE SITUATION KEPT SHIFTING, I COULDN'T BE COMPLETELY SURE.
ALL I WAS SURE OF WAS THAT NOTHING WAS AS IT SEEMED.
...AND THEN, THE WATER ROLLED OUT OF THE PYRAMID, DOWN ONTO THE PLAINS. I SAW A COUPLE OF MARTIAN ARMY GUYS GET SWEPT AWAY BY THE FLOOD. NOT A GOOD WAY TO GO BUT BETTER THEM THAN ME.
IN OTHER WORDS, THERE'S WATER EVERYWHERE AND THE COHAAGENS CAN'T CONTROL US ANYMORE.
WORD'S COMING THROUGH THE GRAPEVINE THAT MARS NOW HAS A TWO OR THREE MAJOR OCEANS, PLUS SOME RIVERS AND STREAMS.
I WOULDN'T SAY THAT, TONY. WITH THE APPEARANCE OF FREE FLOWING WATER, THE NEW ADMINISTRATORS MAY FEEL LIKE THEY ARE ABOUT TO LOSE EVERYTHING. DESPERATE PEOPLE TAKE EVEN MORE DESPERATE ACTIONS.
THAT MAKES THE COHAAGENS MORE OF A THREAT, NOT LESS IN MY VIEW.
WELL, NOBODY ASKED YOU, "QUAID."
SO FAR, YOU HAVEN'T DONE MUCH OF ANYTHING BUT REACT. AT LEAST HAUSER WAS A REAL MAN OF ACTION, NOT A DAYDREAMER LIKE YOU.
AS A MATTER OF FACT, I'VE HAD ENOUGH OF YOU, 'QUAID'. I'M GONNA--

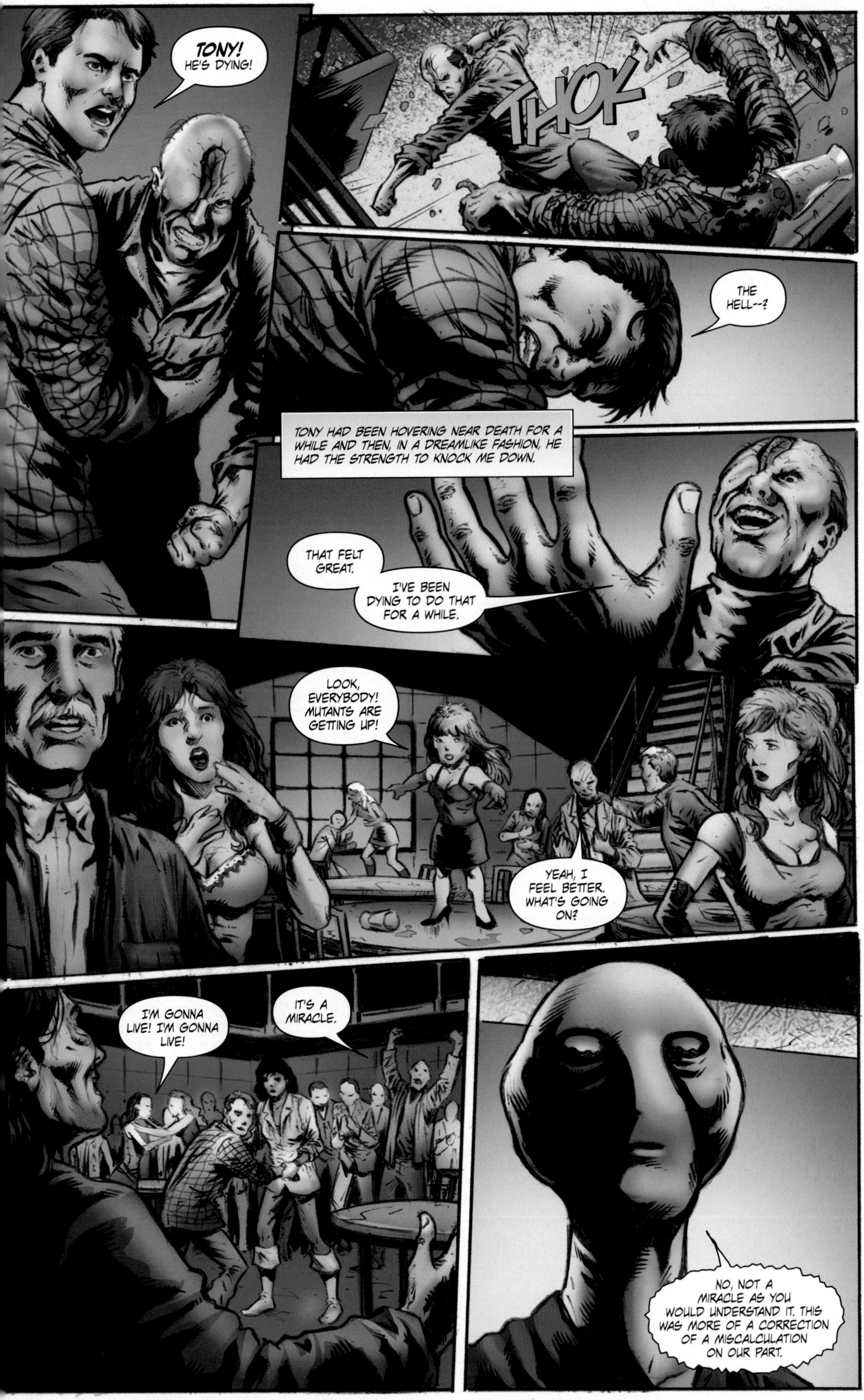
TONY! HE'S DYING!
THOK
THE HELL--?
TONY HAD BEEN HOVERING NEAR DEATH FOR A WHILE AND THEN, IN A DREAMLIKE FASHION, HE HAD THE STRENGTH TO KNOCK ME DOWN.
THAT FELT GREAT.
I'VE BEEN DYING TO DO THAT FOR A WHILE.
LOOK, EVERYBODY! MUTANTS ARE GETTING UP!
YEAH, I FEEL BETTER. WHAT'S GOING ON?
I'M GONNA LIVE! I'M GONNA LIVE!
IT'S A MIRACLE.
NO, NOT A MIRACLE AS YOU WOULD UNDERSTAND IT. THIS WAS MORE OF A CORRECTION OF A MISCALCULATION ON OUR PART.

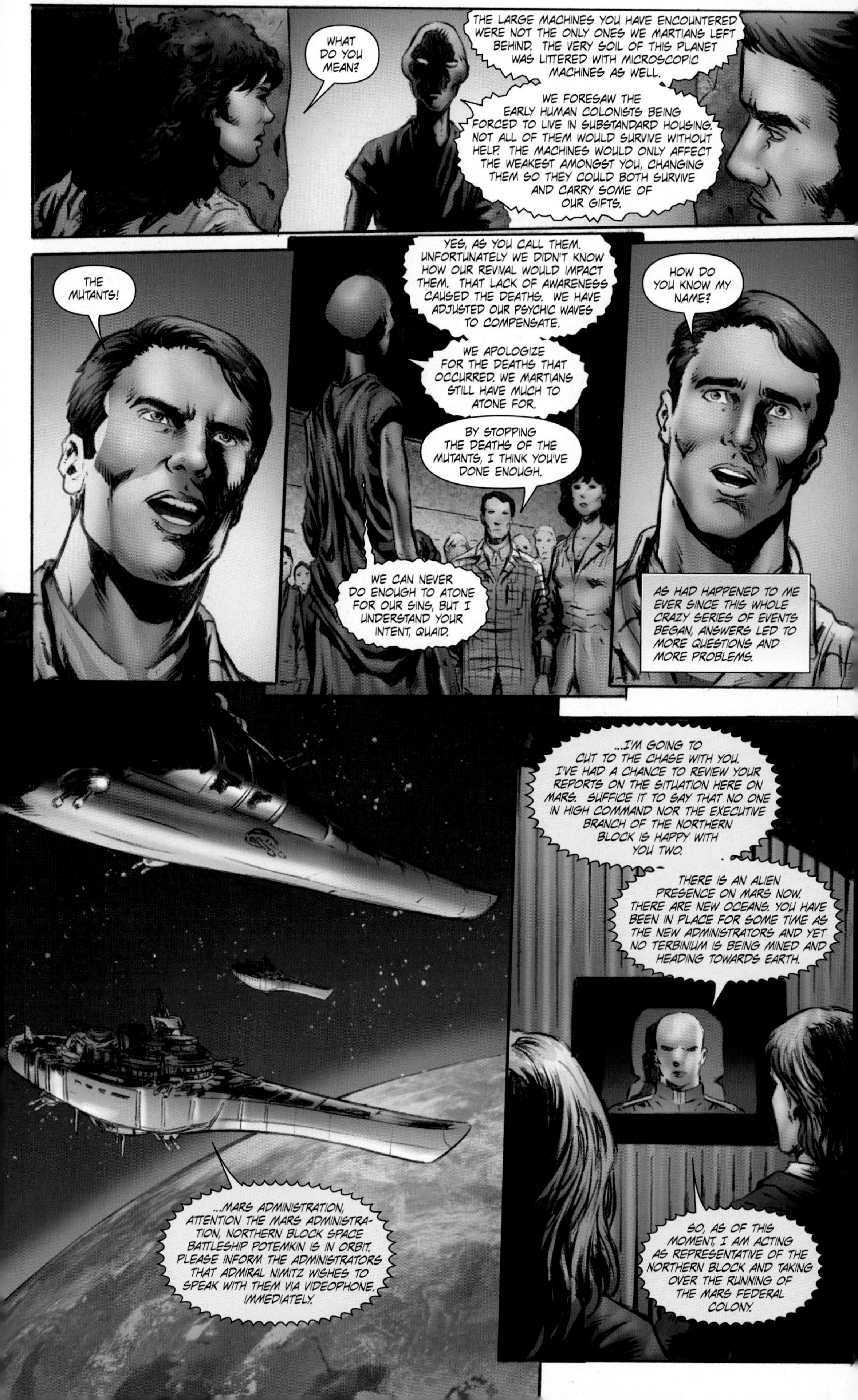
WHAT DO YOU MEAN?
THE LARGE MACHINES YOU HAVE ENCOUNTERED WERE NOT THE ONLY ONES WE MARTIANS LEFT BEHIND. THE VERY SOIL OF THIS PLANET WAS LITTERED WITH MICROSCOPIC MACHINES AS WELL.
WE FORESAW THE EARLY HUMAN COLONISTS BEING FORCED TO LIVE IN SUBSTANDARD HOUSING. NOT ALL OF THEM WOULD SURVIVE WITHOUT HELP. THE MACHINES WOULD ONLY AFFECT THE WEAKEST AMONGST YOU, CHANGING THEM SO THEY COULD BOTH SURVIVE AND CARRY SOME OF OUR GIFTS.
THE MUTANTS!
YES, AS YOU CALL THEM. UNFORTUNATELY WE DIDN'T KNOW HOW OUR REVIVAL WOULD IMPACT THEM. THAT LACK OF AWARENESS CAUSED THE DEATHS. WE HAVE ADJUSTED OUR PSYCHIC WAVES TO COMPENSATE.
WE APOLOGIZE FOR THE DEATHS THAT OCCURRED. WE MARTIANS STILL HAVE MUCH TO ATONE FOR.
BY STOPPING THE DEATHS OF THE MUTANTS, I THINK YOU'VE DONE ENOUGH.
WE CAN NEVER DO ENOUGH TO ATONE FOR OUR SINS, BUT I UNDERSTAND YOUR INTENT, QUAID.
HOW DO YOU KNOW MY NAME?
AS HAD HAPPENED TO ME EVER SINCE THIS WHOLE CRAZY SERIES OF EVENTS BEGAN, ANSWERS LED TO MORE QUESTIONS AND MORE PROBLEMS.
...MARS ADMINISTRATION, ATTENTION THE MARS ADMINISTRATION, NORTHERN BLOCK SPACE BATTLESHIP POTEMKIN IS IN ORBIT. PLEASE INFORM THE ADMINISTRATORS THAT ADMIRAL NIMITZ WISHES TO SPEAK WITH THEM VIA VIDEOPHONE. IMMEDIATELY.
...I'M GOING TO CUT TO THE CHASE WITH YOU. I'VE HAD A CHANCE TO REVIEW YOUR REPORTS ON THE SITUATION HERE ON MARS. SUFFICE IT TO SAY THAT NO ONE IN HIGH COMMAND NOR THE EXECUTIVE BRANCH OF THE NORTHERN BLOCK IS HAPPY WITH YOU TWO.
THERE IS AN ALIEN PRESENCE ON MARS NOW. THERE ARE NEW OCEANS. YOU HAVE BEEN IN PLACE FOR SOME TIME AS THE NEW ADMINISTRATORS AND YET NO TERBINIUM IS BEING MINED AND HEADING TOWARDS EARTH.
SO, AS OF THIS MOMENT, I AM ACTING AS REPRESENTATIVE OF THE NORTHERN BLOCK AND TAKING OVER THE RUNNING OF THE MARS FEDERAL COLONY.

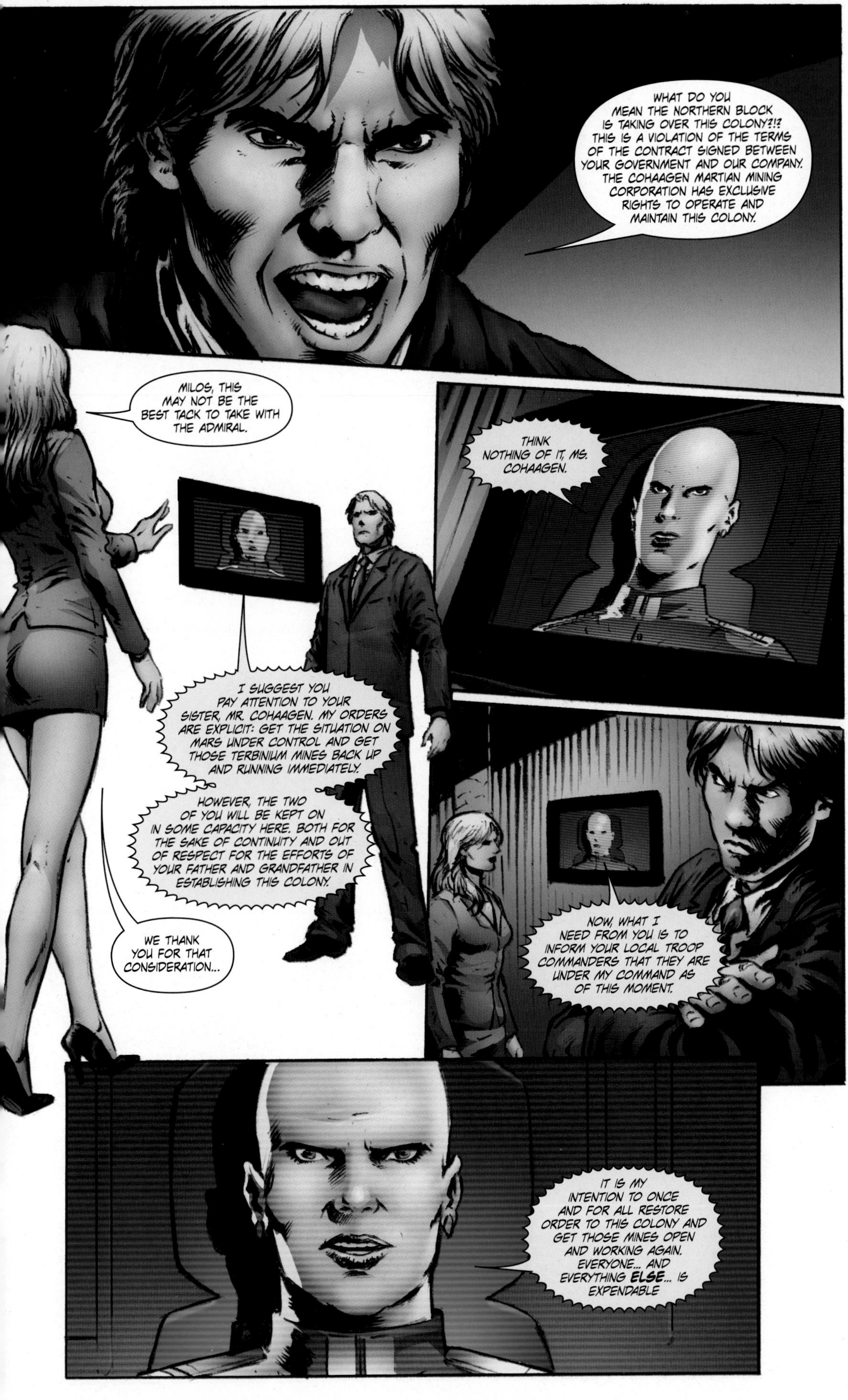
WHAT DO YOU MEAN THE NORTHERN BLOCK IS TAKING OVER THIS COLONY?!? THIS IS A VIOLATION OF THE TERMS OF THE CONTRACT SIGNED BETWEEN YOUR GOVERNMENT AND OUR COMPANY. THE COHAAGEN MARTIAN MINING CORPORATION HAS EXCLUSIVE RIGHTS TO OPERATE AND MAINTAIN THIS COLONY.
MILOS, THIS MAY NOT BE THE BEST TACK TO TAKE WITH THE ADMIRAL.
THINK NOTHING OF IT, MS. COHAAGEN.
I SUGGEST YOU PAY ATTENTION TO YOUR SISTER, MR. COHAAGEN. MY ORDERS ARE EXPLICIT: GET THE SITUATION ON MARS UNDER CONTROL AND GET THOSE TERBINIUM MINES BACK UP AND RUNNING IMMEDIATELY.
HOWEVER, THE TWO OF YOU WILL BE KEPT ON IN SOME CAPACITY HERE. BOTH FOR THE SAKE OF CONTINUITY AND OUT OF RESPECT FOR THE EFFORTS OF YOUR FATHER AND GRANDFATHER IN ESTABLISHING THIS COLONY.
WE THANK YOU FOR THAT CONSIDERATION...
NOW, WHAT I NEED FROM YOU IS TO INFORM YOUR LOCAL TROOP COMMANDERS THAT THEY ARE UNDER MY COMMAND AS OF THIS MOMENT.
IT IS MY INTENTION TO ONCE AND FOR ALL RESTORE ORDER TO THIS COLONY AND GET THOSE MINES OPEN AND WORKING AGAIN. EVERYONE... AND EVERYTHING ELSE... IS EXPENDABLE

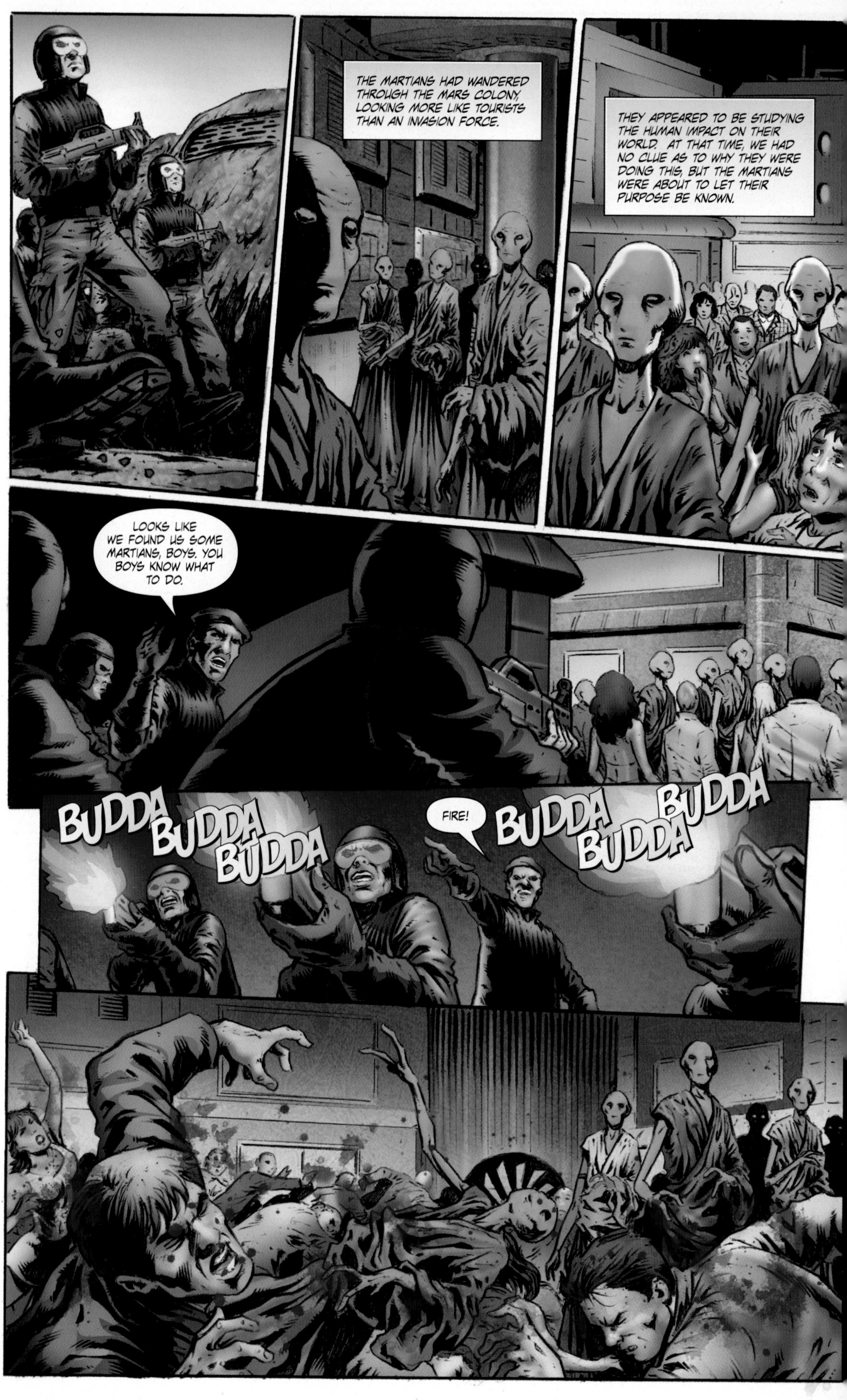
THE MARTIANS HAD WANDERED THROUGH THE MARS COLONY, LOOKING MORE LIKE TOURISTS THAN AN INVASION FORCE.
THEY APPEARED TO BE STUDYING THE HUMAN IMPACT ON THEIR WORLD. AT THAT TIME, WE HAD NO CLUE AS TO WHY THEY WERE DOING THIS, BUT THE MARTIANS WERE ABOUT TO LET THEIR PURPOSE BE KNOWN.
LOOKS LIKE WE FOUND US SOME MARTIANS, BOYS. YOU BOYS KNOW WHAT TO DO.
BUDDA BUDDA BUDDA
FIRE!
BUDDA BUDDA BUDDA

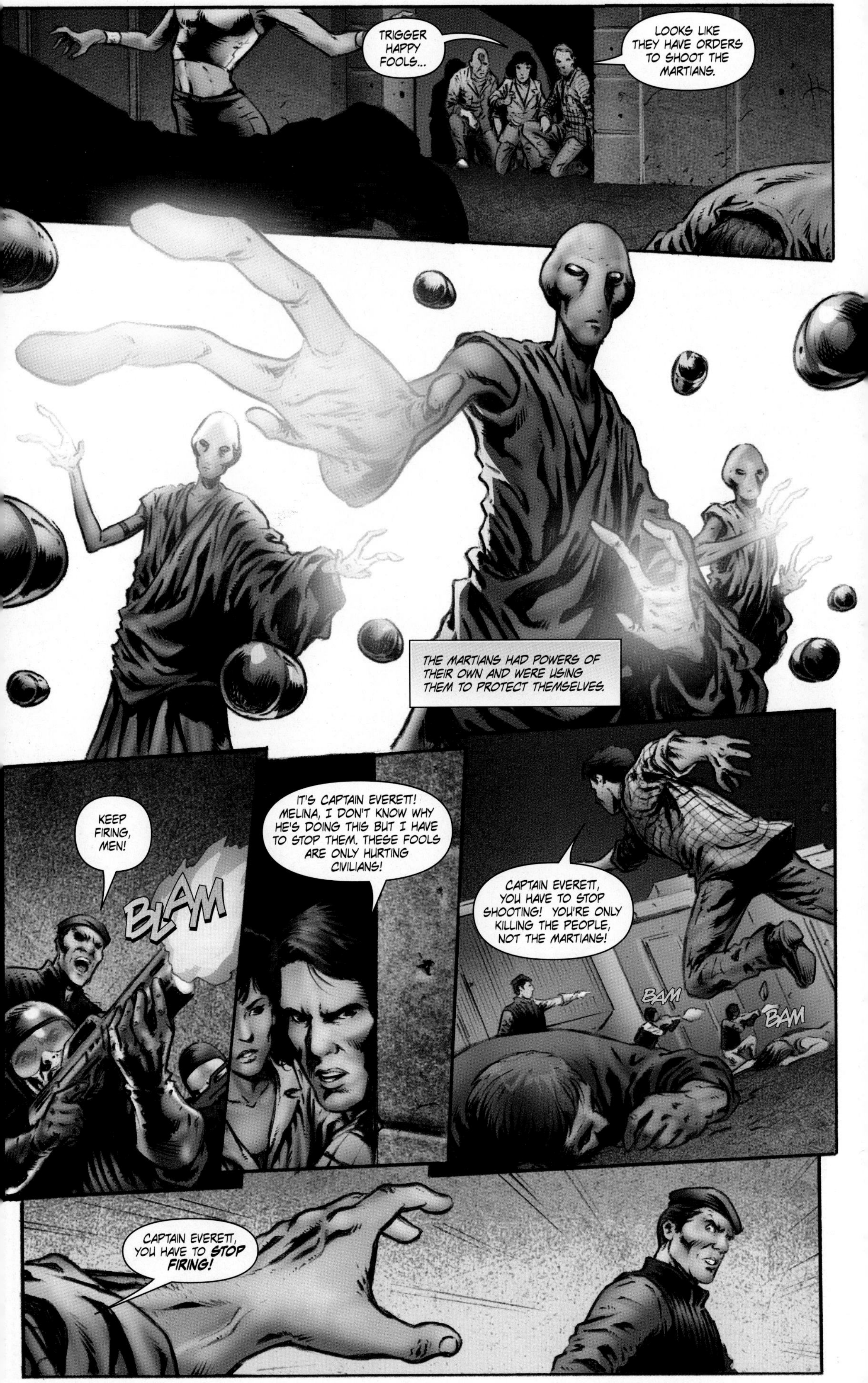
TRIGGER HAPPY FOOLS...
LOOKS LIKE THEY HAVE ORDERS TO SHOOT THE MARTIANS.
THE MARTIANS HAD POWERS OF THEIR OWN AND WERE USING THEM TO PROTECT THEMSELVES.
KEEP FIRING, MEN!
BLAM
IT'S CAPTAIN EVERETT! MELINA, I DON'T KNOW WHY HE'S DOING THIS BUT I HAVE TO STOP THEM. THESE FOOLS ARE ONLY HURTING CIVILIANS!
CAPTAIN EVERETT, YOU HAVE TO STOP SHOOTING! YOU'RE ONLY KILLING THE PEOPLE, NOT THE MARTIANS!
BAM
BAM
CAPTAIN EVERETT, YOU HAVE TO STOP FIRING!

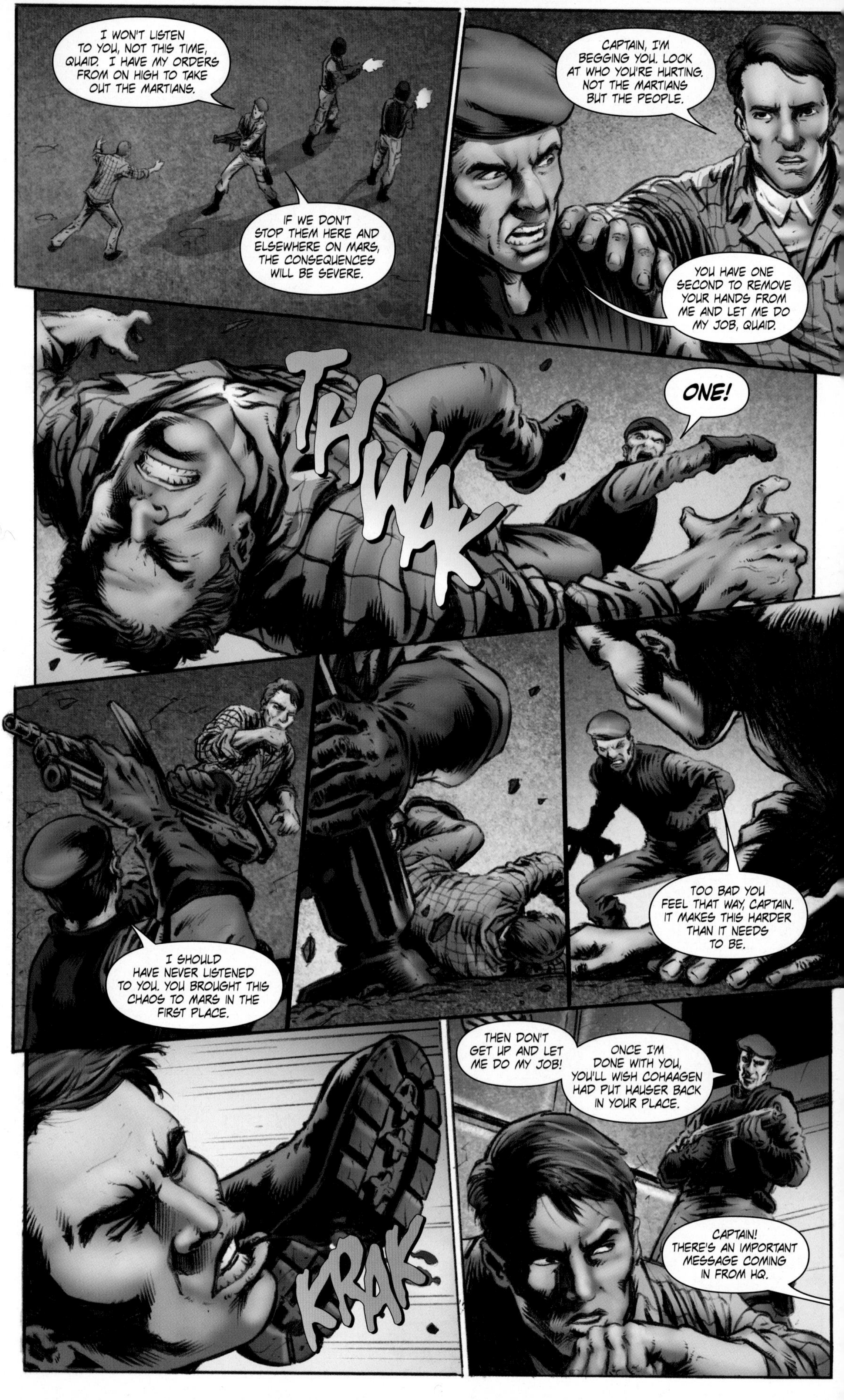

I WON'T LISTEN TO YOU, NOT THIS TIME, QUAID. I HAVE MY ORDERS FROM ON HIGH TO TAKE OUT THE MARTIANS.
IF WE DON'T STOP THEM HERE AND ELSEWHERE ON MARS, THE CONSEQUENCES WILL BE SEVERE.
CAPTAIN, I'M BEGGING YOU. LOOK AT WHO YOU'RE HURTING. NOT THE MARTIANS BUT THE PEOPLE.
YOU HAVE ONE SECOND TO REMOVE YOUR HANDS FROM ME AND LET ME DO MY JOB, QUAID.
THWAK
ONE!
I SHOULD HAVE NEVER LISTENED TO YOU. YOU BROUGHT THIS CHAOS TO MARS IN THE FIRST PLACE.
TOO BAD YOU FEEL THAT WAY, CAPTAIN. IT MAKES THIS HARDER THAN IT NEEDS TO BE.
KRAK
THEN DON'T GET UP AND LET ME DO MY JOB!
ONCE I'M DONE WITH YOU, YOU'LL WISH COHAAGEN HAD PUT HAUSER BACK IN YOUR PLACE.
CAPTAIN! THERE'S AN IMPORTANT MESSAGE COMING IN FROM HQ.

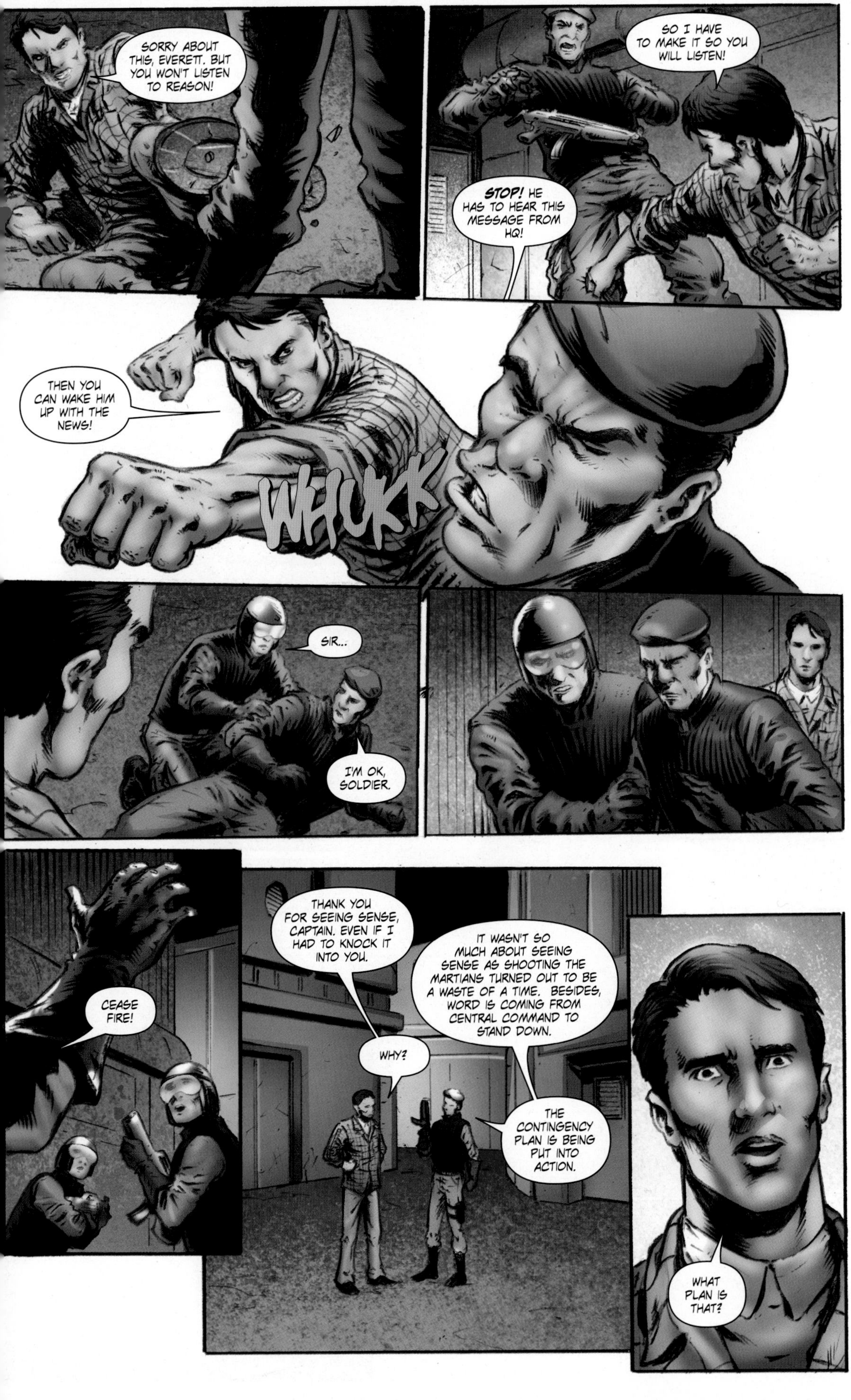
SORRY ABOUT THIS, EVERETT. BUT YOU WON'T LISTEN TO REASON!
SO I HAVE TO MAKE IT SO YOU WILL LISTEN!
STOP! HE HAS TO HEAR THIS MESSAGE FROM HQ!
THEN YOU CAN WAKE HIM UP WITH THE NEWS!
WHUKK
SIR...
I'M OK, SOLDIER.
CEASE FIRE!
THANK YOU FOR SEEING SENSE, CAPTAIN. EVEN IF I HAD TO KNOCK IT INTO YOU.
IT WASN'T SO MUCH ABOUT SEEING SENSE AS SHOOTING THE MARTIANS TURNED OUT TO BE A WASTE OF A TIME. BESIDES, WORD IS COMING FROM CENTRAL COMMAND TO STAND DOWN.
WHY?
THE CONTINGENCY PLAN IS BEING PUT INTO ACTION.
WHAT PLAN IS THAT?

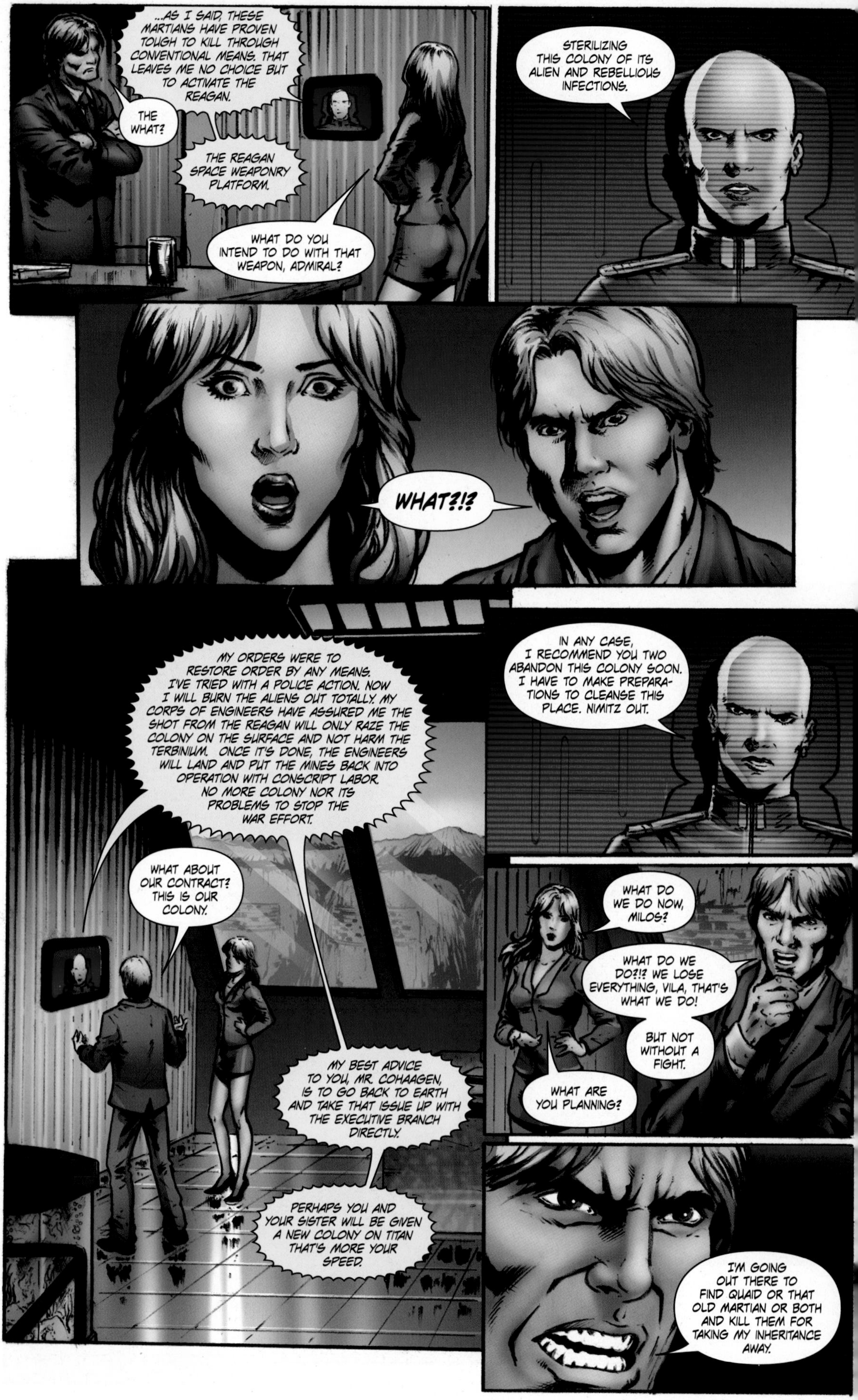
...AS I SAID, THESE MARTIANS HAVE PROVEN TOUGH TO KILL THROUGH CONVENTIONAL MEANS. THAT LEAVES ME NO CHOICE BUT TO ACTIVATE THE REAGAN.
THE WHAT?
THE REAGAN SPACE WEAPONRY PLATFORM.
WHAT DO YOU INTEND TO DO WITH THAT WEAPON, ADMIRAL?
STERILIZING THIS COLONY OF ITS ALIEN AND REBELLIOUS INFECTIONS.
WHAT?!?
MY ORDERS WERE TO RESTORE ORDER BY ANY MEANS. I'VE TRIED WITH A POLICE ACTION. NOW I WILL BURN THE ALIENS OUT TOTALLY. MY CORPS OF ENGINEERS HAVE ASSURED ME THE SHOT FROM THE REAGAN WILL ONLY RAZE THE COLONY ON THE SURFACE AND NOT HARM THE TERBINIUM. ONCE IT'S DONE, THE ENGINEERS WILL LAND AND PUT THE MINES BACK INTO OPERATION WITH CONSCRIPT LABOR. NO MORE COLONY NOR ITS PROBLEMS TO STOP THE WAR EFFORT.
WHAT ABOUT OUR CONTRACT? THIS IS OUR COLONY.
MY BEST ADVICE TO YOU, MR. COHAAGEN, IS TO GO BACK TO EARTH AND TAKE THAT ISSUE UP WITH THE EXECUTIVE BRANCH DIRECTLY.
PERHAPS YOU AND YOUR SISTER WILL BE GIVEN A NEW COLONY ON TITAN THAT'S MORE YOUR SPEED.
IN ANY CASE, I RECOMMEND YOU TWO ABANDON THIS COLONY SOON. I HAVE TO MAKE PREPARATIONS TO CLEANSE THIS PLACE. NIMITZ OUT.
WHAT DO WE DO NOW, MILOS?
WHAT DO WE DO?!? WE LOSE EVERYTHING, VILA, THAT'S WHAT WE DO!
BUT NOT WITHOUT A FIGHT.
WHAT ARE YOU PLANNING?
I'M GOING OUT THERE TO FIND QUAID OR THAT OLD MARTIAN OR BOTH AND KILL THEM FOR TAKING MY INHERITANCE AWAY.

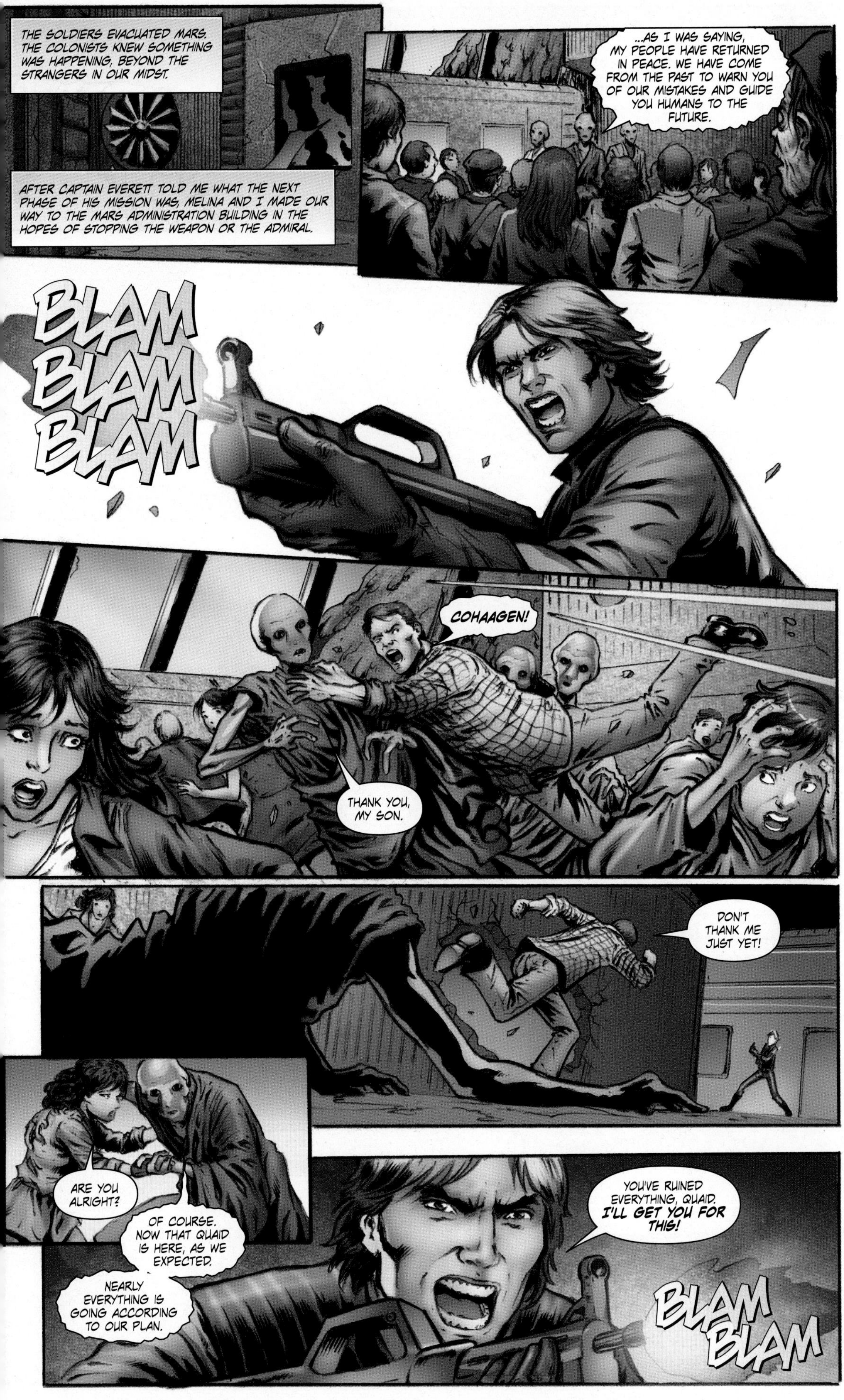
THE SOLDIERS EVACUATED MARS. THE COLONISTS KNEW SOMETHING WAS HAPPENING, BEYOND THE STRANGERS IN OUR MIDST.
AFTER CAPTAIN EVERETT TOLD ME WHAT THE NEXT PHASE OF HIS MISSION WAS, MELINA AND I MADE OUR WAY TO THE MARS ADMINISTRATION BUILDING IN THE HOPES OF STOPPING THE WEAPON OR THE ADMIRAL.
...AS I WAS SAYING, MY PEOPLE HAVE RETURNED IN PEACE. WE HAVE COME FROM THE PAST TO WARN YOU OF OUR MISTAKES AND GUIDE YOU HUMANS TO THE FUTURE.
BLAM BLAM BLAM
COHAAGEN!
THANK YOU, MY SON.
DON'T THANK ME JUST YET!
ARE YOU ALRIGHT?
OF COURSE. NOW THAT QUAID IS HERE, AS WE EXPECTED.
NEARLY EVERYTHING IS GOING ACCORDING TO OUR PLAN.
YOU'VE RUINED EVERYTHING, QUAID. I'LL GET YOU FOR THIS!
BLAM BLAM

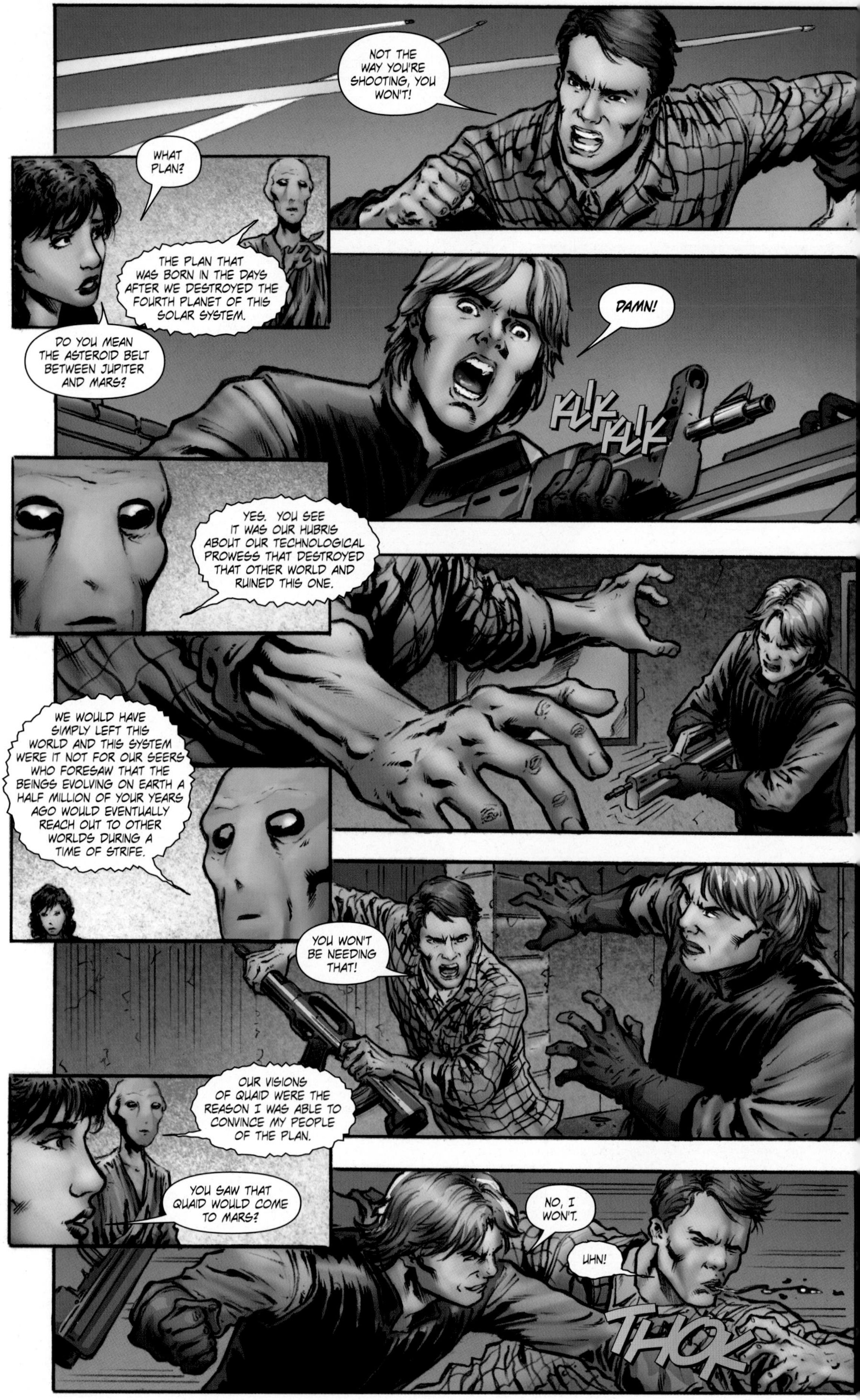
NOT THE WAY YOU'RE SHOOTING, YOU WON'T!
WHAT PLAN?
THE PLAN THAT WAS BORN IN THE DAYS AFTER WE DESTROYED THE FOURTH PLANET OF THIS SOLAR SYSTEM.
DO YOU MEAN THE ASTEROID BELT BETWEEN JUPITER AND MARS?
DAMN!
KLIK KLIK
YES. YOU SEE IT WAS OUR HUBRIS ABOUT OUR TECHNOLOGICAL PROWESS THAT DESTROYED THAT OTHER WORLD AND RUINED THIS ONE.
WE WOULD HAVE SIMPLY LEFT THIS WORLD AND THIS SYSTEM WERE IT NOT FOR OUR SEERS WHO FORESAW THAT THE BEINGS EVOLVING ON EARTH A HALF MILLION OF YOUR YEARS AGO WOULD EVENTUALLY REACH OUT TO OTHER WORLDS DURING A TIME OF STRIFE.
YOU WON'T BE NEEDING THAT!
OUR VISIONS OF QUAID WERE THE REASON I WAS ABLE TO CONVINCE MY PEOPLE OF THE PLAN.
YOU SAW THAT QUAID WOULD COME TO MARS?
NO, I WON'T.
UHN!
THOK

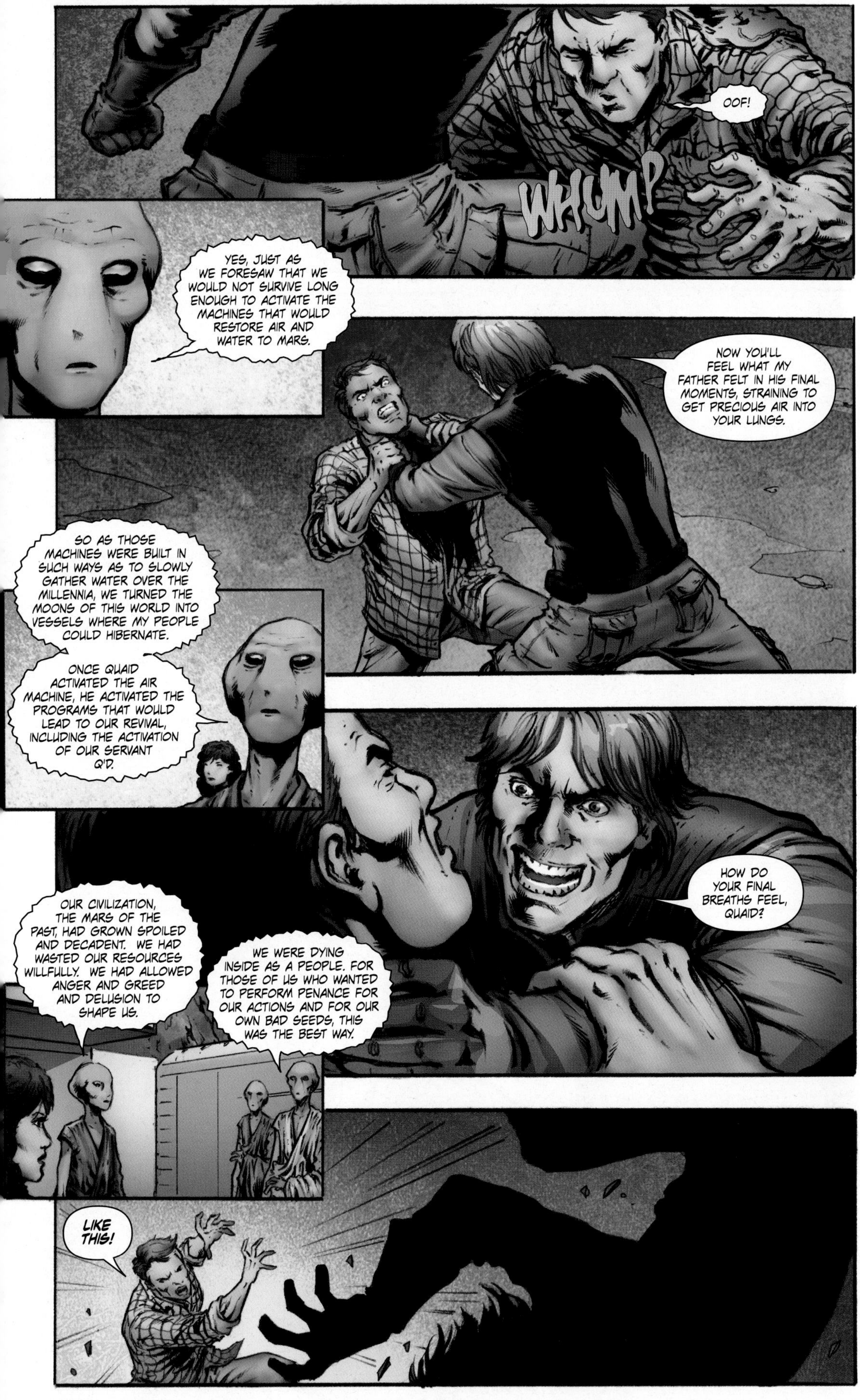
OOF!
WHUMP
YES, JUST AS WE FORESAW THAT WE WOULD NOT SURVIVE LONG ENOUGH TO ACTIVATE THE MACHINES THAT WOULD RESTORE AIR AND WATER TO MARS.
NOW YOU'LL FEEL WHAT MY FATHER FELT IN HIS FINAL MOMENTS, STRAINING TO GET PRECIOUS AIR INTO YOUR LUNGS.
SO AS THOSE MACHINES WERE BUILT IN SUCH WAYS AS TO SLOWLY GATHER WATER OVER THE MILLENNIA, WE TURNED THE MOONS OF THIS WORLD INTO VESSELS WHERE MY PEOPLE COULD HIBERNATE.
ONCE QUAID ACTIVATED THE AIR MACHINE, HE ACTIVATED THE PROGRAMS THAT WOULD LEAD TO OUR REVIVAL, INCLUDING THE ACTIVATION OF OUR SERVANT Q'D.
HOW DO YOUR FINAL BREATHS FEEL, QUAID?
OUR CIVILIZATION, THE MARS OF THE PAST, HAD GROWN SPOILED AND DECADENT. WE HAD WASTED OUR RESOURCES WILLFULLY. WE HAD ALLOWED ANGER AND GREED AND DELUSION TO SHAPE US.
WE WERE DYING INSIDE AS A PEOPLE. FOR THOSE OF US WHO WANTED TO PERFORM PENANCE FOR OUR ACTIONS AND FOR OUR OWN BAD SEEDS, THIS WAS THE BEST WAY.
LIKE THIS!

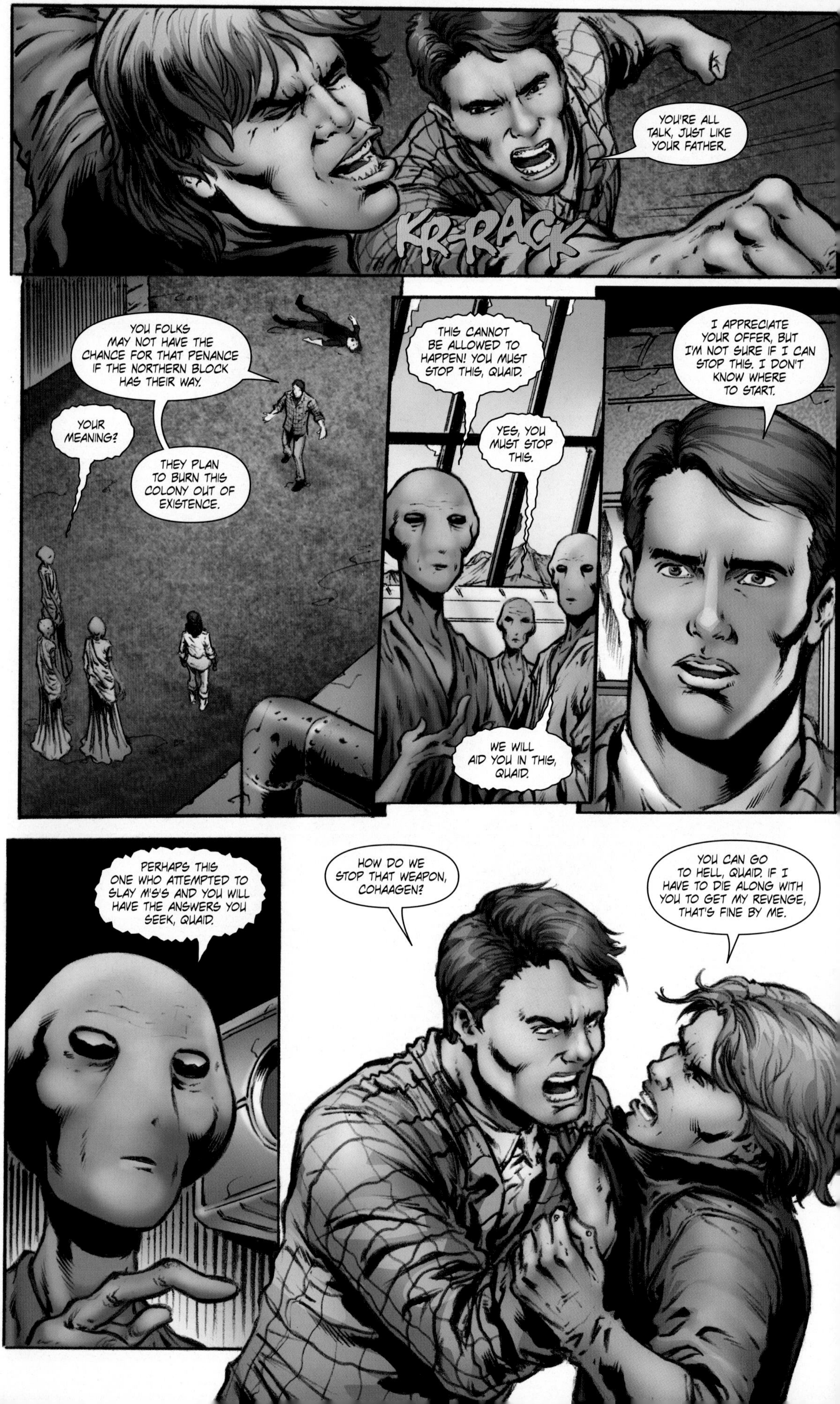
YOU'RE ALL TALK, JUST LIKE YOUR FATHER.
KR-RACK
YOU FOLKS MAY NOT HAVE THE CHANCE FOR THAT PENANCE IF THE NORTHERN BLOCK HAS THEIR WAY.
YOUR MEANING?
THEY PLAN TO BURN THIS COLONY OUT OF EXISTENCE.
THIS CANNOT BE ALLOWED TO HAPPEN! YOU MUST STOP THIS, QUAID.
YES, YOU MUST STOP THIS.
WE WILL AID YOU IN THIS, QUAID.
I APPRECIATE YOUR OFFER, BUT I'M NOT SURE IF I CAN STOP THIS. I DON'T KNOW WHERE TO START.
PERHAPS THIS ONE WHO ATTEMPTED TO SLAY M'S'S AND YOU WILL HAVE THE ANSWERS YOU SEEK, QUAID.
HOW DO WE STOP THAT WEAPON, COHAAGEN?
YOU CAN GO TO HELL, QUAID. IF I HAVE TO DIE ALONG WITH YOU TO GET MY REVENGE, THAT'S FINE BY ME.

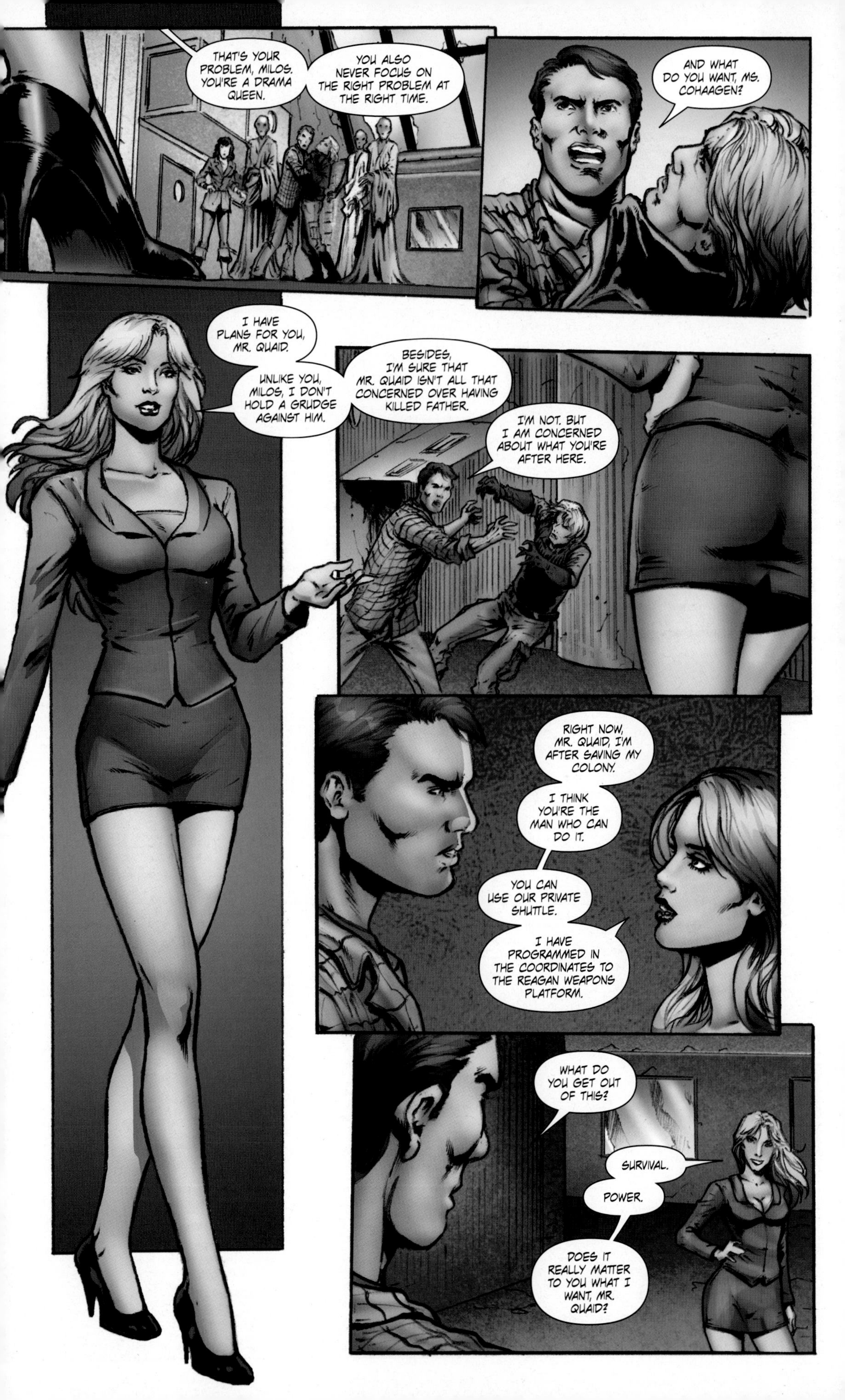
THAT'S YOUR PROBLEM, MILOS. YOU'RE A DRAMA QUEEN.
YOU ALSO NEVER FOCUS ON THE RIGHT PROBLEM AT THE RIGHT TIME.
AND WHAT DO YOU WANT, MS. COHAAGEN?
I HAVE PLANS FOR YOU, MR. QUAID.
UNLIKE YOU, MILOS, I DON'T HOLD A GRUDGE AGAINST HIM.
BESIDES, I'M SURE THAT MR. QUAID ISN'T ALL THAT CONCERNED OVER HAVING KILLED FATHER.
I'M NOT. BUT I AM CONCERNED ABOUT WHAT YOU'RE AFTER HERE.
RIGHT NOW, MR. QUAID, I'M AFTER SAVING MY COLONY.
I THINK YOU'RE THE MAN WHO CAN DO IT.
YOU CAN USE OUR PRIVATE SHUTTLE.
I HAVE PROGRAMMED IN THE COORDINATES TO THE REAGAN WEAPONS PLATFORM.
WHAT DO YOU GET OUT OF THIS?
SURVIVAL.
POWER.
DOES IT REALLY MATTER TO YOU WHAT I WANT, MR. QUAID?

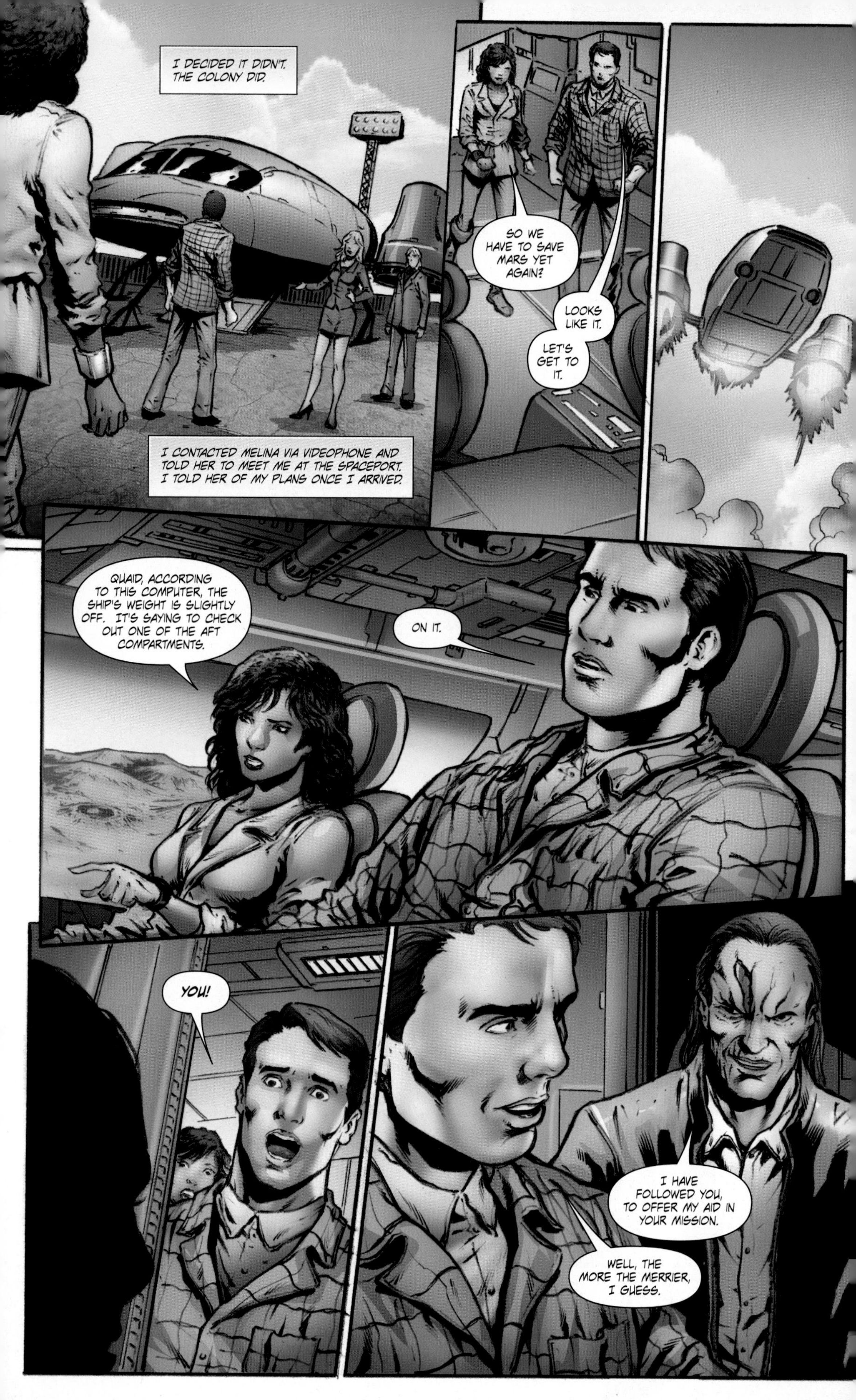
I DECIDED IT DIDN'T. THE COLONY DID.
I CONTACTED MELINA VIA VIDEOPHONE AND TOLD HER TO MEET ME AT THE SPACEPORT. I TOLD HER OF MY PLANS ONCE I ARRIVED.
SO WE HAVE TO SAVE MARS YET AGAIN?
LOOKS LIKE IT.
LET'S GET TO IT.
QUAID, ACCORDING TO THIS COMPUTER, THE SHIP'S WEIGHT IS SLIGHTLY OFF. IT'S SAYING TO CHECK OUT ONE OF THE AFT COMPARTMENTS.
ON IT.
YOU!
I HAVE FOLLOWED YOU, TO OFFER MY AID IN YOUR MISSION.
WELL, THE MORE THE MERRIER, I GUESS.

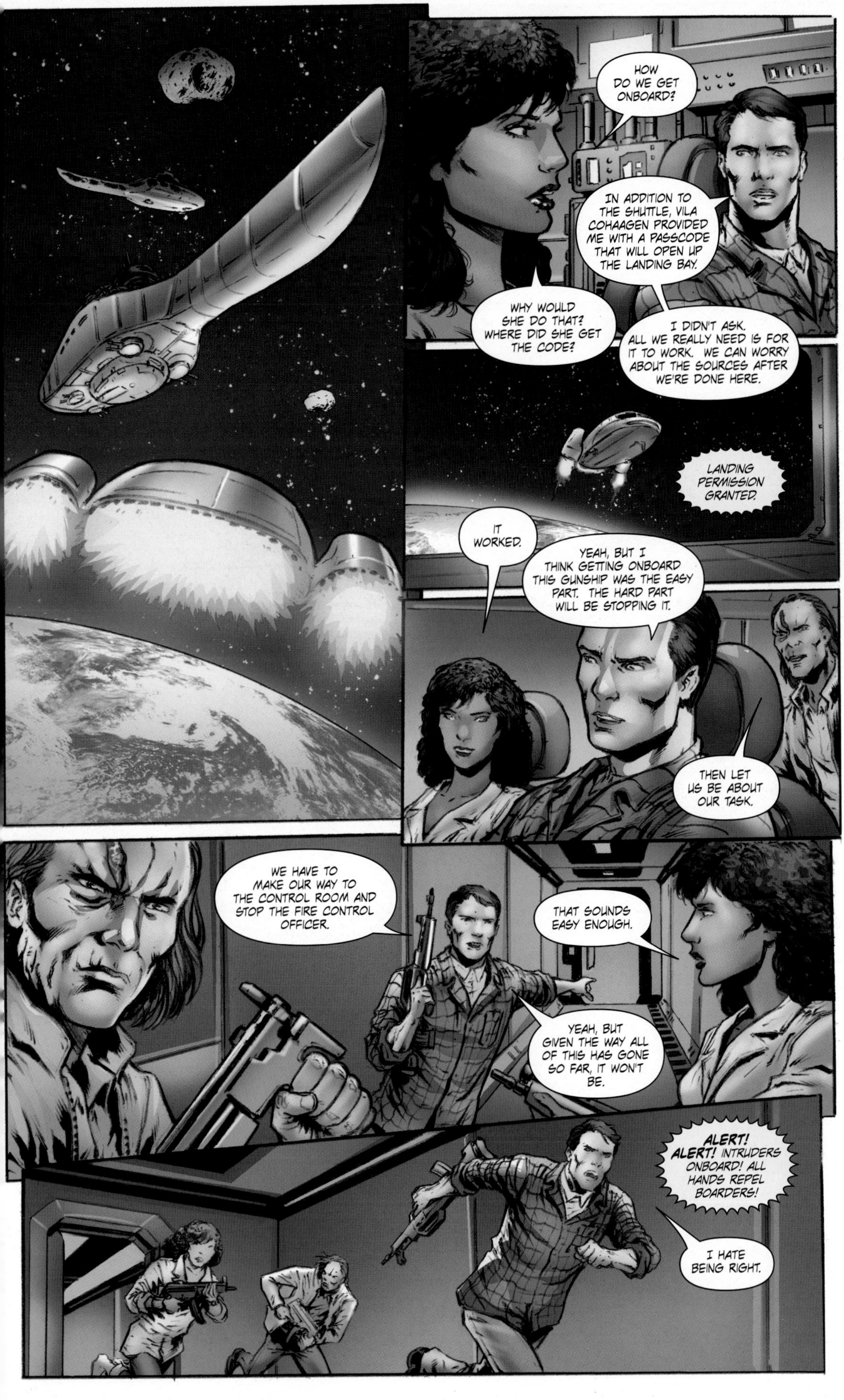
HOW DO WE GET ONBOARD?
IN ADDITION TO THE SHUTTLE, VILA COHAAGEN PROVIDED ME WITH A PASSCODE THAT WILL OPEN UP THE LANDING BAY.
WHY WOULD SHE DO THAT? WHERE DID SHE GET THE CODE?
I DIDN'T ASK. ALL WE REALLY NEED IS FOR IT TO WORK. WE CAN WORRY ABOUT THE SOURCES AFTER WE'RE DONE HERE.
LANDING PERMISSION GRANTED.
IT WORKED.
YEAH, BUT I THINK GETTING ONBOARD THIS GUNSHIP WAS THE EASY PART. THE HARD PART WILL BE STOPPING IT.
THEN LET US BE ABOUT OUR TASK.
WE HAVE TO MAKE OUR WAY TO THE CONTROL ROOM AND STOP THE FIRE CONTROL OFFICER.
THAT SOUNDS EASY ENOUGH.
YEAH, BUT GIVEN THE WAY ALL OF THIS HAS GONE SO FAR, IT WON'T BE.
ALERT! ALERT! INTRUDERS ONBOARD! ALL HANDS REPEL BOARDERS!
I HATE BEING RIGHT.

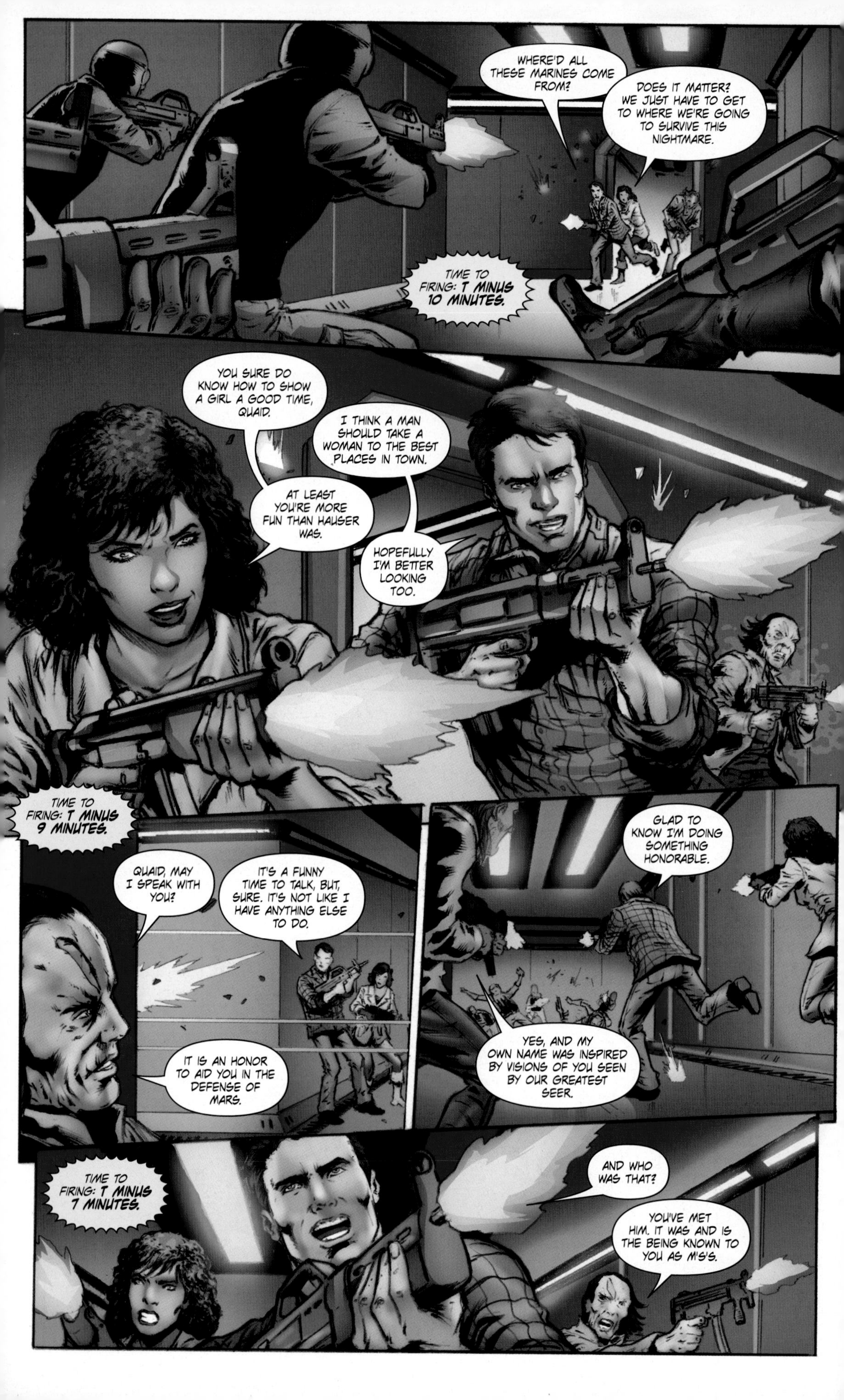
WHERE'D ALL THESE MARINES COME FROM?
DOES IT MATTER? WE JUST HAVE TO GET TO WHERE WE'RE GOING TO SURVIVE THIS NIGHTMARE.
TIME TO FIRING: T MINUS 10 MINUTES.
YOU SURE DO KNOW HOW TO SHOW A GIRL A GOOD TIME, QUAID.
I THINK A MAN SHOULD TAKE A WOMAN TO THE BEST PLACES IN TOWN.
AT LEAST YOU'RE MORE FUN THAN HAUSER WAS.
HOPEFULLY I'M BETTER LOOKING TOO.
TIME TO FIRING: T MINUS 9 MINUTES.
QUAID, MAY I SPEAK WITH YOU?
IT'S A FUNNY TIME TO TALK, BUT, SURE. IT'S NOT LIKE I HAVE ANYTHING ELSE TO DO.
IT IS AN HONOR TO AID YOU IN THE DEFENSE OF MARS.
GLAD TO KNOW I'M DOING SOMETHING HONORABLE.
YES, AND MY OWN NAME WAS INSPIRED BY VISIONS OF YOU SEEN BY OUR GREATEST SEER.
TIME TO FIRING: T MINUS 7 MINUTES.
AND WHO WAS THAT?
YOU'VE MET HIM. IT WAS AND IS THE BEING KNOWN TO YOU AS M'S'S.

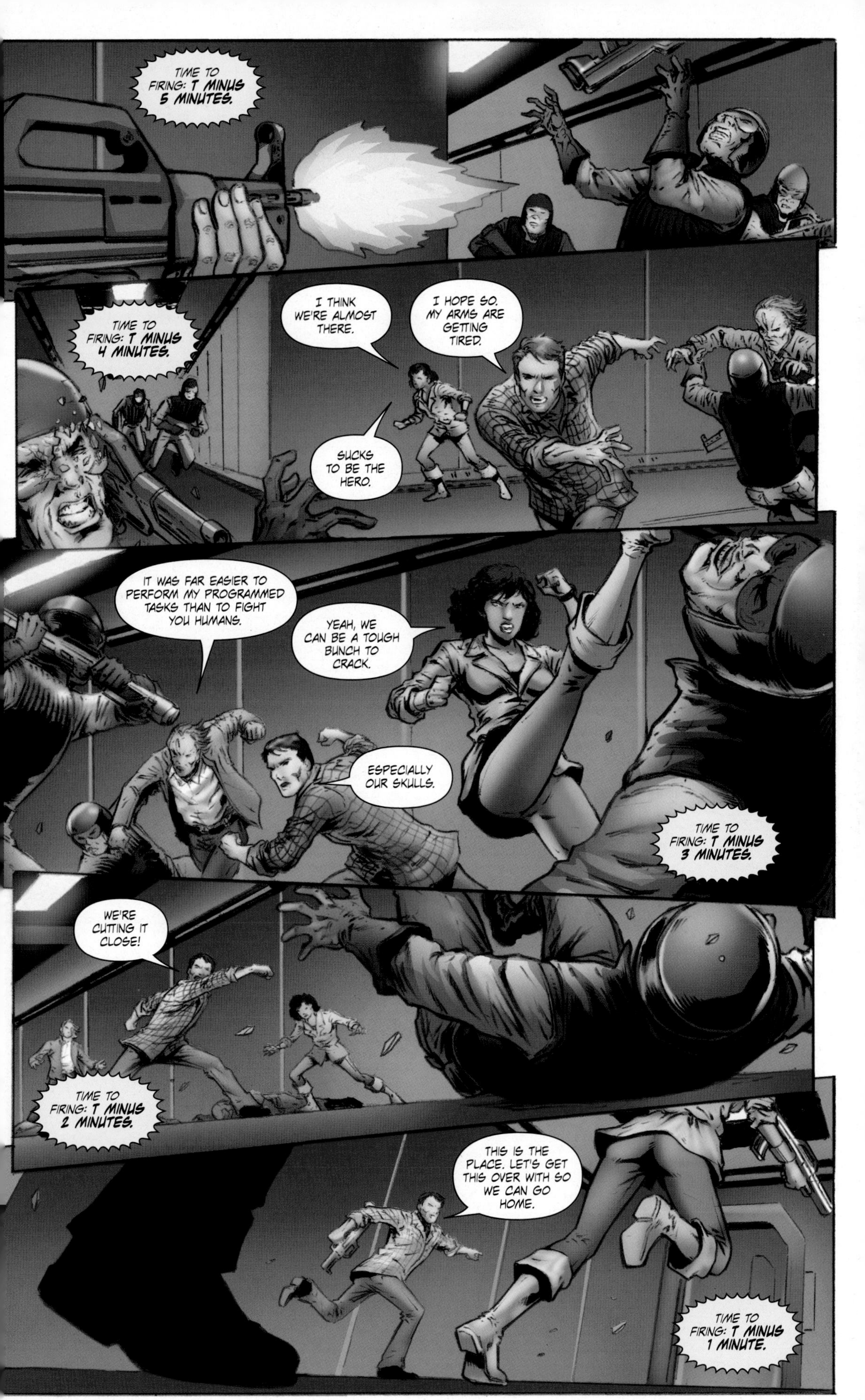
TIME TO FIRING: T MINUS 5 MINUTES.
TIME TO FIRING: T MINUS 4 MINUTES.
I THINK WE'RE ALMOST THERE.
I HOPE SO. MY ARMS ARE GETTING TIRED.
SUCKS TO BE THE HERO.
IT WAS FAR EASIER TO PERFORM MY PROGRAMMED TASKS THAN TO FIGHT YOU HUMANS.
YEAH, WE CAN BE A TOUGH BUNCH TO CRACK.
ESPECIALLY OUR SKULLS.
TIME TO FIRING: T MINUS 3 MINUTES.
WE'RE CUTTING IT CLOSE!
TIME TO FIRING: T MINUS 2 MINUTES.
THIS IS THE PLACE. LET'S GET THIS OVER WITH SO WE CAN GO HOME.
TIME TO FIRING: T MINUS 1 MINUTE.

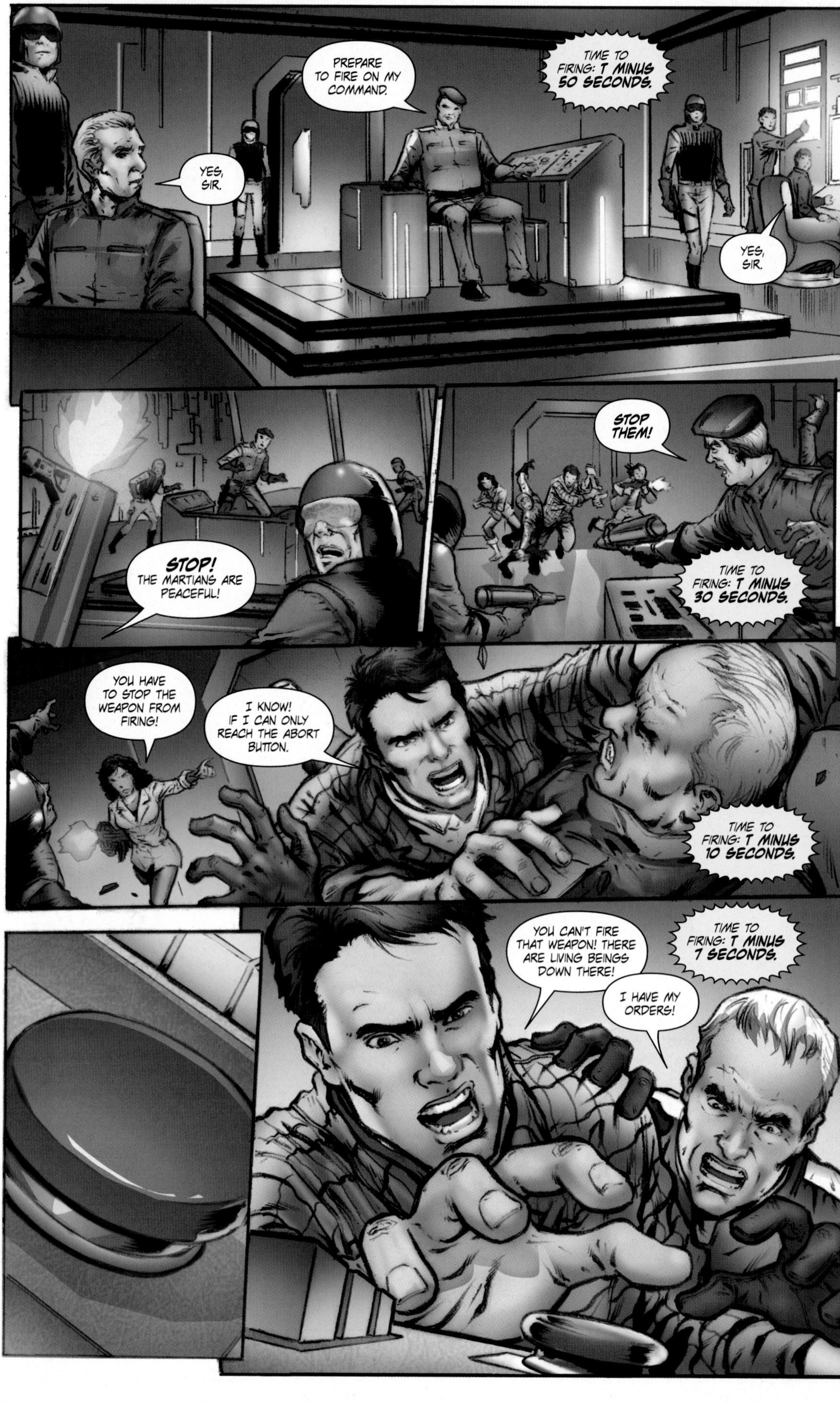
PREPARE TO FIRE ON MY COMMAND.
TIME TO FIRING: T MINUS 50 SECONDS.
YES, SIR.
YES, SIR.
STOP! THE MARTIANS ARE PEACEFUL!
STOP THEM!
TIME TO FIRING: T MINUS 30 SECONDS.
YOU HAVE TO STOP THE WEAPON FROM FIRING!
I KNOW! IF I CAN ONLY REACH THE ABORT BUTTON.
TIME TO FIRING: T MINUS 10 SECONDS.
TIME TO FIRING: T MINUS 7 SECONDS.
YOU CAN'T FIRE THAT WEAPON! THERE ARE LIVING BEINGS DOWN THERE!
I HAVE MY ORDERS!

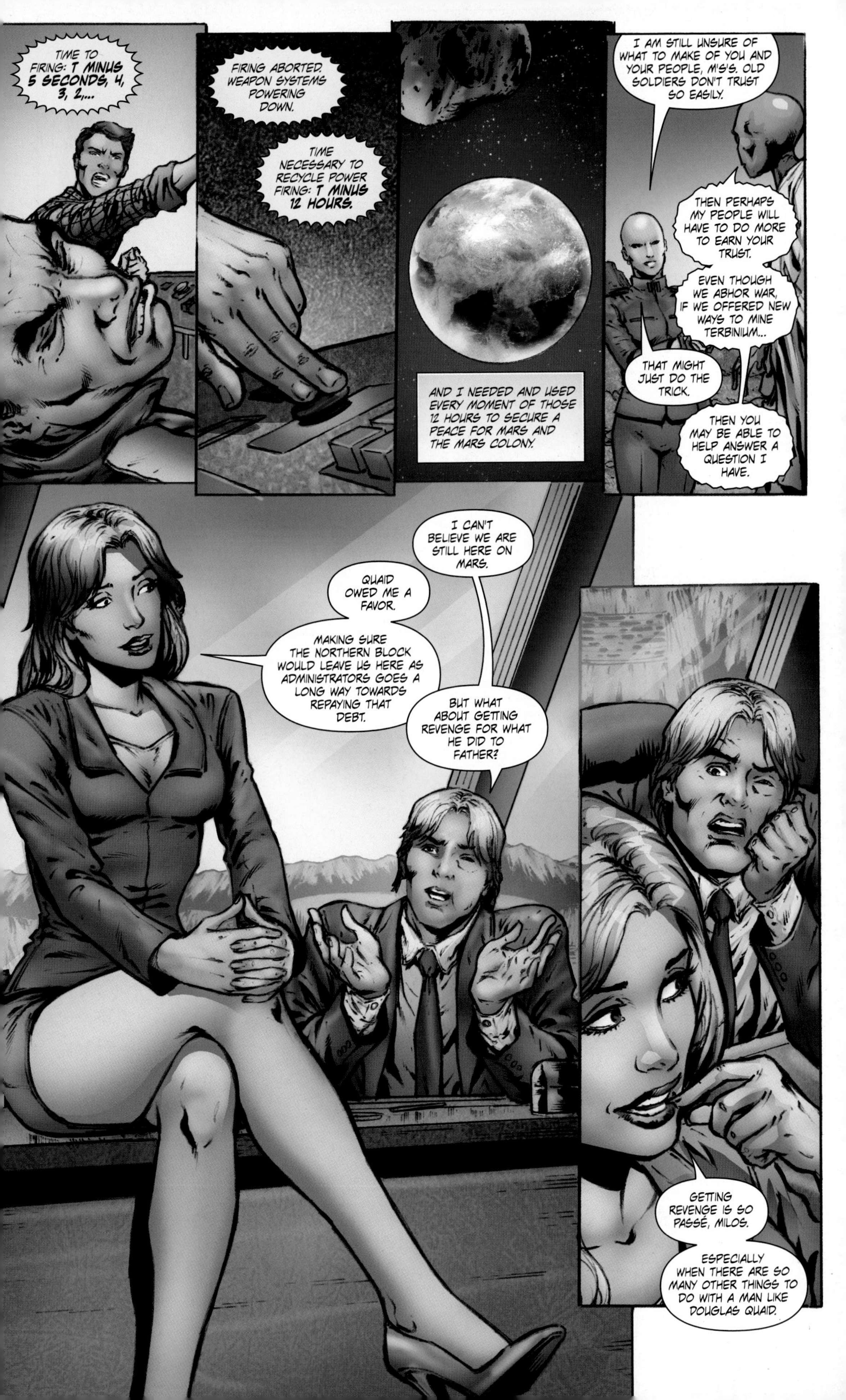
TIME TO FIRING: T MINUS 5 SECONDS, 4, 3, 2,...
FIRING ABORTED. WEAPON SYSTEMS POWERING DOWN.
TIME NECESSARY TO RECYCLE POWER FIRING: T MINUS 12 HOURS.
AND I NEEDED AND USED EVERY MOMENT OF THOSE 12 HOURS TO SECURE A PEACE FOR MARS AND THE MARS COLONY.
I AM STILL UNSURE OF WHAT TO MAKE OF YOU AND YOUR PEOPLE, M'S'S. OLD SOLDIERS DON'T TRUST SO EASILY.
THEN PERHAPS MY PEOPLE WILL HAVE TO DO MORE TO EARN YOUR TRUST.
EVEN THOUGH WE ABHOR WAR, IF WE OFFERED NEW WAYS TO MINE TERBINIUM...
THAT MIGHT JUST DO THE TRICK.
THEN YOU MAY BE ABLE TO HELP ANSWER A QUESTION I HAVE.
I CAN'T BELIEVE WE ARE STILL HERE ON MARS.
QUAID OWED ME A FAVOR.
MAKING SURE THE NORTHERN BLOCK WOULD LEAVE US HERE AS ADMINISTRATORS GOES A LONG WAY TOWARDS REPAYING THAT DEBT.
BUT WHAT ABOUT GETTING REVENGE FOR WHAT HE DID TO FATHER?
GETTING REVENGE IS SO PASSÉ, MILOS.
ESPECIALLY WHEN THERE ARE SO MANY OTHER THINGS TO DO WITH A MAN LIKE DOUGLAS QUAID.

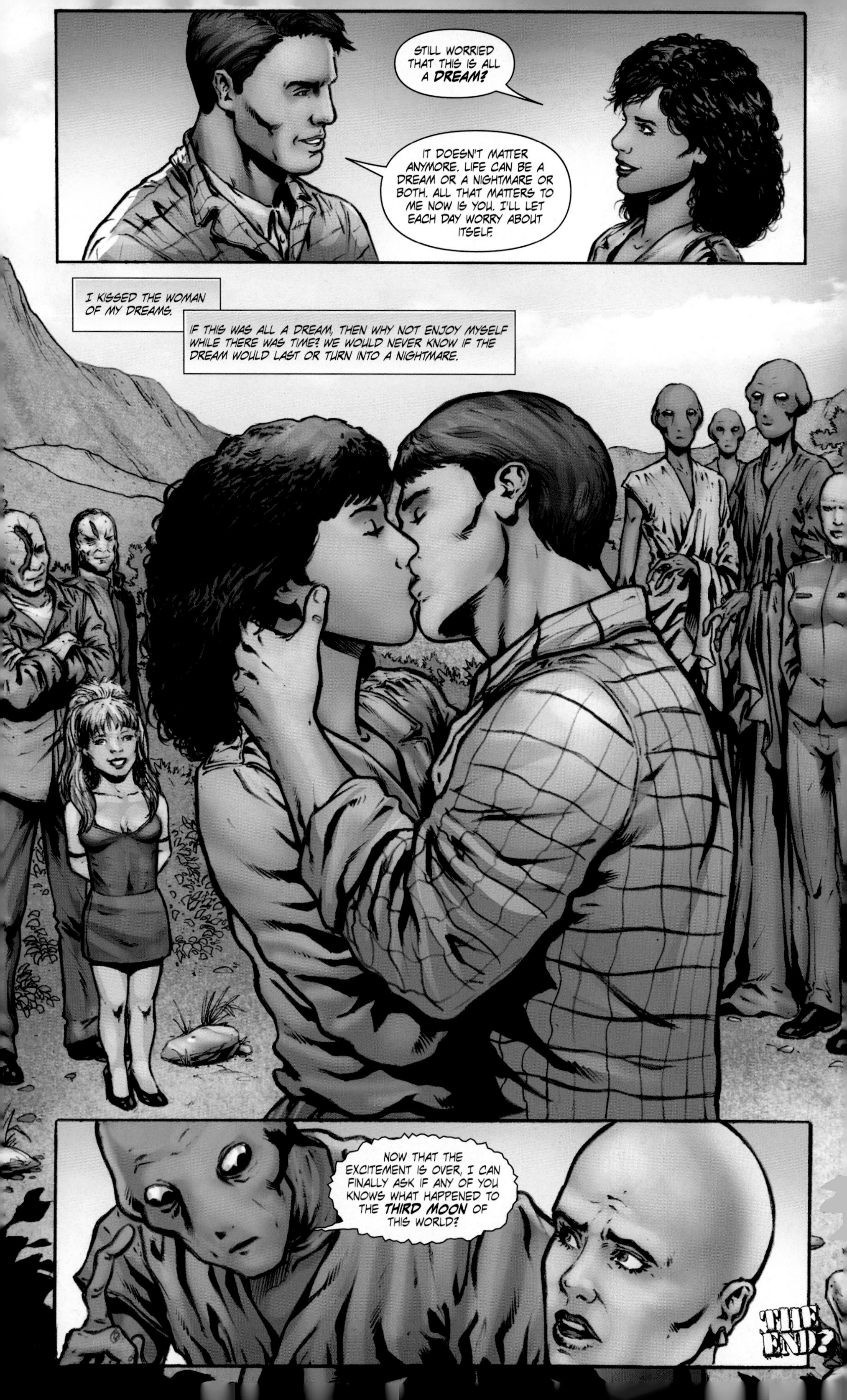
STILL WORRIED THAT THIS IS ALL A DREAM?
IT DOESN'T MATTER ANYMORE. LIFE CAN BE A DREAM OR A NIGHTMARE OR BOTH. ALL THAT MATTERS TO ME NOW IS YOU. I'LL LET EACH DAY WORRY ABOUT ITSELF.
I KISSED THE WOMAN OF MY DREAMS.
IF THIS WAS ALL A DREAM, THEN WHY NOT ENJOY MYSELF WHILE THERE WAS TIME? WE WOULD NEVER KNOW IF THE DREAM WOULD LAST OR TURN INTO A NIGHTMARE.
NOW THAT THE EXCITEMENT IS OVER, I CAN FINALLY ASK IF ANY OF YOU KNOWS WHAT HAPPENED TO THE THIRD MOON OF THIS WORLD?
THE END?

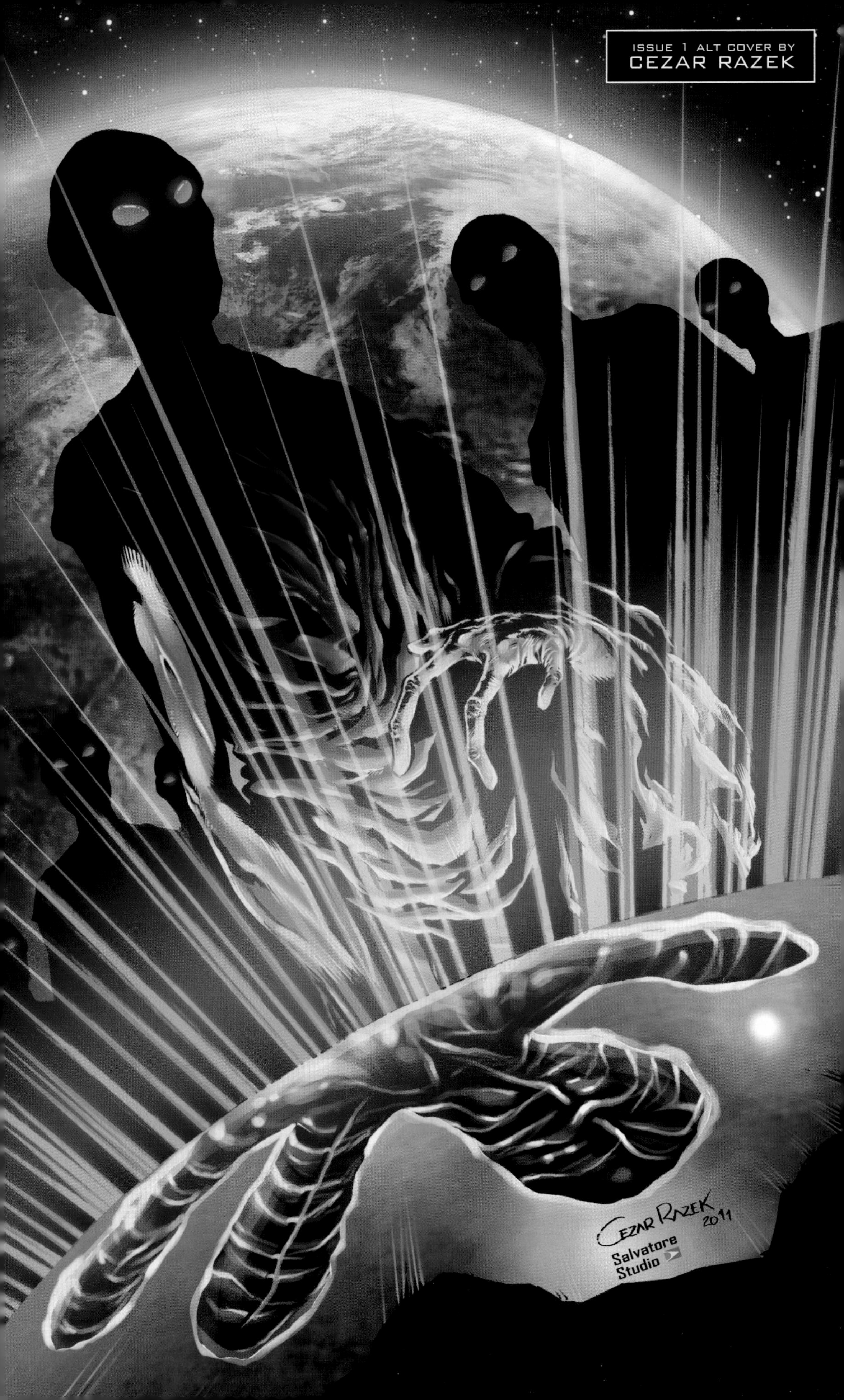

ISSUE 1 ALT COVER BY
CEZAR RAZEK

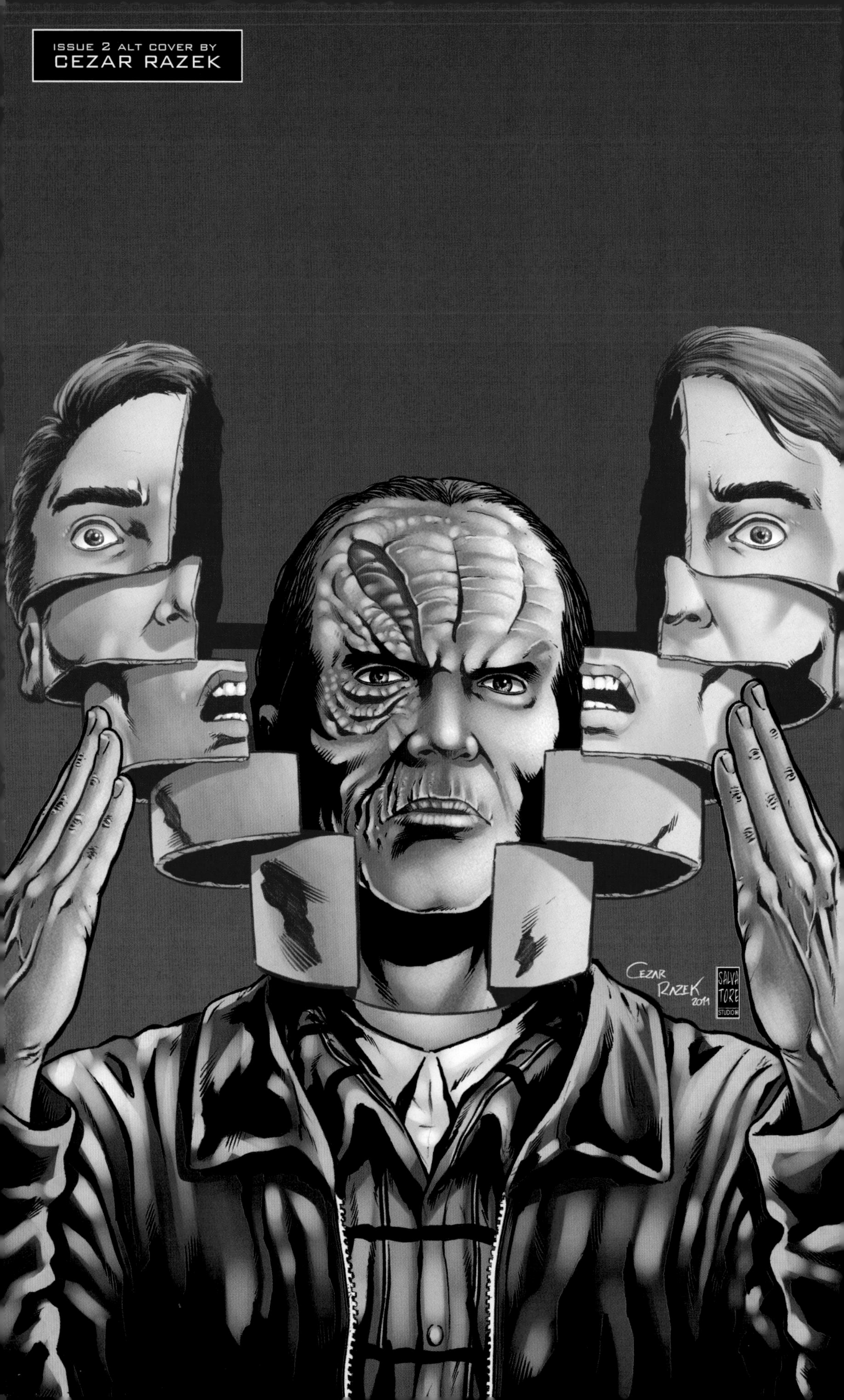

ISSUE 2 ALT COVER BY
CEZAR RAZEK

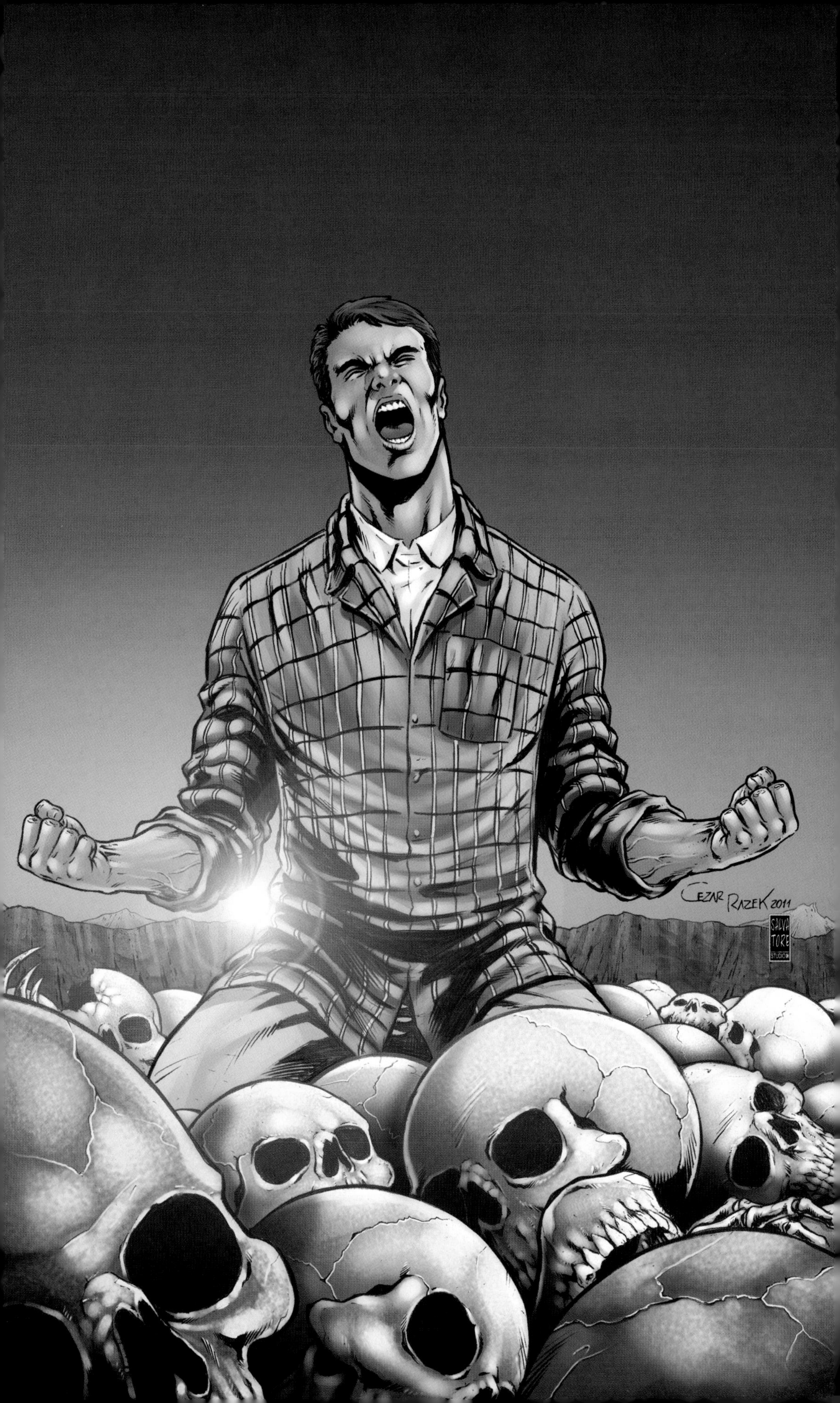
CEZAR RAZEK 2011

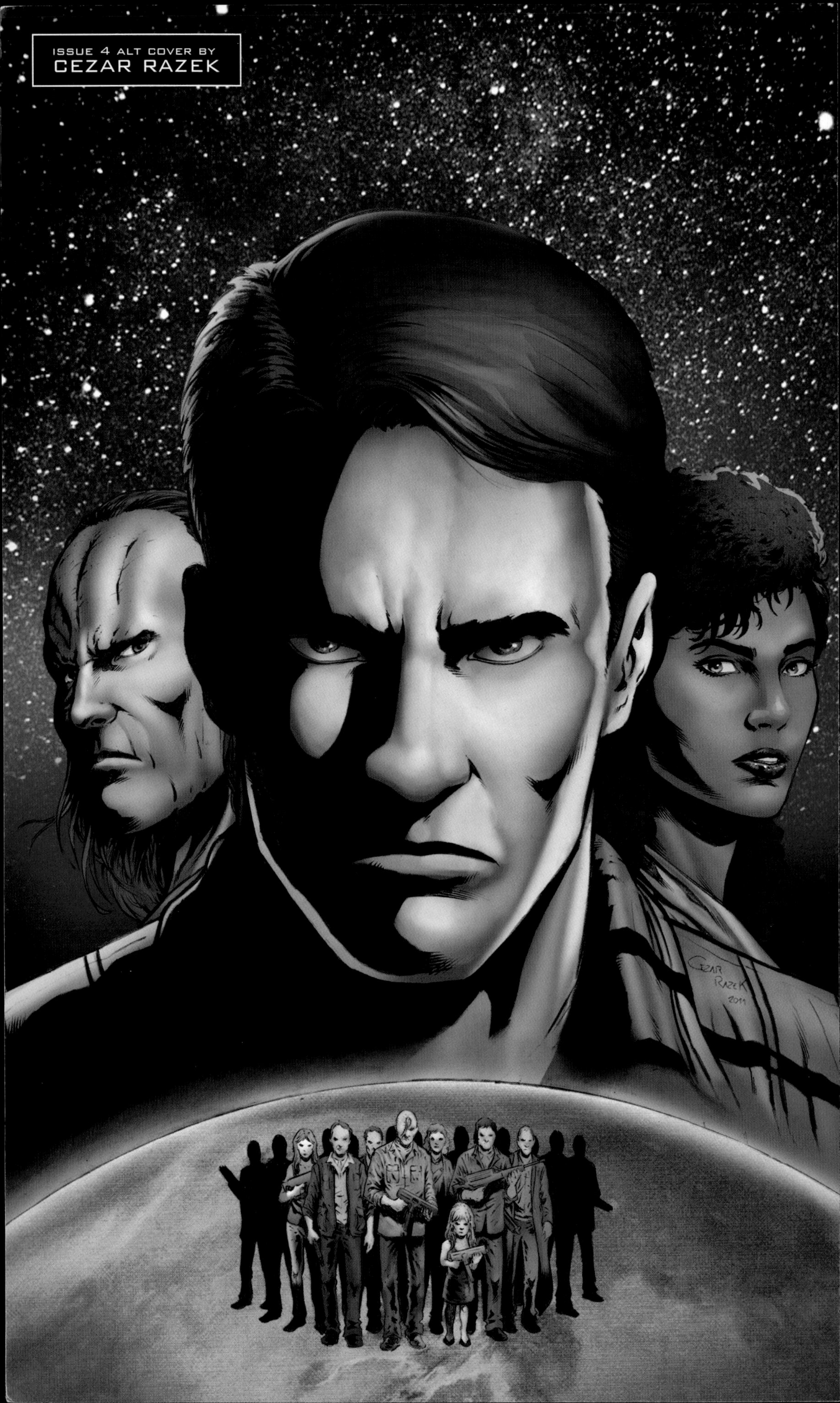
CEZAR
RAZEK
2011
ISSUE 4 ALT COVER BY
CEZAR RAZEK

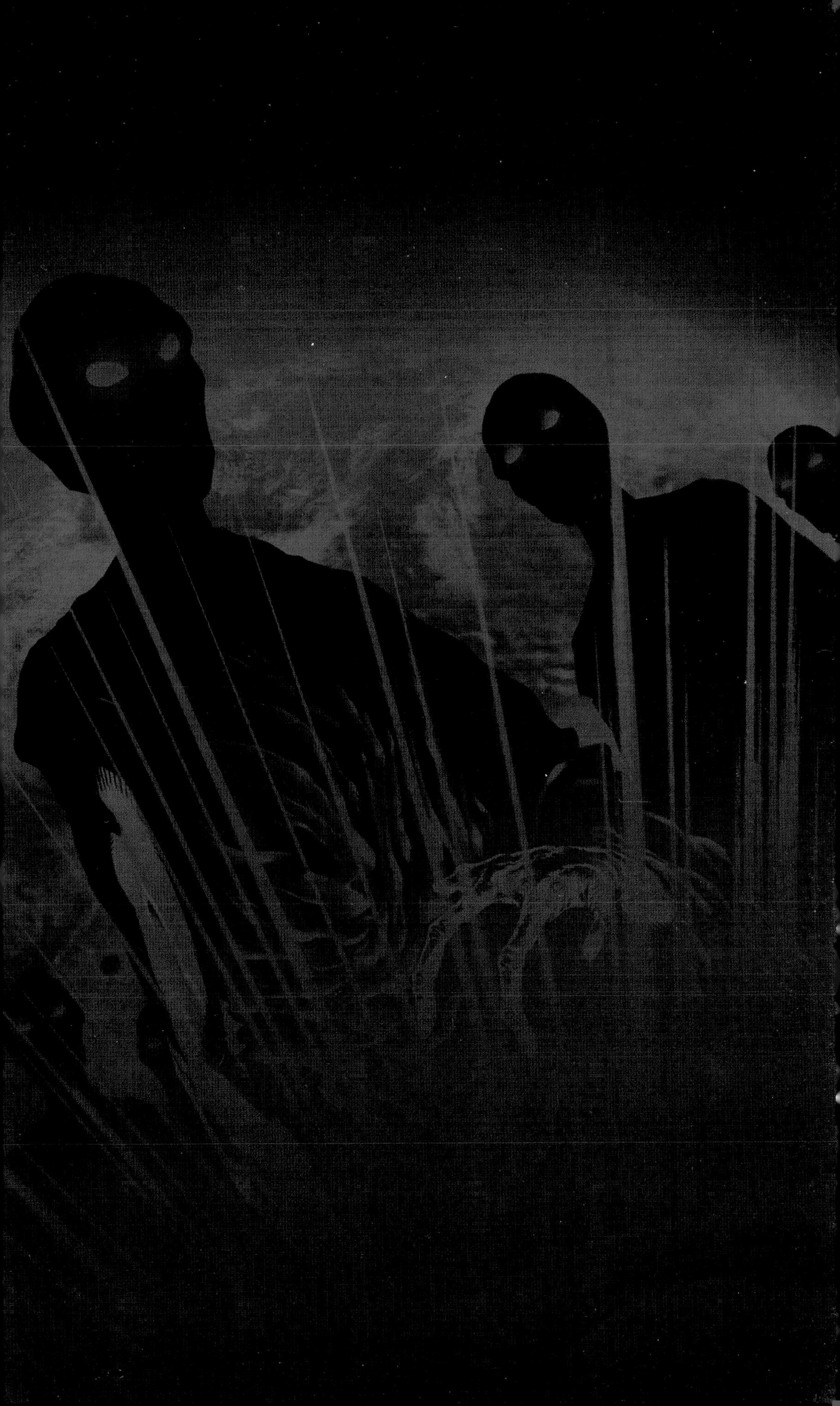